THE POLITICAL BACKGROUND

OF

AESCHYLEAN TRAGEDY

Anthony J. Podlecki

Second Edition

PAPERBACKS

TO MY PARENTS

First published in 1966 by The University of Michigan

Second edition published in 1999 by
Bristol Classical Press
an imprint of
Gerald Duckworth & Co. Ltd
61 Frith Street
London W1V 5TA
E-mail: inquiries@duckworth-publishers.co.uk
Website: www.ducknet.co.uk

Reprinted 2000 (with minor amendments)

© 1966, 1999 by A.J. Podlecki

A catalogue record for this book is available
from the British Library

ISBN 1-85399-573-8

Printed in Great Britain by
Booksprint

Contents

Preface to the Second Edition

This book first appeared over 30 years ago and much has been written since then about the connection between ancient Greek drama and politics. It is not my purpose here to present a thorough review of all that material, but rather to focus on a few items that extend, modify or challenge views which I originally put forward in 1966, and for the most part still espouse.

Much is made by Goldhill (1987, 1990) of the politically charged and often socially and psychologically self-critical nature of Athenian drama; his extreme view should be balanced by the more moderate observations of Griffin (1998). Connor (1989: 23) sees "the importance of the Dionysia as a celebration of civic freedom". Ober and Strauss (1990) attempt to situate Athenian drama within a larger context of "political discourse". Cole (1993) details the social aspects of the processions which preceded the dramatic performances. The wider social context of Greek drama is studied by Green (1994). Hall (1997) gives an overview of various aspects of Greek tragedy that might be termed "sociological". Wise (1998) draws analogies between legal trials in Athens and the agonistic confrontations of Greek tragedy; on this topic, see also Hall (1995).

There are useful surveys of material in Degani (1979) and Sartori (1988). Collections of articles with a distinctly Marxist tinge are presented by Schmidt (1981; with my review [1985]) and Kuch (1983). More recent collections of articles without an ideological slant are Sommerstein et al. (1993) and Pelling (1997).

Politics in Aeschylus have been the subject of some general studies, with a fairly broad (and occasionally rather unfocussed) sweep across all the plays: Miralles (1968), who draws interesting parallels with modern writers like Sartre and Camus; di Benedetto (1978); and more recently Meier (1993). Lampugnani Nigri (1972) pessimistically sees the "death of the *polis*" (i.e. a curtailment of citizens' individual freedoms) running as a leitmotif through the tragedies.

In two articles (1986 and 1993) I have argued that leaders in Aeschylus are portrayed in a way that may reflect the contemporary situation. Rosenbloom (1995) takes the rather implausible view that the playwright is warning the Athenians against the dangers of hubris engendered by their maritime empire.

Persians

As Aeschylus' most overtly historical play this has received a great deal of attention. Relevant material is to be found in the introductions to the texts by Belloni (1988) and Hall (1996). Hall (1989) argues that the Persians in the play are largely constructed as "other" than the Athenians. Vogt (1972) conversely maintains that they are "Hellenized" and assimilated to Greek cultural and religious attitudes. Gellie (1982: 59 and 61) well describes the play as "myth based on real events rather than on a legendary story", containing "the emotional history of the 470s". Di Virgilio proposes (rather unconvincingly, it seems to me) that the Queen's ominous dream (*Persians* 181 ff.) prefigures exclusively the Persian defeat at Plataia (816 ff.), not the campaigns of 480 as a whole (1973: 242 ff.; with review by Salvaneschi [1974]). Paduano (1978) tries to take account of the historical aspects by placing them in a larger, "narratological" discussion of the play. Hahn's view (1981) closely corresponds to mine that the play is strongly pro-Themistocles. Salanitro's thesis (1965) that the play glorifies Aristeides at Themistocles' expense seems to me impossible in the light of the description of the battle of Salamis and its victorious outcome. Péron (1982), in a detailed and wide-ranging study with abundant bibliography, Sartori (1969/70), Petre (1978), and Pelling (1997) all take a more centrist line than I about the political content of *Persians*. Various historical points arising from the play are discussed by Jouanna (1981), Saïd (1981 and 1992/

1993), and Lazenby (1988). According to Goldhill (1988: 193) "Aeschylus' *Persae* seems to suggest that the Greeks are victorious not only because of the gods, not only because of Persian *hubris*, but also because of the values of democratic *collectivity* (his emphasis), embodied in Athens, as opposed to barbarian tyranny". Kuch (1995) surveys three poetic accounts of the battle of Salamis. I have looked again (1998) at some passages in the play and asked why they might have appealed to Pericles, its *chorêgos*.

Seven Against Thebes

Petre (1971: 24) discerns in the fratricidal conflict between Oedipus' sons "l'image mythique de la guerre civile". According to Yaari (1995: 100) "...the setting Aeschylus employs in *Seven against Thebes* expands till it encompasses the geographic space beyond the theatre and turns the entire city of Athens into a setting for the play".

Suppliants

Sardiello (1969-1971) accepts my position that the play is pro-Themistocles. Some of my views (1972) are challenged by Burian (1974: 10), who remarks that "Pelasgus' dilemma is the dilemma of a statesman". Salanitro (1968) believes that the play is a warning to the Athenians not to grant the Libyan rebel Inaros' request for help (so in essence Luppino [1967], who, like Salanitro, accepts Diodorus' date 463 for the Egyptian rebellion). Sommerstein (1997) suggests that *Suppliants*, produced possibly in 461, was an attack on Cimon and his expedition to aid the Spartans.

Oresteia

Salanitro (1966) is unlikely to be correct in arguing that in the trilogy Aeschylus is approving Athenian expansion by land but warning against the dangers of expanding their maritime empire. Parallels between *Eumenides* and Solon's teaching in his poem on civil order, *Eunomiê* (fr. 4 West^2), are drawn in detail by Ameduri (1970/71). Cole (1977) believes that the trilogy represents "a plea for reconciliation" between radicals and conservatives. According to Nichols (1980: 91), "the *Oresteia* develops the possibility of a middle ground where the two spheres [public/male and private/female] can meet without mutual destruction or dissolution". Beer (1981) detects a "passionate plea" that the Areopagus use its powers to forestall an attempt at tyranny. Macleod (1982/1983) agrees that there are "politics" in the trilogy but he defines the term in a much more general sense than the one in which it is normally understood: "a concern with human beings as part of a community." Euben (1990: 91) believes that "inspired by the goddess [Athena] and assuming the Solonic mantle of poet-sage, the playwright joins with both the goddess and lawgiver in contributing to the city's political self-education, its wisdom, and its justice". Bearzot (1992) argues against Meier that Aeschylus supported the reforms of 462. Suardi (1994) shows how the various levels of meaning intersect within the trilogy. Griffith (1995) maintains (somewhat implausibly, it seems to me) that Aeschylus' message to the Athenian *demos* was that they should acquiesce in leadership by the leading families who were, for all their flaws, "irreplaceable".

Conacher (1987) reviews various positions taken about the political import of *Eumenides*. Sommerstein (1989: 32) thinks that, while Aeschylus supported the foreign policy advocated by the reformers, the poet's main message regarding domestic politics was "the vital importance of avoiding anything that might lead to internal conflict". In the introduction to my edition of the play (1989) I have restated the case I try to make in chapter V of the present work.

Prometheus

(I prescind here from the matter of the play's authorship.) Saïd (1985; with my review [1988]) explores the characterization of the two central characters and tries to place them in their cultural and philosophical context. Grossmann (1970; with my review [1974]) analyzes cogently the significant and topical themes in *Prometheus* and *Oresteia*. Cerri (1975: 10) sees in Prometheus "una figura di carattere schiettamente aristocratico" but this seems extremely unlikely. Ritoók (1983) detects a "thoroughly Solonian spirit [a call for moderation]" in the way the conflict is presented. The tyrannical aspects of the portrayal of Zeus are examined by Bees (1993: 194-231).

Historical Issues

I have analyzed critically and in detail the sources for Themistocles' life (1975). Marr's recent translation of Plutarch's *Life of Themistocles* (1988) has informative notes. For readable yet well-documented accounts of the Persian Wars, see Lazenby (1993), Hammond (1988), and Green (1996). There are interesting speculations about possible relations between Aeschylus and Simonides in Culasso Gastaldi (1986).

That interest in the subject of politics in Greek drama is still alive is shown by the bibliography here prefixed to the new edition; by the number of conferences and colloquia devoted to the topic, for example, Sommerstein et al. (1993) and Pelling (1997); and by the fact that it has been designated as one of the themes of the forthcoming FIEC Congress to be held in Kavala, Greece, in August 1999.

Friends and associates in various quarters have suggested that a reprint of my book would be of use; I hope they are right.

Vancouver, Canada
November 1998

Select Bibliography

Ameduri, Orlando (1970/71) "L'*Eunomia* di Solone e le *Eumenidi* di Eschilo" *Annali di Facoltà de lettere e filosofia* (University of Naples) 13: 15-22.

Bearzot, Cinzia (1992) "Ancora sulle *Eumenidi* di Eschilo e la riforma di Efialte (in margine ad una pagina di Chr. Meier)" *Prometheus* 18: 27-35.

Beer, D.G. (1981) "Tyranny, *anarkhia*, and the problem of the *Boule* in the *Oresteia*" *Florilegium* 3: 47-71.

Bees, Robert (1993) *Zur Datierung des Prometheus Desmotes* [Beiträge zur Altertumskunde 38] (Stuttgart: Teubner).

Belloni, Luigi (1988) *Eschilo. I Persiani* (Milan: Università Cattolica del Sacro Cuore).

Burian, Peter (1974) "Pelasgus and politics in Aeschylus' 'Danaid trilogy'" *Wiener Studien* N.F. 8: 5-14.

Cerri, Giovanni (1975) *Il linguaggio politico nel Prometeo di Eschilo. Saggi di semantica* (Rome: dell' Ateneo).

Cole, John R. (1977) "The *Oresteia* and Cimon" *HSCP* 81: 99-112.

Cole, Susan Guettel (1993) "Procession and celebration at the Dionysia" in Niall W. Slater and Bernhard Zimmermann (edd.) 1993: 25-38.

Conacher, Desmond J. (1987) *Aeschylus'* Oresteia. *A literary commentary* (Toronto: University of Toronto Press) [especially "Some views on the political and social aspects of the *Eumenides*": 195-222].

Connor, W. Robert (1989) [1990] "City Dionysia and Athenian democracy" *Classica et Mediaevalia* 40: 7-32 [repr. in Fears (ed.) 1990: 7-32].

Corsini, Eugenio (ed.) (1986, 1988) *La polis e il suo teatro* vols. i and ii (Padua: Editoriale Programma).

Culasso Gastaldi, Enrica (1986) "Temistocle, Eschilo, Simonide e il culto della vittoria" in Corsini (ed.) 1986: 31-47.

Degani, Enzo (1979) "Democrazia ateniese e sviluppo del dramma antico. La tragedia" in Nenci et al. (edd.) 1979: 255-310.

di Benedetto, Vincenzo (1978) *L'ideologia del potere e la tragedia greca. Ricerche su Eschilo* (Turin: Einaudi).

di Virgilio, Raffaele (1973) *Il vero volto dei 'Persiani' di Eschilo* [Biblioteca Athena 13] (Rome: dell'Ateneo).

Easterling, Pat (ed.) (1997) *The Cambridge companion to Greek tragedy* (Cambridge: Cambridge University Press).

Euben, J. Peter (ed.) (1986) *Greek tragedy and political theory* (Berkeley: University of California Press).

———(1990) *The Tragedy of political theory. The Road not taken* (Princeton: Princeton University Press).

Fears, J.R. (ed.) (1990) *Aspects of Athenian democracy* (Copenhagen: Museum Tusculanum Press).

Gellie, George (1982) "The *Persians* of Aeschylus" in Horseley (ed.) 1982: 59-62.

Ghiron-Bistagne, Paulette; Moreau, Alain; and Turpin, Jean-Claude (edd.) (1992/1993) "Les *Perses* d'Eschyle" *Cahiers du GITA* 7: 53-69.

Goff, Barbara (ed.) (1995) *History, tragedy, theory. Dialogues on Athenian drama* (Austin: University of Texas Press).

Goldhill, Simon (1987) "The great Dionysia and civic ideology" *JHS* 107: 58-76; revised version in Winkler and Zeitlin (edd.) 1990: 97-129.

———(1988) "Battle narrative and politics in Aeschylus' *Persae*" *JHS* 108: 189-193.

Green, J.R. (1994) *Theatre in ancient Greek society* (London: Routledge).

Green, Peter (1996) *The Greco-Persian Wars* (Berkeley: University of California Press) [new ed. of *The Year of Salamis, 480-479 B.C.* (London: Weidenfeld and Nicolson, 1970)].

Griffin, Jasper (1998) "The Social function of Attic tragedy" *CQ* n.s. 48: 39-61.

Griffith, Mark (1995) "Brilliant dynasts: power and politics in the *Oresteia*" *CA* 14: 62-129.

Grossmann, Gustav (1970) *Promethie und Orestie. Attischer Geist in der attischen Tragödie* (Heidleberg: Carl Winter).

Hahn, István (1981) "Aischylos und Themistokles. Bemerkungen zu den 'Persern'" in Schmidt (ed.) 1981: 173-186.

Hall, Edith (1989) *Inventing the barbarian: Greek self-definition through tragedy* (Oxford: Clarendon Press) [especially "Inventing Persia": 56-100].

———(1995) "Lawcourt dramas: the power of performance in Greek forensic oratory" *BICS* 40: 39-58.

———(1996) *Aeschylus, Persians* (Warminster: Aris & Phillips).

———(1997) "The Sociology of Athenian tragedy" in Easterling (ed.) 1997: 53-126.

Hammond, Nicholas G.L. (1988) "The Campaign and battle of Marathon" in *Cambridge Ancient History* (vol. IV 2nd ed.) (Cambridge: Cambridge University Press) [especially 506-517 and 569-590].

Horsley, Graham H.R. (ed.) (1982) *Hellenika: essays on Greek politics and history* (North Ryde NSW: Macquarie Ancient History Association).

Jouanna, Jacques (1981) "Les causes de la défaite des barbares chez Eschyle, Hérodote et Hippocrate" *KTEMA* 6: 3-15.

Kuch, Heinrich (ed.) (1983) *Die griechische Tragödie in ihrer gesellschaftlichen Funktion* (Berlin: Akademie-Verlag).

———(1995) "La tradizione poetica sulla battaglia di Salamina" *Lexis* 13: 145-155.

Lampugnani Nigri, Arrigo (1972) "KAIROS è libertà in Eschilo" *Acme* 25: 229-262.

Lazenby, John F. (1988) "Aischylos and Salamis" *Hermes* 116: 168-185.

———(1993) *The Defence of Greece, 490-479 B.C.* (Warminster: Aris and Phillips).

Luppino, Emma (1967) "L'intervento ateniese in Egitto nelle tragedie eschilee" *Aegyptus* 47: 197-212.

Macleod, Colin W. (1982) "Politics and the *Oresteia*" *JHS* 102: 124-144 [repr. in Macleod, *Collected Essays* (Oxford:

Clarendon Press,1983): 20-43].

Marr, John L. (1998) *Plutarch: Lives – Themistocles* (Warminster: Aris and Phillips).

Meier, Christian (1993) *The Political art of Greek tragedy* tr. by Andrew Webber (Baltimore: Johns Hopkins University Press) [especially "Aeschylus": 62-165].

Miralles, Carlos (1968) *Tragedia y política en Esquilo* (Barcelona: Ariel).

Nenci, Giuseppe et al. (edd.) (1979) *La Grecia nell'età di Pericle. Storia, letteratura, filosofia* [Storia e civiltà dei Greci 3] (Milan: Bompiani).

Nichols, D.K. (1980) "Aeschylus' *Oresteia* and the origins of political life" *Interpretation* 9: 83-91.

Ober, Josiah; and Strauss, Barry (1990) "Drama, political rhetoric, and the discourse of Athenian democracy" in Winkler and Zeitlin (edd.) 1990: 237-270.

Paduano, Guido (1978) *Sui Persiani di Eschilo: problemi di focalizzazione drammatica* (Rome: dell'Ateneo).

Pelling, Christopher B.R. (1997) "Aeschylus' *Persae* and history" in Pelling (ed.) *Greek tragedy and the historian* (Oxford: Clarendon Press): 1-19.

Péron, Jacques (1982) "Réalité et au-delà dans les Perses d'Eschyle" *Bulletin de l'Association Guillaume Budé* Mars 1982: 3-40.

Petre, Zoe (1971) "Thèmes dominants et attitudes politiques dans les Sept contre Thèbes d'Eschyle" *Studii Classice* 13: 15-28.

———(1978) "Eschyle, Salamine et les épigrammes de Marathon" *Revue romaine d'histoire* 17: 327-336.

Podlecki, Anthony J. (1972) "Politics in Aeschylus' *Supplices*" *Classical Folia* 26: 64-71.

———(1974) rev. of Grossmann (1970) in *Classical Journal* 70: 84-87.

———(1975) *The Life of Themistocles* (Montreal: McGill-Queen's University Press).

———(1985) "A contribution to the Aeschylus-Pindar-Jubilee 524-1977 [rev. of Schmidt (ed.) 1981]" *Philologus* 129: 308-312.

Podlecki, Anthony J. (1986) "*Polis* and monarch in early Attic tragedy" in Euben (ed.) 1986: 76-100.
———(1988) rev. of Saïd (1985) in *JHS* 108: 224-226.
———(1989) *Aeschylus*, Eumenides (Warminster: Aris and Phillips) [especially "Philosophy – and politics": 17-21].
———(1993) "*Kat'archês gar philaitios leôs*: the concept of leadership in Aeschylus" in Sommerstein et al. (edd.) 1993: 55-79.
———(1998) *Perikles and his circle* (London: Routledge) [especially "Entry into public life, Aischylos (and Themistokles)": 11-16].
Ritoók, Zsigmond (1983) "Die Prometheus-Gestalt in der griechischen Tragödie" in Kuch (ed.)1983: 85-101.
Rosenbloom, David (1995) "Myth, history, and hegemony in Aeschylus" in Goff (ed.) 1995: 93-130.
Salvaneschi, Enrica (1974) rev. of di Virgilio (1973) in *Maia* 26: 358-361.
Saïd, Suzanne (1981) "Darius et Xerxès dans les *Perses* d'Eschyle" *KTEMA* 6: 17-38.
———(1981) "Concorde et civilisation dans les *Euménides*" in *Théâtre et spectacles dans l'antiquité* [Publications du Centre de Recherche sur Proche-Orient et la Grèce antiques, Univ. de Strasbourg II] (Strasbourg) 96-121.
———(1985) *Sophiste et tyran, ou le problème du Prométhée enchaîné* (Paris: Klincksieck).
———(1992/93) "Pourquoi Psyttalie" in Ghiron-Bistagne et al. (edd.)1992/93: 53-69.
Salanitro, Giovanni (1965) "Il pensiero politico di Eschilo nei Persiani" *Giornale Italiano di Filologia* 18: 193-235.
———(1966) "'L'Orestea' e la politica estera di Atene" *Siculorum Gymnasium* n.s. 19: 155-173.
———(1968) "La data e il significato politico dell 'Supplici' di Eschilo" *Helikon* 8: 311-340.
Sardiello, Rosanna Elena (1969-1971) "Il problema della datazione e il significato politico delle 'Supplici' di Eschilo" *Annali della Facoltà di Lettere di Lecce* 5: 5-36.
Sartori, Franco (1969/70) "Echi politici ne 'I Persiani' di Eschilo" *Atti dell'Istituto Veneto di Scienze, Lettere ed Arti* 128:771-797.

Sartori, Franco (1988) "Teatro e storia nella Grecia antica: opinioni recenti su vecchi problemi" in Corsini (ed.) vol. ii (1988): 11-48.

Schmidt, Ernst Günther (ed.) (1981) *Aischylos und Pindar. Studien zu Werk und Nachwirkung* (Berlin: Akademie-Verlag).

Slater, Niall W.; and Zimmermann, Bernhard (edd.) (1993) *Intertextualität in der griechisch-römischen Komödie* [Drama. Beiträge zum antiken Drama und seiner Rezeption, Band 2] (Stuttgart: M & P).

Sommerstein, Alan H. (1989) *Aeschylus, Eumenides* (Cambridge: Cambridge University Press).

———(1997) "The Theatre audience, the *demos*, and the *Supplices* of Aeschylus" in Pelling (ed.) 1997: 63-79.

Sommerstein, Alan H.; Halliwell, Stephen; Henderson, Jeffrey; and Zimmermann, Bernhard (edd.) (1993) *Tragedy, comedy and the* Polis. *Papers from the Greek drama conference, Nottingham, 18-20 July 1990* (Bari: Levante Editori).

Suardi, Laura (1994) "Tempo mitico, tempo storico e tempo tragico nell' Orestea di Eschilo" *Dioniso* 64: 33-54.

Vogt, Joseph (1972) "Die Hellenisierung der Perser in der Tragödie des Aischylos: religiose Dichtung und historisches Zeugnis" in Ruth Stiehl and G.A. Lehman (edd.), *Festschrift Hans Erich Stier* [Fontes et Commentationes Suppl.-Bd. 1] (Münzter Westfalen: Aschendorff): 131-145.

Winkler, John J.; and Zeitlin, Froma I. (edd.) (1990) *Nothing to do with Dionysos? Athenian drama in its social context* (Princeton: Princeton University Press).

Wise, Jennifer (1998) *Dionysus writes. The Invention of theatre in ancient Greece* (Ithaca: Cornell University Press) [especially "Courtroom drama": 119-168].

Yaari, Nurit (1995) "Anchoring Thebes: defining place and space in ancient Greek theatre" in B. Zimmermann (ed.) *Griechisch-römische Komödie und Tragödie* [Drama. Beiträge zum antiken Drama und seiner Rezeption, Band 3] (Stuttgart: M & P): 94-110.

Preface to the First Edition

The contemporary French theater provides many examples of political drama, among which Anouilh's *Antigone* and Giraudoux's *Tiger at the Gates* are perhaps the best known in this country. Dramatists writing in English have done less with the genre, but Arthur Miller's *The Crucible* comes to mind as a play with a political theme. These works have a contemporary relevance and often a "message" whose meaning is clear to us because we know the political context—occupied France, Europe between the wars, or McCarthy's America—in which they were written.

It is otherwise with Greek drama. The subtleties of Greek history are largely lost to us; only the most important names and a few main trends survive. Because the contemporary background is for the most part hidden, any relevance the plays might have to that background generally eludes us. It is only the more marked allusions in some of Euripides' plays that have drawn the notice of scholars. Unless we are prepared to entertain the idea that less obvious reflections of the contemporary scene are *possible* in Greek tragedy, we shall not think of questioning the plays about their political background.

The first step, then, is to recognize that dramas written in a particular historical context may also reflect that context.

The issues and personalities with which the dramatist is involved in his public life can impinge on his art in various ways. Themes of political importance—matters, say, of legal and civic justice—may be translated into dramatic terms. Again, the dramatist may, by his choice of subject and by his handling of it, show that he is vitally concerned with, indeed even taking sides in, a current controversy. Or, more rarely, he may place specific persons and historical events in a dramatic setting.

When we have satisfied ourselves that these contemporary influences are possible, we must guard against the prejudice that such works would be necessarily inferior *as art*. Whatever may be said about the value of modern attempts to write "committed" drama, on only very narrow aesthetic canons about the purity of art can their success be predetermined. It would be fairer to examine them individually before deciding whether they are good or bad. If a bad play is not made better because of its message, neither is a good one made worse. It might even be argued that our appreciation of it is enhanced when we discover that the dramatist has not sealed off his political interests in a separate compartment, but has transformed and brought them to life on the stage. And if any period in the history of the world was apt to provide a setting conducive to such a transformation it was fifth-century Athens, where generals could be dramatic critics and dramatists served as generals.

The last and greatest need is to ask the right questions. What these are will necessarily differ with each play, but in general they will be questions like the following: What is the background of this play? What were the issues being discussed when the playwright molded his idea and cast it into final shape? Are these issues reflected—in a general or in some specific way—in his work? (It is easier to show what a wrong question is: What historical persons do we see posing as fictional characters in the drama?) Almost as important as the kind of question is the tone in which we ask it. It must be relaxed and unanxious: sometimes, although we can be fairly sure that there is a meaning deeper than meets the eye, its exact nuance is irrecoverable. Often it refuses to expose itself because of the very stridency and insistence of our demand for an answer.

In the study which follows I have examined the extant plays of Aeschylus in a chronological order which is now, for all practical purposes, secure. I have tried to ask the right questions about them—often different questions of different plays—and in what I hope is a suitably civil tone. I have kept firmly before me the double truth that they are both works of art and products of a historical context. If their artistic qualities have often been taken for granted in what follows, it is because these have received most critical attention elsewhere; if, to my historical questions, the plays remain largely silent or the answers are thought unconvincing, I can only hope that with additional discoveries and further refinement of critical methods they can someday be coaxed into yielding up their secrets.

There remains the pleasant duty of thanking those who have made this study possible. Professors M. E. White of Trinity College, Toronto, D. de Montmollin of Victoria College, and the late W. P. Wallace of University College read most of the chapters in their earliest and roughest form and made many helpful suggestions. Professor C. J. Herington, then of University College, also read these chapters, and, in addition, read and criticized a later draft of the chapter on the *Prometheus* and put at my disposal his deep knowledge of that play, as of the rest of the Aeschylean *corpus*. Professor D. J. Conacher of Trinity College, who supervised my research, deserves my deepest gratitude; his patient and kindly counsel has improved every page of the manuscript.

The guiding force behind my work has been Mr. W. G. Forrest of Wadham College, Oxford. He discussed the topic with me in 1959, read Aeschylus with me in 1960–61, and encouraged me in the early stages; many of my own theories are merely the growth of ideas planted by him, verbally or in print. My thanks are also due Professor K. J. Dover of St. Andrew's University, who read the typescript and suggested numerous improvements, and Professor E. R. Dodds, whose seminar on the political background of Greek tragedy at Oxford in Hilary term, 1960, exposed me to the wide literature on the subject and to the exciting possibilities of further research. Professor Dodds, in addition, read the typescript and offered criticisms which were often salutary.

To all of these I am most grateful, as well as to my family and friends for their tacit support. I reserve special thanks for my wife, whose gentle encouragement was essential to the work's completion, and for my parents, to whom, as a partial and imperfect repayment of the large debt of *pietas,* this book is respectfully dedicated.

ABBREVIATIONS

AJA   *American Journal of Archaeology*

CP   *Classical Philology*

CQ   *Classical Quarterly*

CR   *Classical Review*

FGH   (*F Gr Hist*)   Felix Jacoby, *Die Fragmente der griechischen Historiker*

GGL   Schmid-Stählin, *Geschichte der griechischen Literatur*

Gomme, *Commentary*   A. W. Gomme, *A Historical Commentary on Thucydides*

HSCP   *Harvard Studies in Classical Philology*

IG   *Inscriptiones Graecae*

JHS   *Journal of Hellenic Studies*

LSJ   Liddell-Scott-Jones, *A Greek-English Lexicon* 9 ed.

Mette   H. J. Mette, *Die Fragmente der Tragödien des Aischylos*

R-E   *Pauly's Real-Encyclopädie der classischen Altertumswissenschaft*

REA   *Revue des Etudes Anciennes*

Rose, *Commentary*   H. J. Rose, *A Commentary on the Surviving Plays of Aeschylus*

TAPA   *Transactions and Proceedings of the American Philological Association*

CHAPTER I

Introduction: Life of Aeschylus

Our sources for the life of Aeschylus are few and defective. Chief among them is the anonymous *Life* prefixed to the Medicean manuscript of the plays. It is a more or less continuous narrative of eighteen short paragraphs, or "chapters," some of which can only have found their way into it thanks to a later scribal compilator. To accept all that the *Life* offers as trustworthy is obviously hazardous, for, as Dindorf reminds us, at the best of times "the ancient Greek biographers were a very lying lot."[1] Nor can it safely be assumed that what we have goes back substantially to one biographical source, however tempting it may be to seize upon one of these biographers whom we know to have written on Aeschylus and attribute the bare facts in the *Life* to him. The shadowy Chamaeleon has been a favorite candidate.[2]

It seems safe to posit, with Dindorf,[3] as a distant archetype for the *Life* the work of some editor in that great repository of fact and fancy, the library at Alexandria. We may wonder what materials were available to *him*, that is, after we have discarded the obvious or assumed errors of later "editors" and interpolators, how much of the *Life* can be trusted as coming from reputable, pre-Alexandrian, sources? The answer must be: discouragingly little. The Alexandrian scholar

1

would have had the above-mentioned Chamaeleon's treatise *On Aeschylus*. The fragments of it which can be recovered from Athenaeus[4] show that it contained, alongside serious information about Aeschylus' technique of composition (as, for example, that he was his own choreographer), the most absurd trivia—he composed his tragedies while drunk. This may serve to remind us that the late Peripatetic "biographies" of great poets of an earlier age were not biographies at all: they were, on the one side, theoretical and highly schematic studies of artistic technique, and, on the other, grab bags of highly spiced bits of gossip. Factual details of a man's life, if any come through, do so almost entirely by accident.

We know the names of many of these Peripatetics who busied themselves writing such studies of the poets: Phanias of Eresus, Dicaearchus of Messene, Aristoxenus, Duris of Samos, Satyrus. Some of these must have been general works, treatises *On Poets* in imitation of Aristotle's lost dialogue. And some of these general and comparative studies would have contained details of Aeschylus' technique, and perhaps of his life as well; the story (with suspiciously picturesque embroidery) of Aeschylus' trial before the Areopagus for betraying secrets of the Mysteries is definitely ascribed to the first book of Heracleides Ponticus' work *On Homer*. It is noteworthy that, whereas we have notices of several of these Peripatetic "biographies" of individual poets (like Duris' works on Sophocles and Euripides) and even the tattered remains of one of them, Satyrus' *Life of Euripides*, Aeschylus seems to have been unpopular as a subject of individual biography: we hear only of the work of Chamaeleon already discussed, and reference to an earlier treatise, *On the Poetry of Aeschylus*, by Glaucus of Rhegium.

The earlier sources which these late fourth- and third-century writers drew upon seem themselves to have been heavily preoccupied with literary criticism or "appreciation" on the one hand and titillating gossip on the other. The line between the two is not always clearly drawn: the delightful goings-on in the *Frogs* suggest what Pherecrates' *Crapatali*, which also brought Aeschylus on the stage, must have been like. Beyond this—what? It would be comforting to think that Ion of Chios, Aeschylus' younger contemporary, gave a full-scale portrait of the tragedian, replete with factual material, in the *Epidêmiai*. What little we have to connect Ion and Aeschylus suggests very faintly that those travelers' tales may have been the source of much in the later tradition. Finally, there is that last haven of desperate historians, "oral tradition." The probability is higher for Aeschylus than for other figures of antiquity that clusters of anecdotes about him (some perhaps even containing factual information about his life) may have been passed from generation to generation by word of mouth, to find their way ultimately into an Alexandrian biography. Such, at any rate, is suggested by his fame during his lifetime and by the unique honor of *ad lib.* public performance of his works after his death.

These, then, were the components of the biographical tradition on which our *Life of Aeschylus* may have been based: the written reminiscences of contemporaries, accounts of his dramatic technique and the *personalia* of his life beginning in the next generation and coming to full fruit in the late Lyceum, passing references in later authors, oral tradition. Besides these sources, a chronological scheme was introduced at some stage: the dates in the Parian Marble seem internally consistent and therefore not open to serious doubt. What absolute dates or synchronisms the later tradition provides may go back to a basically trustworthy chronographic source like Apollodorus, but these have to be judged individually, and acceptance or rejection will often depend only on the unstable criterion of plausibility.

The altogether inadequate materials for a life of Aeschylus have been outlined. It is now time to turn to the *Life*,[5] to see what nuggets of historical fact can be mined from it.

Aeschylus was born in 525/4[6] at Eleusis,[7] "of the nobility" as the *Life* avers. His father was Euphorion, and we know the names of several of his brothers: Cynegeirus, Euphorion, perhaps Ameinias. He had, in addition, a sister, several of whose descendants followed in their uncle's footsteps and gained reputations as tragic poets.[8] Aeschylus was, as the *Life* points out, a contemporary of Pindar's, and it is perhaps inevitable that the Theban poet should have been said to have associated with Aeschylus, his senior by seven years, and to have been influenced by the dramatist's grandiloquence.[9]

Inevitable, too, is the connection of Aeschylus' name with several battles of the Persian Wars. The entry in the *Life* reads as follows: "They say . . . that he took part in the battle of Marathon with his brother Cynegeirus, and in the sea fight at Salamis with Ameinias the youngest of his brothers, and in the land battle at Plataea."[10] For Aeschylus' presence at Marathon we have excellent confirmation, for the "epitaph" which the *Life* says stood on his grave at Gela singles out his services at Marathon for special mention.[11] No less certain is his presence at Salamis, which is attested by Ion of Chios, his younger contemporary.[12] For Aeschylus' presence at the battle of Plataea we have only the unsupported witness of the *Life*, and the invariable attraction of great names for great events is shown by Pausanias' passing reference to "Aeschylus, who fought in the naval battle *off Artemisium* and at Salamis." Wilamowitz may have been right in maintaining that "Artemisium was added by sheer conjecture, just as Plataea in the *Life*."[13] We find the names of Aeschylus' brothers connected with several of these battles. Herodotus, in his account of the battle of Marathon, records that "Cynegeirus, son of Euphorion, fell there, his hands cut off with an axe when he was holding onto a ship's stern."[14] Herodotus also tells of the daring exploits of a certain Ameinias during the engagement at Salamis, but twice describes him as "of Pallene";[15] if that is correct, we must suppose that this Ameinias and Aeschylus' brother of the same name were erroneously identified at some stage in the tradition.[16]

There is no way of knowing exactly when Aeschylus entered upon his dramatic career. According to "Suidas'" notice of Pratinas, that dramatist's competitors "in the seventieth Olympiad" (499–6) were Aeschylus and Choerilus. This may refer to a first production by Aeschylus;[17] the *Life* simply records that he "began tragedies as a young man."[18] It is possible that Aeschylus began to write tragedies about 500 B.C., although according to the Parian Marble he did not win his first victory until the spring of 484.[19]

The *Life* gives us some information about Aeschylus' trips to Sicily, but the account is extremely confused. "He went off to Hiero, according to some because he had been oppressed[20] by the Athenians and had been defeated by the young Sophocles, although others say because he had been defeated by Simonides in the elegy for those who had died at Marathon." (The next sentence contains a "critical" comment on the unsuitability of Aeschylus' talents for elegy, and Section 9 reports that the chorus of the *Eumenides* had a violent effect on pregnant women.) The *Life* then continues: "Having gone therefore to Sicily, since Hiero was at that time founding Aetna, he exhibited the *Aetnaean Women* as an augury of a good life for the city's settlers. And, held in high esteem by the tyrant Hiero and the people of Gela, he lived three years more and died an old man" (*Life* 9–10).

The first thing to note is that the *Life* is here conflating at least two certain visits of Aeschylus to Sicily, that which came at the end of his life, and an earlier one, during which he presented the *Aetnaean Women*. That he went west after the *Oresteia* and died in Gela in 456/5 seems assured by the "epitaph" and by the notice in the Parian Marble.[21] But this visit can hardly be connected with the hospitality afforded him, probably at Syracuse, by Hiero, who died in 467/6. That visit, during which Aeschylus produced his *Aetnaean Women*, must have been some time around 475, when Hiero founded his new city.[22] Neither of these visits can be connected with Aeschylus' defeat by the neophyte Sophocles, for we know from Plutarch that Sophocles' victory took place in the archonship of Apsephion, that is, March 468. Our suspicions ought to be aroused by a similar confusion in Plutarch's account of the incident. There, too, the period between Aeschylus' defeat by Sophocles and his death is truncated. "It is said that, when Sophocles won, Aeschylus became greatly distressed and bore it heavily; he passed no long time in Athens, and then went in anger to Sicily, where he died and was buried in the neighborhood of Gela."[23] At some stage in the tradition a motive involving personal pique at a defeat by Sophocles in the dramatic contests was devised to explain Aeschylus' one visit to the West which was beyond dispute, his last. But what of the *Life*'s alternative explanation, that Aeschylus went to Sicily because he lost the Marathon-epigram contest to Simonides? The epigram controversy is a Pandora's box which fortunately need not be opened here. Whether or not such a contest was ever held, it is enough to note, with Kiehl, that Aeschylus' departure for Sicily to produce the *Aetnaean Women* soon after an outstanding victory by Simonides in the *dithyrambic* contest may have given rise to the story.[24]

At least two Sicilian visits are assured. The number could be raised to three if we could accept the reported testimony of Eratosthenes that Aeschylus presented the *Persians* in Sicily at Hiero's request.[25] The matter of a third sojourn, presumably between 472 and 467, when Aeschylus was back in Athens to produce the *Seven Against Thebes*, is unaffected by a lingering doubt over whether it was the *Persians* as we have it or a revised version that Aeschylus presented in Sicily.[26] Further than this we cannot go; it would be unsafe to put any faith in the stories of Aeschylus' departure for the West after his loss to Simonides for the honor of composing the elegy for the dead at Marathon—a story not itself above suspicion—or after his defeat by the parvenu Sophocles. Later writers knew that, but not when, Aeschylus had gone to Sicily, and they would go to any lengths to devise a motive for these visits. Witness the comment of "Suidas": ". . . having fled to Sicily because the benches fell when he was exhibiting."[27] It must have been a favorite tale to associate with the name of any well-known dramatist, for we are told in that same lexicon, under the entry "Pratinas," that "when this man was exhibiting, the benches on which the spectators were standing fell. . . ."[28]

Why Aeschylus left Athens is uncertain. Aristophanes said "Aeschylus did not get along with the Athenians,"[29] but this need not have a specific reference. According to the *Life,* he was killed by a falling tortoise which an eagle had dropped on his head.[30] "The people of Gela buried him in honor" says the *Life,* and appends the epitaph:

> Aeschylus son of Euphorion deceased
> This monument of wheat-growing Gela covers;
> Of his glorious strength Marathon's grove could tell
> And the long-haired Mede knows it well.[31]

Wilamowitz did not believe that this was a genuine epitaph on the grounds that "a monument set up at Gela would not name Gela,"[32] but the very rarity of the formulation "monument . . . of Gela" makes it unsafe to draw such a generalization.[33]

Aeschylus' death at the age of sixty-nine in the archonship of Callias (456/5) is attested by the Parian Marble.[34]

The total number of his compositions is variously given. According to the *Life* "he composed seventy dramas and about five satyr plays in addition. He received thirteen victories in all."[35] The figure seventy seems rather too low, for the Catalogue of titles which follows the *Life* in the Medicean contains seventy-two or seventy-three (if *"Phrygians"* be admitted as a separate title), and this has been supplemented with as many as nine other titles. The notice in "Suidas" mentions ninety tragedies and twenty-eight victories. The discrepancy between thirteen and twenty-eight victories may result, as many have thought, from the inclusion in the latter figure of posthumous victories.[36] "The Athenians so admired Aeschylus that a decree was passed after his death that whoever wished to present Aeschylus' plays should receive a chorus";[37] and, the *Life* adds, "he won not a few victories after his death."[38] Greek idiom notwithstanding, the phrase does not seem to justify the incredibly high figure of fifteen posthumous victories.

CHAPTER II

Persians

Aeschylus' *Persians* is unique in the history of Greek drama, for it is the only surviving example of a *genre* which can never have been large, historical tragedy.[1] Its tragic hero was a living person whom disaster had overtaken not in the misty past of saga and myth, but eight years before the play was produced; the agents of his downfall were many of the same men who sat in the theater in 472. In choosing this contemporary subject, Aeschylus ran a risk: he had to engage the audience in the tragic fate of Xerxes, and this would require a nearly total abstraction from natural stirrings of pride at their own part in bringing about the defeat of this bitter enemy. They had almost to forget who they were and to concentrate on the common humanity which they shared with their former enemy, a man subject, as are all men, to the *phthonos* of heaven and the vicissitudes of fortune.

The playwright found himself with another limitation arising from his subject. Writing for men who had fought in the battle, as he himself had done, it was impossible for him to depart from the main outlines of known fact or even from such minor details as a substantial part of his audience would have remembered. This was drama concerned with the living past, in which he and his audience had been and continued to be intimately concerned, and so the picture of recent events which the play gives must have been substantially true to life. Lattimore puts it well:

> It is useless to argue that Aeschylus was a poet, not a historian, and therefore did not feel himself bound by the actualities. Dramatic foreshortening may be conceded, but we have no right to assume that the Athenians would award first prize to a tragic poet for dealing wildly with known facts in a contemporary theme. . . .[2]

But, within the limits of substantial accuracy, a wide choice of detail and emotional coloring was possible. A poet could emphasize or suppress features of the defeat as it suited his dramatic (or other) purposes. Thus, there seems to be a consistent suppression of historical details which show Darius to have been as violent and warlike as his son;[3] Xerxes' hybris is in this way thrown into sharper relief. On the side of emphasis, Aeschylus was an Athenian, writing for an audience of his compatriots, and the name of Athens and its citizens is brought to the center of the stage again and again. Atossa has just retailed at some length her portentous dream, and the chorus of elders advises her to make libations and avert the evil omen. "I will do what you say . . ."—and then, with no previous connection of thought, "This is what I want to know, where on earth do they say Athens is located?" (230–231). They have not even been talking of Greece, or the expedition. Atossa continues: "Why does my son desire to hunt down this city?" Note the chorus' reply: "For all Hellas would be subject to the King" (234). What of the Spartans? the Corinthians? It is Athens that is the cornerstone of Hellas' defense. "What shepherd have they? What lord of the troops?" the Queen asks. No, Athens is not a nation of sheep, "slaves of no one nor subject to any man," as the chorus says (242). How could the audience not have thrilled to those words?[4]

"We cannot fail to see here the glorification of a victory which is, as far as Aeschylus can make it so, *Athenian*," as Lattimore well remarks.[5] But he does not bring out adequately the dramatist's persistence in keeping not simply Athens, but, more particularly, Salamis, before his audience. The fatal name is made to ring through the lines again and again. After entering and reporting that the "whole barbarian force has been destroyed" (255), the messenger engages in an exchange with the chorus in which he interposes pairs of iambic trimeters to their lyric iambics. His first two sets of lines add no new information. The chorus bewails the "many and sundry weapons" which have been lost (text corrupt) "in the hostile land of Hellas."[6] At this the messenger interjects:

> The shores of Salamis and all the space around
> Are full of corpses miserably destroyed.   (272–273)

His next lines are again general, "the whole force has perished, defeated by the rammings of ships" (278–279). Then,

> O most hateful name of Salamis to hear!   (284)

He opens his long list of the slain at 302 ff. by saying that "Artembares, commander of ten thousand horse, is being dashed along the hard shores of Sileniae" (303), that part of Salamis' coast, according to the Scholiast, near Cape Tropaea, "Victory Point."[7] The island's central position in the Persian defeat continues to be kept before the audience throughout this sad litany. Tenagon, the Bactrian commander, "frequents (or 'smites') the sea-beaten isle of Ajax" (307), and Lilaios, Armenes, and Argestes are said to "batter the island nurse of doves" (309), taken by the Scholiast to refer yet again to Salamis. In the first stasimon the chorus reflects on and laments the naval disaster in a balanced triple refrain whose effect can hardly be captured in translation:

> Xerxes led forth, oh oh
> Xerxes destroyed, woe woe
> Xerxes administered evilly
> And barques of the sea.   (550–553)

This is echoed in the antistrophe by

> Ships led forth, oh oh
> Ships destroyed, woe woe

Ships with rams all destructively
In Ionian hands.   (560—563)[8]

In the next strophe they bewail "Those who fell first, caught
by Ananke, around Cychreian shores" (568—570), another
periphrasis for Salamis, so called after its mythical hero-king
Cychreus (or Cenchreus), who is said by Pausanias (1.36.1)
to have appeared to the Greeks during the battle in the form
of a snake. In their very first lines in this stasimon the Persian
elders once again allude to Salamis:

> The blood-stained soil
> of Ajax' sea-washed isle
> holdeth all that once was Persia.
>
> (595—597, trans. Smyth)

In the stasimon which follows the appearance of Darius'
ghost the chorus bemoans the impending loss of Lesbos, Chios,
Samos, and the Cyclades; moving westward it mentions Lemnos, Icarus, Rhodes, Cnidus, and the three cities of Cyprus,
among which is Salamis, "whose mother-city is now the cause
of our lament" (895—896, trans. Smyth). Even now, the main
disaster over and the tragedy about to be resolved with the
appearance of the defeated prince, Aeschylus forces the hated
name to his characters' lips. The shattered Xerxes appears and
the play closes with a long and sorrowful *kommos*. This time
it is Xerxes who reminds the elders of the scene of destruction
and "Ares turning the tide and cutting a wide swathe through
the gloomy sea and the ill-starred shore" (953, 954). One final
time is the island mentioned, by Xerxes in his next strophe,
when he laments:

> Wretched were those I lost
> From a Tyrian ship,
> Destroyed on the shores
> Of Salamis, striking
> Against the hard shore   (962—966),

a bitter echo of the messenger's description earlier in the play
(303).

The audience is never allowed to forget that it was at Salamis that the Persian might was broken; on Salamis' shores the tides wash up heaps of floating corpses; the hateful name punctuates the tragedy throughout. It is as if Aeschylus were compressing the whole agonized resistance of Hellas to the barbarian invader into this one engagement. Where are Artemisium? Thermopylae? Marathon is dismissed in a line-and-a-half: "The barbarians whom Marathon destroyed before were not enough" (474–475). Even if Aeschylus does not, as Lattimore maintained, reduce Plataea to an "insignificant mopping-up operation,"[9] that battle must take second place. The Persian force was shattered at Salamis and the "Dorian spear" had only to administer the coup de grace.

A detailed account of the battle itself occupies the whole central portion of the play; its name recurs throughout in a grim refrain. What can have prompted Aeschylus to write a tragedy which must have reminded the Athenians of their glorious victory over the invader at Salamis? Why at this time, eight years after the event? We are told in the Hypothesis that Aeschylus won the tragic competition with a tetralogy which included the *Persians* in the archonship of Menon, that is, 472 B.C., the very time when Themistocles' political existence in Athens was being seriously threatened. When the actor who portrayed the Persian messenger began his account of the battle with the words, "there was a man, a Greek, who came from the Athenian camp . . . ," and then proceeded to relate how the Persian fleet was lured to its destruction by a false message that the Greeks would flee under cover of night,[10] who in the audience would not have thought of Themistocles, the author of the trick? We can hardly avoid the conclusion that now, probably on the eve of Themistocles' ostracism,[11] Aeschylus is taking special pains to remind the Athenians that the victory of Salamis was almost single-handedly Themistocles' doing. His enemies were to charge collusion in the alleged Medizing activities of Pausanias the Spartan. Aeschylus here presents a stirring retelling of the way in which the Persian might was shattered in the engagement which had had Themistocles as its mastermind. Could the dramatist have demonstrated his support of Themistocles more forcefully?[12]

There is a convergence of scattered lines of evidence to show that in the decade after 480 a controversy arose over which victory over the Persian—Marathon or Salamis—was the more important. A propaganda battle seems to have developed between Cimon, whose father Miltiades had been the hero of Marathon, and Themistocles, author of the victory of Salamis. Each side enlisted the help not only of poets, but also of painters and sculptors, to impress its own version of the facts on public opinion.

Plutarch tells how Cimon rode to the forefront of popular favor by "discovering" the bones of the hero Theseus on the island of Scyros and having them transported to Athens in accordance with an oracle; they were then enshrined with great pomp in the newly built Theseion (*Cimon* 8.6). Plutarch tells the same story in his *Life of Theseus*, where he dates the oracle to 476/5 and includes the significant detail that the main reason why the Athenians honored Theseus as a demigod was for the assistance which he was believed to have rendered to the fighters *at Marathon*; many veterans of the battle claimed to have seen an apparition of Theseus, clad in full armor and charging ahead of them against the barbarians (*Thes.* 35, *ad fin*). It is of some interest to remember that Theseus was a favorite subject of the painter Polygnotus, whose connections with Cimon were very close.[13] He appeared in Polygnotus' *Nekyia* at Delphi, according to Pausanias (10.29.9), and several vase representations of the hero seem to have been influenced by murals of the painter.[14] Later, the victory at Marathon figured prominently in Polygnotus' mural in the Stoa Poikile, where it appeared in conjunction with the victory of Theseus and Herakles over the Trojans and Amazons (Pausanias 1.15.3). The Trojan story is also brought into close connection with the victory of Marathon in an early work ascribed by Pausanias to the sculptor Pheidias, whose bronze grouping of Miltiades and other heroes with Athena and Apollo, near the wooden horse, was set up at Delphi as a tithe-offering after Marathon (10.10.1).[15] The appearance of Trojan motifs and the victory over the Amazons in many of these contexts is curious: can Cimon have been fostering an image of his father's victory at Marathon as a repeat performance of earlier Greek conquests of barbarians, but this time on Greek soil? Was Miltiades being sold to the Athenians as a second Theseus?

It is in this context that the prominence Aeschylus gives to Salamis finds its real importance: he is helping Themistocles in a contest of mythological propaganda and artistic motif. It would be of considerable interest in this connection to know how closely Aeschylus followed his predecessor, Phrynichus, whose play the *Phoenician Women* had also dealt with Xerxes' defeat, for Themistocles himself had acted as choregus for Phrynichus when the play was produced four years before.[16] It is even possible that this production had been used to solemnize a restoration of the theater of Dionysus by Themistocles and the resumption of dramatic contests after the Persian invasion.[17]

We may stop to focus on an instructive case of poetry in the service of politics. The friendship between Themistocles and Phrynichus was one of long standing; the tragedian's earlier historical play, *The Capture of Miletus*, had been produced in the late 490's probably in the very year of Themistocles' archonship, 493/2.[18] It is highly probable that Themistocles inspired and encouraged the dramatist on that earlier occasion as well, perhaps as part of a program of support of the Ionian revolt against reactionary, isolationist forces at home. The performance achieved a result which neither the poet nor the politician could have foreseen: Herodotus tells how the audience broke into tears at the spectacle of "sufferings which touched themselves," and fined Phrynichus 1,000 drachmas.[19]

When Aeschylus came to write a play on the Salamis theme, to lend support to the architect of the victory in his hour of greatest need, it was natural for him to turn to Phrynichus' *Phoenician Women.* He did not hesitate to borrow from his predecessor not only content, but even matters of phrasing. The Hypothesis of the *Persians* informs us that "Glaucus (of Rhegium, late fifth century B.C.) says in his treatise on Aeschylus' poetry that the *Persians* is adapted from Phrynichus' *Phoenissae*"; the first line of Phrynichus' play is then quoted, and its close resemblance to the opening of the *Persians* is striking. How the play developed we cannot tell in any detail, but a papyrus fragment seems to come from a messenger's speech relating the defeat at Salamis.[20]

The parallelism between the productions of 476 and 472 is not yet complete. For, just as Themistocles had served as choregus for Phrynichus, Aeschylus had as his choregus for the *Persians* the young Pericles.[21]

Through the entire central section of the *Persians*, all of the audience's attention must have been focused on Themistocles. But the hero of Salamis, whose political future in Athens was now being put in jeopardy, impinges on the drama in other places as well. After recounting her dream, the Queen asks the chorus about Athens. Where is it? By whom are the Athenians ruled? The size of their army and their weapons? She then asks about the sources of their wealth[22] and the messenger replies, "they have a fount of silver, the earth's treasure." "This reference to the mines would have had a deep significance for the audience," Broadhead remarks. Indeed it would, when we remember Herodotus' account of Themistocles' connection with the Laureion mines. In 483, when the Athenians were about to divide the increased revenues from a newly discovered vein among the whole population,[23] "Themistocles convinced the Athenians that they should stop this division and use this money to build 200 ships for the war" (7.144). Herodotus goes on to explain that this was the war against the Aeginetans, but it is clear that, even if the Aeginetans provided Themistocles with a pretext, he had his eye on larger prey. The messenger's report of a "fount of silver" would have served to remind the audience of another of the benefactions of the man who was now threatened with disgrace.

In Herodotus' confused and somewhat implausible details

of the various war councils before Salamis, one anecdote deserves closer attention than the rest for the light it may throw on another line in the play. The wrangles between Adeimantus the Corinthian, the Spartan admiral Eurybiades, and Themistocles smack of elaboration as a result of animosities later in the century, and the chronological difficulties which these councils present count against their genuineness. But, based on camp gossip as they undoubtedly are, some of the tales may be valuable as reflecting what was actually being whispered in the various contingents. Now, one of the charges Herodotus reports as having been laid against Themistocles by Adeimantus was that as the Athenians had abandoned their city and fled to Salamis and elsewhere, the Athenian general "had no fatherland"; he should be allowed to cast his vote only if he could "provide himself with a city." The Corinthian made this charge, Herodotus notes, because Athens had already been captured and occupied by the Persians. To this taunt Themistocles had much abuse to offer in return, "and he made it plain to them that the Athenians would have a city and a fatherland greater than Corinth, as long as they had two hundred ships full of men . . ." (8.61.2). In the Queen's interrogation of the messenger after he has announced the defeat and chanted the names of the fallen, she asks with astonishment, "What, is the city of Athens still unsacked?," and the messenger replies: "As long as there are men, a city's wall is safe."[24] It may be that Aeschylus is here alluding to an actual retort used by Themistocles to silence those—perhaps his fellow countrymen—who charged that the Athenians would "have no city" once they abandoned Athens to the invader. And the audience would probably have remembered in this context the lengths to which Themistocles had gone to give a "correct" interpretation to Delphi's oracle which contained the lines:

> . . . wide seeing Zeus grants to Tritogeneia that
> the wooden wall
> Alone will be unsacked, which will benefit you
> and your children. . . .
> (7.141.3)

Themistocles "advised the Athenians to prepare for a naval battle, and consider this (namely, their ships) to be the wooden wall" (7.143).[25]

There are two other themes in the play which may have some connection with Themistocles. A close reading shows that Aeschylus is at some pains to cover up the fact that Xerxes' fleet included a contingent of Ionian Greeks (one hundred ships, according to Herodotus, 7.94). In its description of the variegated Persian host in the Prologue, the chorus mentions the "throng of luxurious Lydians, who control the entire mainland folk" (42–43). Broadhead's note on the passage deserves to be quoted:

> Since the poet wished, for obvious reasons, to avoid direct mention of the Ionian Greeks in his catalogue of races, he has, by inserting a somewhat vague reference to "continental-born races" . . . disguised, as Paley, following Blomfield, says, the humiliating fact that the Ionians were compelled to fight against their kinsmen the Athenians.[26]

Later in the play, when the Ghost of Darius appears and enumerates the past kings of Persia, he mentions the conquests of Cyrus: "He acquired the folk of Lydians and Phrygians, and all Ionia he attacked by force" (770–771). The difference in the two verbs is significant: the Lydians and Phrygians were "acquired" while Ionia was "driven forcefully," a phrase which, as Broadhead notes, "here suggests rather than states subjection . . . implying that the Ionian Greeks put up a stern fight for their independence."[27]

The Ghost scene is followed by a stasimon in which the chorus sings about the past glories of the Persian Empire; the Elders describe the broad geographical areas under the Great King's control, with an implication that Xerxes' defeat will lead to a break-up of this vast territory. In the third pair of strophes they list the Greek islands: Lesbos, Samos, Chios, Paros, Naxos, Myconos, Tenos, Andros, Lemnos, Icarus, Rhodes, Cnidus, and Cyprus. Broadhead explains the pertinence of the catalogue:

All the Aegean islands that had been subject to the Persians were by 472 B.C. members of the confederacy for the preservation of freedom from Persian domination. . . . They had been compelled to send contingents to Xerxes' fleet, and, as we have seen, Aesch. does his best to disguise this humiliating fact.[28]

Besides these passages in which Aeschylus glosses over the fact that the Ionians fought on the Persian side against their kinsmen on the mainland, or implies the enforced nature of their service in Xerxes' navy, there are several places in the closing sections of the play where he makes use of ambiguous terminology to achieve this same effect of obscuring the true Ionian role. For Herodotus, the term "Ionia" is almost always used to denote the Greek settlement on the southwestern coast of Asia Minor and the offshore islands, while he uses "Hellene" to describe an inhabitant of the mainland. This distinction Aeschylus for the most part preserves. But at the beginning of the epode of the stasimon discussed above, immediately after the list of Greek islands, the chorus remarks, "even over the wealthy populous <cities> of Hellenes throughout the Ionian land [Darius] held sway by force of will" (897–901). Broadhead remarks that elsewhere in the play "Hellenes" refers to mainland Greeks; he suggests that its use here of the Ionians "may be taken to imply that the cause of the Ionian colonists of Asia Minor was regarded by the poet as identical with that of the mainland Greeks." The converse change occurs at lines 1011 ff., where the tattered Xerxes laments the defeat of his men, "who met—not happily—Ionian sailors." At 1025 he comments, "the Ionian folk are not deserters." "Ionian" was one of the labels by which the Athenians were sometimes called, after Ion, the son of Xuthus,[29] and may be explained as simply a poetic variant for "Athenian." But at a deeper level "the Ionian folk don't turn their backs" seems to be part of the same complex attempt of the poet to absolve the Ionians of responsibility for having fought on Xerxes' side; in using this ambiguous term, he associates, at least by name, the "real" Ionians with the victory which belonged particularly to Athens.

What connection does all this have with Themistocles? It will be remembered that among the events which occurred after the battle of Artemisium, Herodotus describes an attempt of Themistocles to secure the defection of the Ionian contingent from Xerxes' forces. "Themistocles took it into his head that, if the Ionian and Carian division could be broken away from the Barbarian, [the Greeks] might be able to win superiority over the rest" (8.19). When the news of Leonidas' disaster at Thermopylae came to the Greeks at Artemisium, the others returned south, led by the Corinthians, but the Athenians lagged behind and Themistocles made his way to the springs of drinking water "and engraved in the rock lines which the Ionians read when they came to Artemisium on the following day. . . . 'Men of Ionia, in fighting against your forefathers and attempting to enslave Hellas, you act unjustly. [Either join us or withdraw from the battle.] But if neither of these is possible, and Necessity's yoke is too heavy for you to withdraw, fight halfheartedly in the action when we cross arms, and remember that you are our descendants and that right in the beginning your hostility towards the Barbarians spread to us'" (8.22). The terminology is reminiscent of the excuse Aeschylus seems to be making in the *Persians*: "Persia's yoke on Ionia was too heavy for them to withdraw." And well might Themistocles remind the Ionians of Athenian support for their earlier attempt to revolt from Persia, for he seems to have been the leading proponent of Athenian assistance to the Ionians even after this policy had become unpopular. The "kinship" between Attica and Ionia became the subject of intense interest later in the century, when Athens was eager to foster solidarity within her empire,[30] but it is possible that the traditional links between Athens and Ionia may have been emphasized for propaganda value as early as the beginning of the century. Herodotus reports that when the allied Greek fleet sailed to Samos after Mycale and the Spartans proposed deporting the Medizing states in mainland Greece and settling the Ionians there, the Athenians did not think it right that "the Ionian empire be disrupted nor that the Peloponnesians make proposals about their (that is, the Athenians') colonists" (9.106.3). The tragedian Phrynichus was fined for portraying *oikêia kaka* in "The Capture of Miletus," probably, as we saw above, in the year of Themistocles' archonship. It is altogether likely that Athens' responsibility for Ionia's safety was a part of Themistocles' program of resistance to Persia, and that, as How and Wells comment, Phrynichus' play "may have contained reproaches of Athens for the desertion of Miletus . . . and have been intended to awaken the national spirit and inspire resistance to Persia, perhaps by sea, since Themistocles, choregus for Phrynichus in 476 B.C. (Plut. *Them.* 5) is said to have begun the building of Piraeus as archon in 493 B.C."[31]

Themistocles' attempt to play on the larger loyalties of the Ionians seems to have been only moderately successful at Salamis. Herodotus notes that "only a few of them fought halfheartedly in accord with the behests of Themistocles, but the majority did not" (8.85). But in the course of the battle some Phoenicians who had lost their ships came to Xerxes and accused the Ionians of treason (8.90). This may indicate that the Ionians (on the east wing of the Persian line, according to Herodotus, opposite the Spartans) were behindhand in the fighting or gave way at a crucial point; in other words that they hung back more than Herodotus thought. No credence need be put in Diodorus' story that before the battle the Ionians sent a Samian swimmer across to the Greeks to promise that the Ionians would defect in the course of the fighting (11.17.3), although Herodotus reports that at some unspecified time before the battle four Naxian ships had come over to the Greeks (8.46) and one ship from Tenos during the night before it broke out (8.82).

Themistocles' efforts to pry loose the Ionians achieved their end, if not at Salamis, in the course of the following winter and spring. When the Greek fleet was at Aegina in the early spring of 479, a group of Chian exiles came to them and asked for help in "setting Ionia free." This seems to have been a private enterprise, and did not achieve its purpose immediately, for the Greeks brought them only as far as Delos

(Herodotus 8.132). Another embassy, this time an official one from Samos, came to the fleet while it was at Delos. Their leader, Hegesistratus the son of Aristagoras, promised that "if only the Ionians see you, they will desert the Persians. . . . And calling on common gods, he urged them to free from slavery men who were Hellenes and to repel the Barbarian" (9.90). This promise was kept at Mycale. Before the battle Leutychides, the Spartan commander, appealed to the Ionians in the same tone and with the same purpose (as Herodotus remarks, 9.98.4) as Themistocles had at Artemisium; in the battle itself the other Ionians followed the lead of the Samians and Milesians and either deserted or did what they could to aid the Greek cause (9.103–106). After the battle the Greek fleet held a council at Samos and there "they admitted into alliance the Samians, Chians, Lesbians and other islanders who were fighting on their side, binding them by pledge and oath 'to abide and not to withdraw' " (9.106)—the alliance which was to become the "Delian League."

Like so many of his other policies, Themistocles' advances to Ionia—his support of the Ionian revolt and his attempts to dislodge the Ionians before Salamis—were brought to fruition only by his successors. Of the full-blown "alliance against the Mede," of which the Ionians and islanders were charter members, the first seeds must be sought in Themistocles' efforts, throughout the conflict, to play on the sense of solidarity and identification with mainland Greece which the Ionians had preserved through long decades of Persian domination. By 472 Themistocles' dream had become a reality and the League had won its first successes at Eion, Scyros, and Carystus, and it seems that Aeschylus, by several subtle touches, is reminding the Athenians to what a large extent these were due to the man whose patriotism was now being called into question.

Another theme which runs through the play may also have reminded the audience of Themistocles, but the connection here is more tenuous. As is usual in Aeschylean tragedy, action on the human plane is paralleled by causation on the divine: "When a man himself presses eagerly, God, too, lends a hand" Darius' ghost observes (742). But this theme of divine causality keeps recurring and is given more than usual prominence. Thus, the messenger, before beginning his account of the battle, remarks, "some *daimon* destroyed the army" (345), and he prefaces his report of Themistocles' stratagem with the words

> An avenger or evil *daimon* appeared from somewhere,
> My lady, and began the whole disaster. (353–354)

A few lines later he says that Xerxes responded at once when he heard Themistocles' message "not recognizing the guile of the Greek or the envy of the gods" (361–362). "Thus God gave glory for the naval battle to the Hellenes," he says during his description of the action on Psyttaleia (454–455), and when he has finished, Atossa cries out, "O hateful *daimon*, how truly you cheated the Persians' wits!" (472–473). The chorus echoes the sentiment at 515–516, "O miserable *daimon*, how heavily, too heavily, you leapt on all the Persian race!" When the Queen tells her husband's ghost that their son dared to bridge the Hellespont, and he expresses amazed disbelief, she replies, "It's true; some *daimon*, I suppose, assisted his intent" (724), and Xerxes' first words when he appears are:

> Ah!
> Miserable am I who have obtained
> This hateful lot all unexpectedly;
> With what a savage will the *daimon*
> Trampled on the Persian race. . . . (908–912)

It may be thought that Aeschylus, by emphasizing that the tragedy was due to divine wrath for Xerxes' hybris, thereby diminishes the glory to which the human agent of the victory is entitled. Will a vote for the *daimon* be, in effect, a vote against Themistocles? Not at all, for it is now commonly recognized that when the Greek poets, from Homer on, attribute happenings to the gods, they do not thereby intend to diminish human responsibility. Causality on the divine level is generally paralleled by culpability on the human. Moreover, if we can trust a report in Herodotus, Themistocles himself insisted that it was the gods who brought about Xerxes' downfall. After Salamis, the allied fleet pursued the escaping Persians as far as Andros, but would go no farther. When Themistocles saw that he could not sail to the Helles-pont (so Herodotus tells the story), he spoke privately to the Athenian contingent. Herodotus gives his words at some length, and, in the course of Themistocles' address, we find the following:

> It is not I who have accomplished this, but the gods and heroes who grudged one man to be king of Asia and Europe, an unholy and an impious man at that, who treated sacred and private dwellings in the same way, burning and overturning the gods' images. . . . (8.109.3)

These last words are (as Broadhead notices) very close to Darius' lines in the *Persians:*

> When they came to the land of Hellas the gods' statues
> They did not shame to sack, nor shrink from burning temples;
> Altars were destroyed, and statues of *daimones* pried up
> From their foundations and in confusion overturned.
>
> (809–812)

It is unlikely that Herodotus is here reporting Themistocles' precise words on this very occasion, but it remains possible that he has got hold of so much historical truth: Themistocles may have made a point of transferring responsibility for the victory from himself to the gods and heroes of the Greeks, who laid the Persians low in retribution for their king's impiety. If this were a well-known Themistoclean sentiment, then the theme of "divine cooperation" in the *Persians* might have reminded the audience of him.

The subject of Themistocles' position in the *Persians* cannot be left without a brief mention of the episode of Psyttaleia. The Persian messenger saves it for the climax of his account of the disaster, which will "twice outweigh" what horrors have gone before (437). Those men who were "naturally superior, of outstanding character and conspicuous for noble birth" lost their lives on the island, he says (441–442). He then describes how it happened; beginning with the celebrated passage "there is an island . . ." (447 ff.). The Persians had stationed these men there to save their friends and slay their foes, but when the tide of battle turned in favor of the Greeks, the latter landed a force which encircled the Persians and cut them all to pieces (446–464). In a very short chapter (8.95) Herodotus says that "Aristeides . . . took many of the hoplites who were drawn up along the shore of Salamis— men whose nationality was Athenian—and led them across into Psyttaleia; these slaughtered all the Persians on the island." Now it has been supposed[32] that Aeschylus is here throwing into special prominence an exploit of Aristeides precisely because it was Aristeides', and that he is therefore, so far from reminding his audience of their debt to Themistocles, in reality holding up to popular acclaim his arch-competitor.[33] But several considerations militate against such a view. In the first place, the theory of "Themistocles the Wily vs. Aristeides the Just," with intense and lasting opposition between them, has no factual foundation. It is as old as Herodotus, who never tires of retailing anecdotes to illustrate the hostility between the two men: "There crossed over from Aegina Aristeides son of Lysimachus. . . . He called Themistocles out of the council, although the latter was not his friend but his chiefest enemy . . . and said, 'We must put our strife to good use . . .'" (8.79). The origin of this legend can be traced in part to Herodotus' strong anti-Themistocles bias, probably fostered by his Alcmeonid informants at Athens.[34] The truth of the matter seems to be rather that the disagreement between the two men turned simply on whether Athens was to become a naval power in the 480's,[35] and that their rivalry was buried once and for all when Aristeides returned with the others who had been ostracized in the political amnesty of 481/0. Although Aristeides appears in Herodotus' pages completely unannounced in the passage quoted above,

Bury argued cogently that he must have been recalled and duly elected general—doubtless with Themistocles' blessing —in the spring before Salamis.[36] Certainly, it is highly significant that we find the two men cooperating closely in the winter and spring of 479/8 to put off Sparta until Athens' walls can be rebuilt. Thucydides describes in detail Themistocles' delaying tactics on that occasion; among his colleagues we find "Habronichus son of Lysicles and Aristeides son of Lysimachus" (1.91.3). Gomme's note draws the obvious moral: "It was not necessary to wait for the discovery of Aristotle's Ἀθηναίων Πολιτεία to be sure that the conventional picture of Themistocles, all guile, restless, and democratic, and Aristeides, honest as the day, the dignified conservative (Plutarch's picture), was a false one. They had worked well together, though they may have been rivals."[37] And if it was Themistocles' policy of fortification of the Peiraeus and his foresighted attempt to convince the Athenians that their destiny lay on the sea which set the stage for the later greatness of the Delian League, it was Aristeides who carried out the first tribute assessment and made Athens' new allies swear to uphold the alliance, according to Plutarch (*Aristeides* 25).

We need not suppose, then, that Aristeides contrived the Psyttaleia escapade to outdo Themistocles and that Aeschylus' audience in 472 would have thought of it as precisely Aristeides' *aristeia* as against Themistocles'. Indeed, as the overall plan for the Greek defense at Salamis was Themistocles', that part of it which entailed landing a force on Psyttaleia to face the Persians sequestered there must have been part of his total strategy, even though he entrusted it to his "rival" to carry out.

Nothing has been said of the structure of the play, of the success of Xerxes as a tragic hero, of the strange and moving lamentations which bring the drama to a close. If the battle of Salamis stands at the center of the play, it is only one part of the tragic conception. It is perhaps impossible to establish priority of motives in any work of art, and only the critic who is very sure of himself (or very foolhardy) will assert firmly that the political timeliness of a tribute to Themistocles was the dominant factor which determined Aeschylus to write the *Persians* when and in the form he did. It is sufficient to bear in mind that the tragedy of Xerxes cannot be separated from the victory of Athens, that Athens' victory was due mainly to the near-prophetic foresight and political maneuvering of one man, and that a retelling of the events leading up to the victory would have reminded the Athenians of their debt to him at a time when his enemies were calling his loyalty into question and threatening ostracism or worse. In light of this, it would take an even more self-assured (or foolhardy) critic to maintain that political factors played no part in Aeschylus' motivation in writing the play.

CHAPTER III

Seven Against Thebes

The opening scenes of the *Seven Against Thebes* more than justify Aristophanes' description of the play as a "drama full of Ares" (*Frogs* 1021). Thebes is encircled by the invading Argive host. Eteocles, successor to the throne of Oedipus, appears before his people to bring the city to order and a state of psychological readiness for battle. So far the affairs of war have gone well for Thebes, but now the city must face the greatest challenge of the campaign: "The greatest assaulting force of Achaeans is gathering by night and making plans to attack the city" (28–29).

A scout arrives breathless on the scene. The Argive force has chosen seven warriors to assault each of the seven gates, men even now in the act of dipping their hands in bull's blood, "whose lips spoke not of relenting. Their iron-hearted spirit breathed fiery blasts of manhood, lions with Ares in their looks" (51–53). The tension mounts as the scout pours on gruesome details; Eteocles reacts instinctively to the messenger's news by invoking "Zeus, and Earth, and gods guardians of the city, and the Curse, mighty Erinys of my father" to defend the city and preserve it from annihilation.

Before the balanced measures of the *parodos,* proper, various members of the chorus, young Theban women, utter some twenty-five lines of frenzied dochmiacs, presumably rushing to and fro wildly in the orchestra as they sing. In these and the strophes which follow the frightening details are put on in layer after layer, to achieve the total impression of a city caught in war panic, men and women to whom everything seems hopeless; for such as these there is nothing left but to throw themselves down before the shrines and statues of the gods and pray for a miracle. For the space of some one hundred lines, in a stark antiphony of contrast, the poet plays the grim details of war and the girls' mounting fright against their more and more desperate invocations of all the gods they can think of to save them from disaster.

A desperate situation requires drastic measures. Eteocles reappears and attempts to quiet the Theban women and bring a measure of good sense and forethought to the city's defense. A surprising harshness marks the character of the young king, but it is perhaps justified by his motive: he fears that the frenzy of the chorus may infect the rest of the citizens and sink them so deep in despair that they will take no thought of practical means of defense. Eteocles enforces his strictures with a severe reassertion of his authority: if anyone refuses to obey his call to order, he will be executed.

Nothing is settled by the elaborately stylized choral exchange which follows (203–244), and in the stichomythia (245 ff.) the chorus keeps returning to the same themes—I hear the snorts of horses; the city moans to its foundations; the clatter at the gates increases; O assembly of gods, don't betray the city, don't let slavery befall me. Interspersed between the chorus' fear-ridden outbursts are Eteocles' angry attempts to silence the women and restore order—Is it not sufficient that I have taken thought of this matter? No, not *brought* to slavery; you'll bring it on yourselves and on the city. To their anguished prayer to Zeus he retorts sardonically: "O Zeus, what a tribe you've given us in women." Finally, he asks in an acid tone that they grant him a "small favor." "Tell us what it is." "Be silent, don't frighten our own men." And they finally acquiesce: "I am still. With the rest I shall suffer what fate has in store."

The tension is relaxed. The women accept the command of Eteocles, who has tried several means of bringing them to order, from a reasoned explanation that he is in charge and has things under control, to an imperious demand for silence and sarcastic invective. There is very little development in the scene; Eteocles' first words, like his last, are a harsh rebuke of the women's frenzied indiscipline. Instead of progression of plot, the poet gives us a striking exemplification of the psychology of panic, the way in which a distraught mob is quieted and brought to its senses at one point, only to have frenzy break out again at another and require yet another appeal for calmness and good sense. The impact of the scene is achieved mainly through its tripartite structure: the direct address of Eteocles culminating in his threat of execution, followed by the stylized formality of the lyrical exchange of 203–244, and finally the rapid stichomythia which ends in the chorus' promise to be silent. The scene closes as it began, with a speech of Eteocles in which he approves of the women's acquiescence, solemnly vows to dedicate spoil to the gods in the event of victory, and states his intention of choosing seven defenders, including himself, to match the seven Argive attackers. The stasimon which follows consists of a calmer, more moderate prayer to the gods, and a long, exquisitely moving evocation of the ills which befall a captured city and the pathetic sufferings of its captive inhabitants.

Aristophanes has Aeschylus say about his play that "every man in the audience would have longed to be a fighter" (*Frogs* 1022), but this need not be taken seriously either as a sober evaluation of the *Seven* or as an explanation of why Aeschylus wrote it. According to the Hypothesis, the play was produced in 468/7, and so far from being under siege, Athens was riding the crest of success. In the preceding decade she had taken the offensive in external affairs, capturing Eion on the Strymon and the island of Scyros, and waging a successful campaign against the Carystians.[1] A likelier explanation of Aristophanes' comment is that he has been influenced by the condition of Athens in his own day. When the *Frogs* was produced in 405 the Peloponnesian War had been drawn out for some twenty-five years; able-bodied citizens who would already have been discouraged by the bleak pointlessness of it might well have been even more hesitant to fight after the scandal of the execution of the generals after the battle of Arginusae the year before. What better credentials could be offered by the poet who, at the end of the Aristophanic fantasy, was to return to Athens to "save our city with good counsels and teach the ignorant" (*Frogs* 1501–1503) than a "drama full of Ares, whose every viewer would have longed to go to war"?

It seems likely that Aeschylus has achieved the realistic tone of the terror and irresolution which affect a city under siege by a personal reminiscence of the siege of Athens in 480. Tucker in his edition of the play[2] noted that in the mournful picture of a city burnt by its besiegers (lines 340 ff.) "the allusion to the burning of Athens by the Persians is unmistakable." J. T. Sheppard detected further echoes of the Persian siege. "Words and phrases like ἑτεροθρόῳ, φθόγγον Ἑλλάδος, βάρβαρον τρόπον are alive, and suggest no thoughts of ethnology to an audience which remembers the burning of Athens by the Persians."[3] The lines in the play to which Sheppard is apparently referring are the prayer of the chorus in the *parodos* to the gods and goddesses who guard the walls "not to betray the city to an army which speaks a foreign tongue" (169–170). It looks as if Aeschylus were distinguishing the language of the Argives from that of Thebes, which Eteocles refers to as "pouring forth the speech of Hellas" (72–73). Sheppard's point is that Aeschylus, so far from putting forward a recondite theory of racial or linguistic difference between Thebes and Argos in prehistoric times, has simply allowed his contemporary model for the Argive force to show through, and Rose approves of this theory: "The difference between invaders and invaded was but one of dialect, Boiotian as against Doric, but the emphasis on it [at lines 169–170] and the mention of the Greek speech of Thebes, *supr.* 72, incline me to agree with [Sheppard] that Aesch. is thinking of Athens and the Persians not 15 years earlier."[4] Sheppard believes that there are further Persian influences on Aeschylus' portrayal of the Argive siege force, but the evidence he adduces is less convincing.[5]

We may agree that the situation has a general historical analogue in conditions in Athens during the Persian siege of 480, but what of the characters? Is there anyone in the *Seven* whom Aeschylus may have drawn from life? The only serious attempt of any length to discover such a parallel is L. A. Post's article "The Seven Against Thebes as Propaganda for Pericles."[6] Post puts forward the view that "The Seven Against Thebes emphasizes the moral that a man under a curse may by unusual ability and utmost devotion save his city from destruction even though the curse falls upon him personally. The moral . . . is particularly applicable to the case of Pericles as he was situated when the play was first produced in 467 B.C." Post begins by pointing out that Pericles had acted as choregus for Aeschylus, almost certainly for the *Persians* in 472. He further takes the story in Plutarch (*Cimon* 8.7–8) of Cimon's decision in favor of Sophocles at the Dionysia of 468 as indicating a personal relationship between them and infers an equally close personal tie between their respective rivals, Pericles and Aeschylus. Toward the end of his paper he expands his argument to include Aeschylus' full-blown support of Pericles in 467 partly out of pique for his defeat at Cimon's hands the year before. "Aeschylus fought in battle, why not in the political arena?" Post asks.

"When Pericles made his bid for power, not long before 467, as nearly as we can judge, his opponents had at command an appeal to prejudice that they almost certainly used, the argument that Pericles shared the curse of the Alcmaeonidae, and that it would not be safe for the city to employ him as leader."[7] Pericles' mother Agariste was a niece of the famous Alcmeonid legislator, Cleisthenes, and, in the welter of real and pretended grievances voiced by both sides before the outbreak of the Peloponnesian War, the Spartans could, with some plausibility, demand that the Athenians "drive out the curse of the Goddess," that is, expel Pericles for his connection with the accursed Alcmeonid family.[8] Post maintains that Pericles' enemies made political capital of his Alcmeonid connection at the very beginning of his career and that it was partly to counter such an attack that Aeschylus wrote the *Seven*. "Aeschylus' portrait of Eteocles, who died in accordance with a curse, but neither wavered in his duty nor failed to protect his city, was bound to create a sentiment unfavorable to superstition and in so far helpful to Pericles."

To say that Aeschylus supported Pericles simply by "creating a sentiment unfavorable to superstition" is innocuous enough, but Post goes further and posits a real identity between Eteocles in the play and the real-life Pericles. "To make the audience see in Eteocles a prototype of Pericles the coincidence that both belonged to families that were under a curse was perhaps enough. The similarity of names would also help in the matter of identification. Nor is it merely fanciful to compare the lofty austerity of Pericles, as described by Plutarch, with the austerity and Olympic thunders of Eteocles as seen in Aeschylus' play."

Post's whole attempt to see Eteocles as "representing" Pericles rests on a fundamental error: he has oversimplified the relation between Eteocles and the curse of Oedipus, and has thereby been led to misinterpret the effect of the curse on Eteocles' decision to defend Thebes. Post himself sees that one interpretation, what he calls the "current view" and for which he cites Gilbert Murray, would make his theory untenable: it is plainly impossible to see Pericles masquerading in the disguise of "a desperate man, overmastered by the Curse."[9] On the contrary, the identity between Eteocles and Pericles and the purported propaganda value of the play depend entirely on the view that Eteocles defends the city *in spite of* the Curse: ". . . the moral that a man under a curse may by unusual ability and utmost devotion save his city from destruction *even though the curse falls upon him personally*"; ". . . died in accordance with a curse, but neither wavered in his duty nor failed to protect his city"; "Eteocles is nowhere represented as lacking in personal prowess or impaired in wisdom or patriotism because of his doom." Thus, Post sees Eteocles as an example of "the supreme self-sacrifice of a patriot," the corollary of which is that "in the *Seven* the curse is kept in the background. . . ." But this is simply untrue. On the contrary, the *Ara* and Erinys to whom Eteocles prays, but only partially understands, at line 70, are seen in the end to be completely efficacious: "Now do my father's curses bring fulfillment" he cries at the moment of awareness (655). So far from a play whose hero goes to his death in spite of a curse, or with the curse in the background, what we really have is one whose hero dies—partially, at least—because of one.

Further to enhance his identification of Pericles with Eteocles, Post maintains that the *Seven* is "the only extant Greek tragedy in fact that is concerned entirely with the theme of self-devotion." Eteocles is seen not only as the king who fights for his city and dies in the effort, but as one who *by his very death* preserves the city and its inhabitants: "Laius had been ordered by Apollo to die childless and preserve his city. He had not done so; hence it remained for his grandson Eteocles to end the line and simultaneously to secure the ultimate preservation of Thebes. . . . Eteocles . . . in order to save his city, must not only slay his brother but perish himself." We may agree that Eteocles' decision to defend the seventh gate arises naturally and inevitably out of his series of choices of appropriate opponents for each attacking chief, but to say that Eteocles goes to his death partly from motives which are praiseworthy is very far from calling that death "sacrificial," a view which cannot be substantiated from the text. On the contrary, even allowing for a certain amount of conventional opposition between the chorus and protagonist, the women seek to dissuade him from meeting his brother in single combat and make it quite clear that he *need not die* in order to save Thebes: "There are Cadmeian men enough to meet the Argives hand-to-hand" (679–680); "the god will honor even a cowardly (that is, surrogate) victory" (716). The theory that the brothers by their deaths compensated for Laius' disobedience to the oracle and that the extinction of the family would of itself guarantee the safety of the city cannot be maintained in view of the chorus' words at 840 ff.: "It has been fulfilled. The father's accursed prophecy did not relent. . . . The disobedient will of Laius endured. But I have a care for the city: the edge of oracles is not blunted. . . ." Far from praising Eteocles for his self-sacrifice, they talk of the brothers' "impious intent" (831) and at 881–882 they are called "overthrowers of the house's walls." As much as we may sympathize with, and even admire, Eteocles' determination to fight for Thebes, Post's view that the *Seven* is "concerned entirely with the theme of self-devotion" must be judged to be seriously one-sided.

We may indeed ask ourselves whether this Eteocles is the sort of man who could stand as a vehicle of propaganda in support of *any* contemporary politician. From an examination of Eteocles' exchanges with the chorus and his own remarks about the gods it can be argued that he manifests a strong pragmatic and even atheistic streak, a serious one-sidedness of view which makes him entirely unsuitable as a stage representative for some real person whom the poet wanted to present to the acclamation of his audience.[10]

Another consideration damaging to any theory of the *Seven* as propaganda for Pericles is the complete absence of evidence that his political career had already begun at the time of the play. We do know that he was choregus for the *Persians* in 472, but he need not have been older than eighteen at the time, as Domaszewski points out.[11] His first attested appearance on the political scene was in 463, as one of the accusers of Cimon in his prosecution for failure to attack Macedonia at the time of the campaign against Thasos.[12] Post's contention that "Pericles was, in 467, just at the point of making his original bid for leadership" is based on a schematized "succession" of political leaders in Plutarch and the *Athênaiôn Politeia:* with Themistocles gone and Cimon away campaigning, Pericles had the local scene all to himself.[13] The generally accepted view is that Pericles was born after 495;[14] it would be very odd for someone under thirty to be "making a bid for leadership" and even as late as the Reforms of 462 Pericles' name remains studiously in the background. It turns out that Post's strongest argument for an emergence of Pericles as early as 467 is a circular one: the putative "propaganda" of the *Seven* requires such a view.

Any view which sees "behind" Eteocles a real character is completely untenable. But what of the other characters? May not Aeschylus be alluding to a real person elsewhere in the play? The messenger's account of the first five Argive attackers gives an overwhelming impression of blasphemous arrogance. Tydeus' full moon and stars the messenger describes as an "arrogant device" (387); Capaneus' boast that he would sack the city "whether God willed or no" and that not even Zeus' *Eris* would hold him back (425–429) is more than human. On Eteocles' shield a man with a scaling ladder approaches the walls boasting that not even Ares will dislodge him. Hippomedon's shield is a very complicated affair, a figure of Typhos apparently fastened by an overplate of coiled snakes running around the rim, and its bearer's shouts and Bacchante-like actions show a fierceness to match. Parthenopaeus at the fifth gate "swears that he trusts and reverences the shield he carries more than God and his sight, and that he will sack the city of the Cadmaeans in spite of Zeus" (529–532). On his shield there stands a figure which offers the supreme insult to Thebes, a movable Sphinx with one of the Cadmeians in its jaws.

Aeschylus has taken great pains to draw a composite picture of the insolence and overweening threats of the Argive invaders in vivid, almost frightening, detail. As the messenger catalogues each of the assailants, Eteocles matches against him a Theban defender whose shield device or some other characteristic makes him an appropriate opponent, but who will act as the Argive's very opposite in justice and moderation. But at the sixth gate all is changed. There stands Amphiaraus the seer, "a man most moderate and best in strength" (568–569). So far from hurling an insolent threat at Thebes, he bitterly reproaches Tydeus, one of the Argive attackers, calling him "teacher of evil to Argos, summoner of the Erinys, minister of death, a whole council-chamber of bad advice for Adrastus" (573–575). Amphiaraus' scourge strikes not only Tydeus, but also Polyneices; the messenger reports the seer's charge against the latter of impiously attacking his own fatherland with a foreign armament. "How can your fatherland," asks Amphiaraus, "possibly be your ally if you capture it with your frenzied spear?" (585–586)—a clear echo of Eteocles' reminder to the Thebans of the debt they owe to their Mother Earth. His shield has no device, the messenger says, and then offers an extended tribute to the *sôphrosynê* of the Argive prophet:

> He wants not to seem best, but to be,
> Reaping the fruit of deep-furrowed thought
> From which noble purposes grow.   (592–594)

Eteocles responds with a prolonged general disquisition on the inequity of a good man who suffers misfortune because of involvement with evil company. "In every transaction there is no greater evil than evil companionship, an intolerable harvest. . . ." (599–600). He illustrates his point with the homely example of a pious man who goes on board a ship full of cutthroats and perishes with the god-forsaken crew. He then uses a political example:

> or a just man, with fellow citizens
> themselves inhospitable, forgetful of the Gods,
> has fallen into the same snare as the unrighteous,
> and smitten by the common scourge of God
> has yielded up his life. (605–608, trans. Grene)

As if this were not enough, he goes on to call Amphiaraus

> wise, just, good, and holy,
> a prophet mighty, mingling with the impious—
> against his better reason—with loud-mouthed
> men who pursue a road long to retrace,
> with God's will shall be dragged to their general doom.
>   (610–614, trans. Grene)

Eteocles expresses confidence that Amphiaraus will not even attack the gates (not from cowardice, he is quick to add, but in fulfillment of an oracle).

It is at once apparent that Eteocles here goes out of his way to praise Amphiaraus far in excess of what would be required to achieve the dramatic contrast of making the insolence of five boastful Argives appear the greater by juxtapo-

sing to them one just man. It is odd enough that the Theban
king should praise one whose presence threatened the safety of
Thebes, but the extravagance of the praise which he lavishes
on Amphiaraus' moderation, wisdom, and godliness, and the
care he takes to absolve Amphiaraus of any blame for taking
part in the expedition by descanting on the evil of an honest
man fallen in with scoundrels, must have led the audience to
wonder whether there was not more here than met the ear.
Indeed, this seems to have been the case. Plutarch, toward
the end of chapter three of his *Life of Aristeides*, is praising
his subject's moderation:

> He was not unduly lifted up by his honors, and faced adversity
> with a calm gentleness, while in all cases alike he considered
> it his duty to give his services to his country freely and without
> any reward, either in money, or, what meant far more, in repu-
> tation. And so it befell, as the story goes, that when the verses
> composed by Aeschylus upon Amphiaraus were recited in the
> theater [there follows a citation of lines 592–4 of *Seven*, with
> *dikaios* substituted for *aristos* in line 592] all the spectators
> turned their eyes on Aristeides, feeling that he, above all men,
> was possessed of such excellence.[15]

How far can Plutarch's story be trusted? Was there a stir in
the theater when these lines were declaimed in the spring of
467, and, if so, did Aeschylus intend them to have an extra-
dramatic reference to Aristeides?

Before an answer can be attempted, it must be determined how far Aeschylus went out of his way to bring the
figure of Amphiaraus into prominence. It seems possible that
Aeschylus, in molding the epic and legendary material at his
disposal, put greater emphasis on the individual Argive chieftains than he had found in his "sources" and even did something to adjust their number to the traditional number of
Thebes' seven gates. Pausanias remarks that "Aeschylus had
reduced the Argive heroes to the number of seven only, although there were more chiefs than this in the expedition,
from Argos, from Messene, with some even from Arcadia"
(2.20.5). This testimony of Pausanias is usually contradicted

on grounds that Pindar's *Sixth Olympian*, which must be earlier than the *Seven*,[16] mentions seven funeral pyres, and that Aeschylus himself notes the presence of other Argive warriors, chief among them being Adrastus. Amphiaraus' place among the attackers (albeit unwilling) is assured by the epic tradition; there was a Homeric *Amphiarai Exelasis*, and he must have figured prominently in the Cyclic *Thebais*.[17] But that Amphiaraus was brought to the fore as one of the attackers of the seven gates in the legend before Aeschylus is a gratuitous supposition. As Legras remarks: "One can very well suppose that the differences, often pointed out, between the dramatic poets and the mythographers in the matter of the chieftains' names come precisely from the fact that each one chose rather at random from among the names with which the epic provided him."[18] It is, then, at least arguable that Aeschylus was the first to place Amphiaraus among the seven attackers of the gates, and some slight confirmation of this may perhaps be found in the fact that for Pindar, Amphiaraus, while accompanying the expedition, seems not to have been one of the Seven. At *Olympian* 6.15 there is mention of seven funeral pyres and yet Amphiaraus, who was swallowed alive by the earth, chariot and all, cannot have found a place on any of these.

However that may be, it is clear that Aeschylus goes out of his way to emphasize Amphiaraus' justice and places him in a climactic position at the sixth gate, the next before Polyneices. We may believe that Amphiaraus provides a needed contrast to the impiety of the other attackers, but the excessive length of the reflections which Amphiaraus' character prompts may be thought to indicate a contemporary reference. On the hypothesis that Aeschylus had Aristeides in mind it remains to discover the political context into which the audience would have fitted the lines.

The end of Aristeides' career was, according to Plutarch, shrouded in mystery, but one of the accounts he gives may shed some light on the problem. Plutarch ascribes the following account to the Macedonian historian Craterus:

After the exile of Themistocles . . . the people waxed wanton, as it were, and produced a great crop of sycophants, who hounded down the noblest and most influential men, and subjected them to the malice of the multitude, now exalted with its prosperity and power. Among these Craterus says that Aristides also was convicted of bribery, on prosecution of Diophantus of the deme Amphitrope, for having taken money from the Ionians when he was regulating the tributes; and, further, that being unable to pay the judgment, which was fifty *minae*, he sailed away and died somewhere in Ionia.[19]

Plutarch himself is skeptical of Craterus' story, for, as he notes, "Craterus furnishes no documentary proof of this—no judgment of the court, no decree of indictment,—although he is wont to record such things with all due fulness, and to adduce his authorities." This skepticism has continued to modern times.[20]

If the story were true, the chronological indications would fit together most strikingly: Themistocles was exiled some time after 471 and the spate of accusations which Craterus says followed his exile might well have culminated in charges against Aristeides in 468/7.[21] Aeschylus might then have inserted in his *Seven Against Thebes* a gratuitous reference to a just man unjustly hunted down and destroyed because of his association with "citizens who took no thought of strangers and unmindful of the gods" (605–606), "a modest, just, good, and pious man . . . mixed up with unholy men of boastful speech against his will" and so dragged down (610 ff.). If Aristeides were about to stand trial for alleged injustices concerning the collection of tribute, there would be a special point to Plutarch's story that when the audience heard the line, "he wishes not to seem just but to be," every eye in the theater was on Aristeides.[22]

Although it is not impossible to believe that Aeschylus threw some dramatic support to Aristeides, the man so temperamentally different from Themistocles yet who had worked closely with him at the time of Salamis and afterward, when the two had cooperated in taking the lead away from Sparta

and had laid the foundations for Athens' later greatness in the
Delian League,[23] it must be admitted that the evidence for a
reference to Aristeides in the play does not inspire confidence.[24]
Even if there were such a reference, and it had been intended
by Aeschylus, it must be emphasized that this would in no
sense have formed a major element either in Aeschylus' dramatic conception or in the play's effect on the audience. At
best it would have been a parergon, a political footnote to a
work whose main impact would have been almost entirely
dramatic. And, of course, a possible reference to Aristeides
does not involve the idle task of trying to guess the identity
of other figures in an alleged political masquerade.[25]

There remains to consider a completely different view of
the historical significance of the play. Tucker, in the introduction to his edition, put forward the theory that Aeschylus in the
Seven was speaking out "in behalf of a debated public policy,
or one which at least required the spur. This was a policy
initiated by Themistocles, continued by Cimon, and accomplished by Pericles; namely, the policy of fortifying Athens
with such completeness that it might henceforth be secure
against assault, whether from barbarian or from hostile
Greek."[26] Tucker cites as evidence Chapter 13 of Plutarch's *Life
of Cimon*, where we are told that "by the sale of the captured
spoil [from the Eurymedon victory] the *demos* was financially
strengthened for other expenditures, and it built the south wall
of the Acropolis with its new affluence from that expedition."
In Tucker's opinion "it is manifest that for some time before
and after the production of the *Septem* the question of the
nature and extent of the fortifications of Athens was one of
chief public prominence. . . . In the *Septem* Aeschylus is in-
dubitably lending his aid to the formation of public opinion
in support of the Cimonian policy of fortification" (xliv–xlv).
But Tucker has exaggerated the importance of Cimon's wall
both as a means of fortifying Athens and as a political issue.[27]
There is no evidence that it was a question on which Athenians
were divided, as Tucker supposes. Plutarch's implication is that
it was only lack of funds which had prevented the building,

not party strife. And it is highly misleading to speak of the "Cimonian policy of fortification." For the great wall-builder was Themistocles. He had begun the Peiraeus walls in his year as archon, and had persuaded the Athenians to complete them after the Persians had departed, according to Thucydides (1.93.3 ff.). The historian further recounts at length the ruse Themistocles had used to secure rebuilding of the city walls in the face of intense Spartan opposition (1.89.3–93.2). If there is any truth in the story of the Eurymedon spoils, it indicates rather that Cimon's victory provided the money necessary to continue the Themistoclean policy and any emphasis on the walls in the *Seven* would simply serve to remind the Athenians of that policy and of its author's good services to Athens.[28]

CHAPTER IV

Suppliants

The mystery of the date of the *Suppliants* has now been solved.
From Oxyrhynchus Papyrus XX.2256, fragment 3, published in
1952, it appears that Aeschylus won first prize with a tetralogy
consisting of *Suppliants, Egyptians, Danaids*, and the satyr
play *Amymone*, in a year in which Sophocles placed second.[1]
We know that when Sophocles won the prize in competition
with Aeschylus in the archonship of Apsephion, it was his first
venture in play production, for Plutarch says quite clearly:
"Sophocles, who was still a young man, entered his first plays
in the competition" (*Cimon* 8.8). The year of this victory in
the archonship of Apsephion is given by the Parian Marble
(ep. 56) as 468, and the inference is unavoidable that the
competition in which Sophocles was beaten by Aeschylus'
Danaid-tetralogy must be later than 468.

The limits can perhaps be narrowed still further. Lobel,
first editor of the papyrus, attached to the list of plays and
victors a scrap of papyrus with the letters *epiar* . . . Although
it is possible that the line continued *epi archontos* . . . (with
the archon's name), it seems far likelier that after *epi* in the
papyrus an archon's name beginning with AR is to be restored.[2]
Archedemides, archon in 464/3, is the only name to satisfy
the conditions, and so what we seem to have in the papyrus is

evidence that the *Suppliants* was produced in the spring of 463.

This evidence could not go unchallenged, for the received opinion had been that the play was Aeschylus' earliest to survive and that it was a specimen of "archaic" choral tragedy. Large theories had been built on this assumption: not only that the dramatist's style "must have" evolved in a certain way, but that the origins from which drama as we know it sprang could be discovered by a simple process of extrapolation. One had only to work backward from the *Suppliants*, reduce the actors' importance and emphasize the chorus', and bring the action to an almost complete standstill, in order to arrive quite automatically at a true picture of "primitive" drama. Such a picture may still be true, but the *Suppliants* can no longer be used to prove it. To argue that Aeschylus "reverted" to an earlier technique is still possible, but only at the cost of disturbing the neat "evolutionary" theory of Aeschylus' dramatic development.[3]

One consequence of this upheaval has been to throw doubt on the validity of "stylistic" criteria for dating otherwise undateable tragedies. In F. R. Earp's conscientious study of Aeschylus' style[4] the *Suppliants* places "early" in almost all graphs based on the stylistic phenomena which Earp catalogues. But it should have been obvious even before the papyrus was unearthed that any evaluation of such statistics must depend, as in all experiments, on the interpreter and his presuppositions. A play supposed to be "early" will have its status confirmed by a chart of certain stylistic variations; the importance of features which do not provide such confirmation can be devalued. Thus, Earp notes that "in the dialogue of the *Eumenides* . . . the proportion [of compounds] is virtually identical with that of the *Supplices*." He then adds, quite unhesitatingly, "on whatever principle these variations depend, it is clearly not the date."[5] Statistics, like well-behaved children, speak only when spoken to, and rarely tell us what we are not already expecting to hear.

Old myths die hard. Earp reacted to the new dating by

putting forward once again all the "evidence" for an early date: simplicity of plot, dominance of the chorus, alleged awkwardness of the actors, profusion of images, piling up of adjectives, and so on. His appeal is plaintive: "Scholars have hitherto regarded the *Supplices* as the earliest extant play of Aeschylus; if we now consent to put it late it makes all attempts to study literature futile."[6] This is perhaps excessively pessimistic; in any case, there remained a way out: to suppose either that the play was written in the nineties but not produced until thirty years later, or that the didascalia refers to a posthumous second production, perhaps by Aeschylus' son Euphorion.[7] Either of these possibilities seems extremely remote. All the indications of fifth-century practice are that the plays were produced as soon as they were written. As for posthumous production, Lesky notes that in the "Suidas" notice Euphorion himself is described as the winner when he produced his father's plays, while from the papyrus it appears beyond doubt "that Aeschylus and no one else appears as victor. With that is eliminated the possibility that our didaskalia could have referred to a posthumous production."[8]

Not that the papyrus is without difficulties. Aeschylus, first, and then Sophocles; third place seems to be held by a certain "Mesatos," a very shadowy figure indeed. A tragedian by that name, a contemporary of Sophocles, appears in the fourth of the epistles wrongly attributed to Euripides, and the Scholiast V on Aristophanes' *Wasps* 1502 seems to know of him; there is also a possibility that the name is to be restored in line six of the Athenian victors' list.[9] It is less likely that the papyrus is here distinguishing a particular dramatist by referring to him as "the middle one."[10] The tangle of titles at the end of the fragment creates further problems. As it stands we have

$$\delta\epsilon\acute{\upsilon}\tau[\epsilon]\rho[o]_S \ \Sigma o\phi o\kappa\lambda\hat{\eta}[_S$$
$$M\acute{\epsilon}\sigma\alpha\tau o_S \ [[N \ldots .$$
$$[[B\acute{\alpha}\kappa\chi\alpha\iota_S \ K\omega\phi o\hat{\iota}[_S$$
$$\Pi o\iota]\mu\acute{\epsilon}\sigma\iota\nu \ K\acute{\upsilon}\kappa\lambda[\omega\pi\iota$$
$$\sigma\alpha\tau\upsilon\rho\iota\kappa\hat{\omega}$$

with a parenthesis before *N* ... and *Bacchae*, indicating that
the scribe wished to delete these titles. Lobel pointed out that
Kôphoi and *Poimenes* were "uniquely Sophoclean" titles, the
remainder not Sophoclean at all; and there is some doubt
whether the scribe meant to cancel all the titles in the two
lines, or simply those immediately following the parenthesis.
Whatever the true solution to this puzzle, scribal errors here
and elsewhere in the didascaliai do not impugn the authority
of their Alexandrian sources in matters of fact.

Not all critics have been satisfied with the stylistic arguments. Kitto, for one, although he believed that the *Suppliants*
was Aeschylus' first surviving play, remarked: "If the *Persae*
were our earliest surviving play, who would believe that a play
twenty years older had displayed the purely dramatic assurance that the *Supplices* does? The whole middle part of the
Supplices is, from the dramatic point of view, incomparably
more mature and confident than the *Persae*. . . ."[11] Two earlier
voices crying in the wilderness were those of Walter Nestle
and, before him, Wecklein, who both dated the play to the
mid-460's on purely stylistic grounds.[12]

The plot can be briefly summarized. The fifty daughters
of Danaus are fleeing from their cousins, the fifty sons of
Aegyptus, who want to force the women into marriage against
their will. They arrive in Argos and ask the king for protection
on grounds of descent from Io, whom Hera had driven into
Egypt in anger at Io's liaison, while in the form of a heifer,
with Zeus Taurios. King Pelasgus consults his people, and they
agree to accept the Danaids as suppliants. The Aegyptiads
arrive at Argos in hot pursuit and dispatch a herald who
attempts (in a wild and much-mutilated scene) to drag the
women away. The king interferes and the play closes with
forebodings of evil to come. We are left in the tantalizing
position of not knowing how Aeschylus concluded the story
in the two lost plays of the trilogy, the *Aegyptiads* and the
Danaids.[13]

The *Suppliants* is in many ways a strange play, but one
theme in particular stands out for its oddness. Even a cursory
reading shows that Argos is not the usual absolute monarchy

one would have expected in the twilight of mythical prehistory. Pelasgus, the king of Argos, arrives on the scene and the suppliants ask him who he is—a private citizen, sacred wand-carrier, or leader of the city (248); he obviously wears no distinguishing marks of office and comes unescorted. He, in turn, a few lines later, asks them who they are: "Be brief," he bids them, confirming Danaus' earlier warning that the Argives dislike a "dragging" speech (200–201), "our *polis* does not like long discourse" (273). When they have made their petition that Argos accept their supplication and defend them from their cousins, the king's first worry is that compliance with their request may embroil the city in war. "The *polis*," he adds wryly, "has no need of *that*" (357–358).

> You are not suppliants at my own hearth;
> If the city in common incurs pollution,
> In common let the people work a cure.
> But I would make no promises until
> I share with all the citizens. . . .   (365–369)

It is indeed an unusual place, this prehistoric Argos, where the king will not act without consulting the citizens. The women at once point out that he need not consult the Argive assembly, he is the state: "You are, yes, the city, the people . . .

> A prince subject to no judge,
> You rule the city's altar and hearth;
> With single vote and nod of your head,
> With single scepter enthroned you fill
> Every need. . . .   (370–375)

The king does not—it is important to note—deny his absolute power; a single phrase would have been sufficient: "I *cannot* act without the people. . . ." But he sees danger in aiding these suppliants, for their eager cousins are not far behind. "Without harm I cannot aid you . . . I am at a loss and fearful is my heart. . . ." (379–380). He plays for time; there must be some law in Egypt to provide for a situation like this. No, they will have none of it: "Choose the side of the gods," they bid. "The choice is not easy; choose me not as judge. I said before that never would I act alone, apart from the people, though I am ruler . . ." (397–399) and then, in a fine Aeschylean image:

> We need profound, preserving care
> To plunge down deep like a diver,
> Keen-visioned, unblurred with wine,
> That all might be without harm, first
>   for the city. . . .
>   (407–410)

They press their appeal once more in a choral lyric, increasing the tension they—and we—feel over the king's choice, and once more underlining the reality of the situation, "O you who have full power in the land . . ." (424–425). There is another exchange in which the Danaids play their trump card, not directly, but with grim coyness letting him draw it out: I have bands and halters, fastenings for my robes—right and fitting for women, too, he says—from these know what a clever scheme—go on, get to the end of your speech (we remember Danaus' warning against prolixity and the king's confirmation of it earlier)—if you don't give trusty assurance to our band— what scheme with your attire?—to decorate these statues with new votive offerings—riddles! speak simply—to hang ourselves from these gods with all haste . . . "I have heard a word which scourges my heart!" (466). The king then delivers an anguished soliloquy which he opens with a splendid composite figure:

> Ah!
> These troubles are many and hard to wrestle with,
> A throng of ills has come on like a river,
> This bottomless sea of ruin, not very easy to cross,
> Have I stepped in, and nowhere a harbor from ill. . . .
>   (468–471)

He then voices his dilemma: to deny their prayer, thus offending Zeus Protector of Suppliants, not to mention the sacrilege of their suicide to which he will contribute, or risk bringing war on Argos? He finally decides to support their cause before an assembly of the Argives, but before going off to summon the citizens, he tells Danaus to take from his daughters their boughs and places them on the altars of the common gods of Argos, to give the citizens some proof of their request, which may prevent them from reproaching him, for, as he says, "the people are quick to complain against authority" (485), although the Greek phrase could equally well mean "people always grumble against the magistrates." In the king's explanation of his actions at the end of the scene, the *demos* is again prominent: "If someone should see these branches and take pity on them . . . the *demos* would then be better disposed to you" (486–488). "I am going off to call together the inhabitants, in order to make the commons favorably disposed" (520–521). And this all-important place of the Argive *demos* in the working out of the plot is given an even greater prominence in the scene which follows.

In the king's absence the chorus sings a long ode retelling the details of Io's wanderings. Danaus returns with the news: "the people have passed decrees giving full authority" (601). "For which motion," the Danaids ask anxiously, "was there a fuller show of hands?" (604). Translation cannot reproduce the full effect of the constitutional terminology, δήμου δέδοκται παντελῆ ψηφίσματα, and the even more striking juxtaposition δήμου κρατοῦσα χείρ. Danaus then gives a full description of what might be a fifth-century democratic assembly meeting. "It was decreed by the Argives, with no division of opinion, but so that my aged heart grew young again. Their united mass of people shot up their right hands, the air bristled as they ratified the decree, 'for us to dwell as free residents of this land, not subject to the reclamations or rapine of the men, and none of the citizens or foreigners to lay a hand on us; if anyone uses force, whoever of these property-owners does not lend assistance is to be *atimos* by popular vote of exile.' Such was Lord Pelasgus' speech in our behalf, and he made great proclamation of the wrath of Suppliant Zeus. . . . When the Argive people heard this, they ratified this decree completely and spontaneously.[14] The *demos* of the Pelasgians hearkened to the persuasive harangues, but Zeus accomplished the result" (605–624).

The language is distinctly reminiscent of the procedure of a democratic legislative assembly. Pelasgus acts as spokesman—as *proxenos*, almost—for the Danaids, and does not merely coach Danaus on what arguments to use, as he had promised (519). This is perhaps best accounted for by supposing that the dramatist hoped to retain interest in the king as individual tragic agent, an almost hopeless task once the matter had been referred to the assembly of Argos. For as soon as Pelasgus "takes the *demos* into partnership" (to borrow an appropriate phrase from Herodotus), the audience's attention is centered on the people. It is they who listen to the king's case for the women; they respond unhesitatingly, their hands make the air bristle as they give complete and unqualified support to the women's plea. The effect of the short scene is spectacular: here is a people unfavorably disposed to stumbling utterance and long speeches, and they are ready to respond to a brief but persuasive address with equal speed and decisiveness. The women's case is no sooner put before them than they take it up and make it their own. The Argive *koinon* is thereby brought prominently to the fore, and the play sweeps on to the Danaids' prayer for their benefactors which forms the third stasimon.

This great choral hymn is the heart of the play, a benediction for the prosperity of the Argives: may war, civil strife, and plague leave the land unscathed; may the land swell with fruits of all seasons and the flower of youth remain forever fresh; let the altars groan with offerings to the gods; away with disease and let the city be filled with song; the people have "cast a favorable vote" (640) and "may the people's power, which rules the city, preserve its rights in security," τὸ δάμιον, τὸ πτόλιν κρατύνει (698–699).[15]

Other examples of terminology taken directly from fifth-century legal procedure could be cited: τελεία ψῆφος Ἀργείων (739)[16] and δημόπρακτος ἐκ πόλεως μία ψῆφος (942–943),[17] but the point is sufficiently clear. After a nod or two to what the audience's taste for authenticity would have demanded, the king's absolute power, Aeschylus presents to them a state *very like contemporary Athens*, where decisions are taken by a vote of the people sitting in common assembly; the king, in Danaus' account, might almost be said to abdicate, for he shrinks to the position of a *dêmagôgos*, who wins the Argive assembly to his view with a persuasive speech.

Whatever the reasons for allusions to democratic procedure elsewhere in Greek drama, the chord is struck here too insistently, the details elaborated too carefully, for it to be a mere anachronistic slip. The conclusion can hardly be avoided that, whatever Aeschylus may have been doing artistically, he was also, on another plane, holding up for his audience's admiration a democratic Argos, the Argos of his own day; he praised the Argive people for its vote to receive the suppliants; he offered a solemn prayer to call down heaven's protection and continued blessing on the Argive democracy.

It has been necessary to make this point with some emphasis and to support it with a close examination of the text, because this conclusion—that the Argive democracy, proceeding in orderly fashion to reach a unanimous decision in an Athenian-type assembly, is in some sense the subject of the *Suppliants*—is still sometimes denied. Kitto, in his otherwise penetrating analysis of the play, commented that "it is surely false criticism to see here a naive intrusion of contemporary democracy, or some vague laudation of the ways of Argos."[18] The intrusion is not naive but fully intended and deftly worked out once the reality of the king's power has been made clear; and the eighty-five-line prayer for the safety of Argos can hardly be called vague. Kitto rightly emphasizes the agony of the king's dilemma; he is described as "overwhelmed by the situation" and "growing numb with spiritual pain."[19] He argues that Aeschylus brings Pelasgus to the edge of the abyss, where there is only a possibility of a choice between evils, and that this is "the centre of his tragic idea."[20] What Kitto fails to see is that Aeschylus brings him to the edge and then has him back away, for, instead of deciding the matter on his own authority, he refers it to the Argive assembly for a decision. Kitto notices the difficulty but his explanation is weak: "The reference to the people is a means of emphasizing the seriousness of the dilemma."[21] Reference to the people on the contrary dispels the seriousness of the dilemma as far as the king personally is concerned. The dramatist has simply transferred the mind-numbing decision to the Argive *demos; they* must decide, and when they reach a decision, democratically, aware of the price they may have to pay for protecting the Danaids, it is they who gain the glory for a courageous stand. When the chorus comes to utter its prayer, the king is not mentioned once.[22]

It is worth stopping to point out how little the text justifies Kitto's view of Pelasgus as a center of the tragic action. What Kitto's theory calls for is a Pelasgus who, after some weighing of the dangers involved, says: "I will protect you and the *demos* will ratify my vote"—a Pelasgus, in fact, much like Theseus in Euripides' *Suppliants* (346 ff.). What we are given instead is the portrait of a man riddled with indecision. "Hard words you have spoken," he tells the women at 324, after they have made their request. There follows a long interlude in which they sing their pleas for help while he interposes various evasions. We sympathize with his dilemma:

> I am at a loss and fear grips my heart,
> To act or not to act and seize on chance . . .   (379–380)

and again,

> Judgment is not easy to give; choose me not as judge.
> (397)

Now, a certain amount of hesitation is dramatically justifiable as a means of increasing tension to a point where its release with the final choice would be more effective; but what we have is a king paralyzed with indecision. The soliloquy at 407 ff. is magnificent. What we expect after the choral ode is a firm announcement; what we get is further agonizing (438 ff.). The women threaten suicide and there follows another anguished soliloquy (468 ff.). The king tells Danaus to take up the suppliant branches and place them on altars in a more public place, to assist him in winning over public opinion; the lines in which Pelasgus voices his anxiety about what the people will say (483 ff.) hardly strengthen our impression of him as a forceful ruler. Not until line 510 are we given anything like an announcement of the king's intentions: "We shall not surrender you to the ravages of the winged ones." Line 522 sounds strangely weak: "I shall go to arrange these matters." (Contrast the grandeur of Theseus' avowal in *Oedipus at Colonus*, 631 ff.) Aeschylus has tried to have it both ways: he wanted to provide a focus of tragic emotion, a man faced with a terrifying dilemma, and so went part of the way toward delineating the kind of character Kitto would like to see; but in the end the poet's desire to reserve for the Argive *demos* the glory of making the final decision and so breaking the deadlock seriously debilitates Pelasgus as a tragic agent. That Aeschylus was not entirely happy about having the *demos* simply submerge the king is suggested by the fact that it is Pelasgus who finally moves the decree in the Argive assembly (615 ff.), although he had earlier said that he would prompt Danaus on what arguments to use (519). The glory is shared between king and people with more success later in the play when Pelasgus denounces the Egyptian herald forcefully and in authoritative tones, and yet is careful to point out that he is enforcing "a unanimous vote passed by the *demos*" (942–943).

The Argive people officially receive a band of suppliants and undertake to protect them even at the price of bloody war. A striking contemporary parallel of this dramatic situation is not far to seek. Some years before the production of the *Suppliants*, probably in 471,[23] Themistocles had been ostracized and was living at Argos. Some time later the Spartans came to Athens and demanded his condemnation for treason, on grounds that he had collaborated with Pausanias to betray Hellas to Xerxes. The story is told in a laconic chapter of the first book of Thucydides:

> When Pausanias had been convicted of Medism, the Lacedae-monians sent ambassadors to Athens and laid a charge against Themistocles, saying that they had discovered evidence from their examinations of Pausanias, and they demanded that the

Athenians punish Themistocles. The latter were persuaded
(Themistocles had been ostracized and was at that time resid-
ing in Argos, although he made visits to the rest of the
Peloponnese) and they sent with the Lacedaemonians—who
were ready to join in the pursuit—men with orders to bring
him back from wherever they might find him.

But Themistocles learned about this beforehand and fled
from the Peloponnese to Corcyra. . . .   (1.135.2—136.1)

This very spare account may be contrasted with the circumstantial details in Diodorus (11.54,55). There we are told that
the Spartans "accused Themistocles of treason, saying that he
was a very great friend of Pausanias and that an agreement
had been reached between them to betray Hellas to Xerxes.
They also had parleys with Themistocles' enemies (*sc.* at
Athens[24]), inciting them to make an accusation, and they gave
them money. . . ." The Spartans told the Athenians that
Pausanias had tried to inveigle Themistocles into his project
of betraying Greece, but the latter refused to participate and
yet did not divulge Pausanias' offer. "An accusation was lodged
against Themistocles, but on that occasion ($\tau \acute{o} \tau \epsilon$) he was acquitted." His popularity increased after his acquittal, but after-
wards, "some who feared his pre-eminence and others who
grudged him his reputation, forgot his good services and took
steps to humble his strength and his pride." At the beginning
of Chapter 55, Diodorus relates that Themistocles was ostracized and "he fled to Argos, and when the Lacedaemonians
heard of this . . . they again ($\pi \acute{a} \lambda \iota \nu$) sent ambassadors to Athens
to accuse Themistocles of collusion with Pausanias." They pro-
posed, according to Diodorus, that he be tried before a General
Congress of the Hellenes. Diodorus then relates that Themistocles knew he did not stand a chance if he was to be handed
over for trial to the League (presumably the "Hellenic League"
against Persia) because of the members' resentment against
Athens. "And the Spartans had got material for their later
accusation against Themistocles from the latter's own defense
which he had made at Athens. For Themistocles, in defending
himself, admitted that Pausanias had sent him letters asking

him to take a share in the betrayal; he used this as the strongest evidence to argue that Pausanias would not have urged him if he had not refused his request."

Whatever we think of Diodorus' detail of the proposed trial before a Congress of Hellenes or of the soundness of Themistocles' argumentation, his self-defense seems to be an authentic point missed by Thucydides. The account yields several other pieces of information: two Spartan embassies to Athens and two accusations, one before Themistocles' ostracism which resulted in a trial and acquittal, the other after he had been ostracized; and the very interesting indication that the Spartans (whether or not they resorted to bribery) enlisted support among Themistocles' enemies at Athens. In Chapter 56 Diodorus continues with Themistocles' flight from Argos to Admetus.

Plutarch's account contains several details which supplement, and others which differ from, Thucydides and Diodorus. He gives the name of Themistocles' Athenian accuser as "Leobotes, son of Alcmeon," but seems to place Pausanias' approaches to Themistocles *after* the latter's ostracism.[25] As in Thucydides, the Spartans do not lay their charges until after Pausanias' death, using "evidence" they claim to have discovered among his papers. Although the detail of an earlier trial is not mentioned specifically by Plutarch, he seems to imply some such version of the story: "The Lacedaemonians cried him down, and his envious fellow-citizens denounced him, though he was not present to plead his cause, but defended himself in writing, making particular use of earlier accusations brought against him" (23.3, trans. Perrin).

The only other account to add anything of value (if the detail is not simply a conjecture) is Nepos' statement that while he was in Argos he "lived in great honor because of his many gallant deeds (*virtutes*)" (*Them.* 8.2).

Now it is unknown whether, among the one or more embassies which Sparta sent to Athens, attempts were also made to secure his extradition from Argos before his trial at Athens. Thucydides remarks that he was "visiting other parts of the Peloponnese," and, although no ancient authority tells what Themistocles was doing, the almost universal assumption has been that he was organizing opposition to Sparta, with Argos as his base of operations, in the rest of the Peloponnese. We know that Elis and Mantineia were synoecized, and democratic constitutions apparently installed during this period, and it has been customary to see behind these developments the guiding hand of Themistocles.[26] If this is correct, then the Spartans would almost certainly have made some such demand of Argos, and it seems likely that Athens, too, would have brought some pressure to bear to put a stop to Themistocles' vexatious activities. Whether such demands were made or not, it is certain that Argos offered him safe refuge during his exile and a secure base for his operations in the Peloponnese.

Themistocles had sought and obtained asylum in Argos during the period of his ostracism, and he had loyal friends at Argos even after he had fled from there; Thucydides notes that when he arrived in Ephesus, there came to him money which he had deposited for safekeeping from friends in Athens and from Argos (1.137.3). It is remarkable that within a very few years of this sequence of events the Argive *demos* should be brought to the center of dramatic attention at Athens for its willingness to give protection to a band of suppliants, even at the risk of war.[27] Exigencies of the myth? Not at all, for Aeschylus seems to have reworked the mythical story precisely in this particular. "No authority other than Aeschylus speaks of an appeal by Danaus to the Argive king and people for protection and most accounts make no mention of the former king."[28] It seems a plausible inference that Aeschylus, by throwing into high relief the Argive people's heroic reception of the Danaids, was reminding the Athenians of Argos' good services to Themistocles some years before.

Without more detailed and more reliable information about the sequence of events between Themistocles' ostracism and his flight from Argos, we have no way of knowing how close the parallel between Themistocles and the Danaids was.

It seems from Thucydides' account that the final joint Spartan-Athenian delegation, which pursued Themistocles as far as the Molossians, did not stop at Argos first, for Themistocles fled as soon as he had heard of the demand for his condemnation at Athens: προαισθόμενος φεύγει Thucydides says (1.136.1). Even if new evidence were to come to light showing that an earlier demand for his surrender had been made to Argos by either the Spartans or the Athenians, it would be a mistake to suppose that the sons of Aegyptus in the play were intended to "stand for" Themistocles' enemies. Aeschylus was not writing political allegory. On the contrary, the general similarity of situation between Themistocles and the Danaids would have been all that was necessary to remind the audience that Argos had once sheltered Themistocles, as it was now, in the immediacy of the myth, sheltering the Danaids. And it is this very sufficiency and clarity of the general parallel which makes unnecessary any agonizings over how the trilogy developed; once the similarity of situation had lodged itself firmly in the audience's mind, the dramatist was free to develop his mythical plot however he liked, although the political parallel may have been carried further in the second play: the Argives were somehow forced in the sequel to give up the Danaids; may this not be a reflection of the pressure, already applied or shortly expected, on Argos for the surrender of Themistocles?[29]

The general parallel was noticed and underlined forty years ago by Cavaignac. He remarked on the centrality of the Argive reception of the suppliants: "It is not a single episode of the drama, it is the fundamental *datum*. . . . The poet is frankly and without any possible ambiguity giving his approval to the refusal of extradition by the Argives. And this is the natural repercussion of his sympathy for Themistocles."[30] From this parallel, Cavaignac argued that the play must have been produced about 470, shortly after Themistocles' ostracism. It was with considerable satisfaction that he could remark, after the discovery of the papyrus, that his interpretation had been vindicated, even if his date had to be lowered by several years.[31] The importance of the Argos-theme as a link between

Aeschylus and Themistocles was noted by Stoessl[32] and the political implications have been worked out more recently and much more elaborately in an important article by W. G. Forrest.[33] He notes of the *Suppliants* that "its theme is the dilemma of Argos—should she accept a suppliant even at the risk of war? In 470 Argos had been faced with just this dilemma and had answered it, as she does in the play, by accepting the suppliant and by risking war, with Sparta certainly and perhaps, as it then seemed, with Kimonian Athens as well. This, it seems to me, puts it beyond all possible doubt that the *Supplices* was a political play."[34] "The praise of democratic Argos in lines 605–24, which is totally irrelevant in any mythological situation, completely relevant in the sixties of the fifth century, shows us more clearly than anything else the gratitude of Aeschylus and the other radicals to Argos for her acceptance of and support for Themistokles."[35]

It is true that in the play prehistoric Argos turns out to be a very democratic place indeed, a mirror-image of Athens. The irrelevancy, or "anomaly" it might be better to call it, of Pelasgus' absolute power in a state which apparently formulates policy by assembly vote, has, of course, been noticed before. Ehrenberg analyzed fully the "democratic" references in the play, but interpreted them simply as a projection of the contemporary Athenian situation: "We may safely assume that the picture of democracy is strongly influenced by the democracy of contemporary Athens."[36] Following the traditional dating ("as early as the nineties of the fifth century") he used the play as "documentary" evidence that the concept "democracy" was known in Athens at that date. "Aeschylus would hardly have spoken of the δήμου κρατοῦσα χείρ or the δῆμος κρατύνων unless the idea of δημοκρατία had previously taken shape and found expression."[37] Ehrenberg was concerned to show that the concept of democracy was formulated as a direct result of Cleisthenes' reforms, but, in the light of a date in the sixties, this conclusion cannot be accepted. In addition, Ehrenberg was wrong to maintain that the references to the Argive *demos* are simple "accidental" anachronisms, reflecting merely the new Athenian interest in its own democracy. It was argued above that the care with which the dramatist establishes Pelasgus' full power, and the king's deliberate transfer of the matter to the Argive assembly for decision, rule out mere anachronism as an explanation. Reference to the *demos* in the play is managed adroitly, and the resulting central position of the Argive commons in the audience's attention is entirely natural.[38]

For Forrest the prominence of Argos and its democratic assembly in the play is much more significant. In the first place the courage of the Argive *demos* in receiving the suppliants and the gratitude which the Argives incur from their new charges seem to be looking ahead to the alliance which Athens concluded with Argos in 461. Forrest notes that this alliance was the culmination of a long line of rebuffs to Cimon and his pro-Spartan policy by the radical democrats. Cimon's decline had begun in 465 with the Drabescus disaster, and it ended with his ostracism. "In 462 [the democrats] opposed Kimon's proposal to help Sparta, and, since the Argive alliance was concluded soon after Kimon's failure, we may reasonably suppose that it was already being advanced as an alternative. Can we conjecture, on the strength of the *Supplices*, that it was already public democratic policy in 463, or rather in late 464, that the play was planned and written to commend it?"[39] Further, Forrest uses the evidence of the *Suppliants* in his reconstruction of the political vicissitudes of Argos in the first half of the century. These changes are the subject of a brief but well-known chapter of Herodotus (6.83). In a detailed and generally convincing reconstruction of events, Forrest suggests that the *douloi* mentioned by Herodotus are in fact the democrats ("slaves" being a not unlikely political smear). The "sons of the slain" will then represent the aristocrats who regained control of Argos at some unspecified time after 494. According to Herodotus, when the *douloi* were exiled from Argos, they took over Tiryns; after an again unspecified interval they waged war on Argos in an effort to regain control. The expulsion of the *douloi*, in Forrest's view, marks the return to power of the Argive aristocrats, which he dates "c. 468" ("winter 469 or spring 468," p. 232) and which he sees as responsible for Themistocles' flight from Argos:

> One would imagine (Forrest writes) that it would need more than a joint Spartan-Athenian embassy to make [Argos] give up the refugee. Yet, in the event, Themistokles did not even wait to see what this embassy would accomplish. Was Argos no longer reliable? Were Themistokles' friends, the *douloi*, no longer securely in control or had they perhaps already been expelled?[40]

Now it is true that, as Forrest notes, Themistocles did not wait for the joint Spartan-Athenian embassy to come to Argos to arrest him: "Having learned about it in advance (*proaisthomenos*), he fled . . . ," according to Thucydides (1.136.1). But this can be explained as well by Themistocles' realization (he was nothing if not a political realist) that Argos could not withstand a concerted Atheno-Spartan attempt to secure his surrender, as by an antecedent collapse of the Argive democracy.[41] The Corcyreans wasted no time in depositing him on the mainland, and even the distant and independent Molossian dynast seems to have had misgivings. The other evidence Forrest adduces—the Argive dedication of statues of the Epigonoi at Delphi and a new dating of Pindar's tenth *Nemean* for Theaios the Argive—are inconclusive on this point,[42] and his reconstruction of Arcadian politics in the 460's (Argos aiding Tegea against Sparta and Tegea helping Argos against Mycenae while Argos was still controlled by the *douloi;* Argive absence from Dipaea and the war against the *douloi* at Tiryns indicating a restored Argive aristocracy) offers no support for the sequence which puts the flight of Themistocles after, and as a result of, the collapse of democracy at Argos.[43] Forrest's own view of the *Suppliants* as a thanksgiving to Argos for its protection of Themistocles, coupled with the trouble Aeschylus has taken to emphasize the democratic procedures by which the Argives undertook to protect the women, makes it all but inconceivable that it should have been the collapse of democracy in Argos which caused Themistocles to flee. It seems far likelier that he fled, as Thucydides says, because he was forewarned of his impending arrest, and that his flight was a cause of the Argive democracy's collapse, rather than a consequence of it.

Forrest is on firmer ground when he uses the play's support of the Athenian democrats' program of alliance with Argos (which itself suggests a sympathetic democratic government of Argos) to argue that "the Epigonoi had themselves been ejected by winter 464 or at any rate that they had been forced completely to reverse their policy of 469/468."[44]

The hypothesis of Aeschylean support for a proposed alliance with Argos may throw some light on another passage in the play. When Pelasgus arrives and questions the women, they in turn ask him his identity. He replies that he is "Pelasgus, scion of autochthonous Palaecthon, *archêgetês* of this land" (251). The race, he continues, is named after him "Pelasgian," and he then describes the extent of his territory:

> All the land, through which the holy Strymon flows,
> In the direction of the setting sun I rule.
> I claim as my possessions the land of the Perrhaiboi,
> And the region beyond Pindus, near the Paeonians,
> And Dodona's mountains. Only the boundary
> Of the watery sea cuts me short. Over all this extent I rule.
>
> (254–259)

As Rose notes: "It appears that the Pelasgian territory is about co-extensive with historical Greece."[45] Themistocles after his ostracism seems to have been operating out of Argos to organize opposition to Sparta in the Peloponnese. Aeschylus may here be supporting a recent resurgence of Argos' perennial claims to primacy over Sparta and thereby implicitly refuting the latter's boast of Peloponnesian hegemony.[46]

It now seems impossible to deny that the *Suppliants* was written, not as so many scholars had for so long supposed, early in Aeschylus' career, but in the 460's. It is probable, but

by no means certain, that it was produced in the spring of
463, the year of Archedemides. The Argive alliance which was
to be concluded in 461 would already have been in the air;
political feelings must have been running high, for so drastic
a change in Athens' foreign commitments could only have
been brought about against the bitter opposition of the conservatives and their leading spokesman, Cimon. This was the
very time when Sparta needed help to put down the Helot
revolt and sent to Athens for assistance. Cimon championed
Sparta's cause in the Assembly. The words he is alleged to
have used to support his plea have found their way into a
contemporary account: the Athenians were not "to stand by
and watch Sparta lamed and Athens without its yokefellow."[47]
The conservatives were temporarily successful and help was
sent. But the Spartans played right into the hands of their
enemies at Athens, for Cimon and his troops were sent back
in disgrace. This was the chance his opponents had been waiting for: they publicized the dismissal as a blow to Athens'
national prestige, had Cimon ostracized, and concluded an
alliance with Argos before the end of the decade.

Into this arena of controversy Aeschylus stepped squarely
and vigorously with the *Suppliants*. His chorus' eulogies of
Argos and her democracy make it clear what side of the Argos-
Sparta dispute he was on. But more than that, the whole
dramatic situation provides a mythological paradigm of a
recent event: Themistocles' reception by Argos after his ostracism. Thus Aeschylus is seen to be aiming a blow at the conservatives from another direction. Not only does he hold up
Argos for his audience to admire, but an Argos which gives
shelter to a band of fugitives at the risk of great danger to
itself—precisely as it had recently done for Themistocles when
he fell under attack by Cimon and the Spartans. Aeschylus
takes the dramatic opportunity to remind the Athenians—at
this crucial moment—of the good services of Argos to the hero
of the Persian Wars at a time when he was in trouble. The
great hymn to Argos which the suppliants sing after they learn
that the Argive *demos* has voted unanimously to accept their

petition (625 ff.) can be read as a thanksgiving for services rendered to Themistocles, and the play itself as a two-pronged attack on Cimon and the conservatives for their earlier prosecution of Themistocles and for their current support of Argos' traditional enemy.

One point more. In the light of the new dating of the play and its place in the troubled period preceding Ephialtes' reforms, Ehrenberg's thesis can be modified to yield fruitful results. He argued that the democratic terminology in the *Suppliants* reflected a fully developed concept of democracy at Athens, but his date for the development, in the 490's, was too early. The sixties can now be seen to be a much more natural and explicable time for democratic practice, which was introduced with Cleisthenes' reforms and grew strong after the Persian Wars, finally to become conceptualized and formulated in theory. Nor was it an idle exercise in abstract theorizing. It must have served as a useful watchword and rallying cry—for whom else but for Ephialtes and the democratic reformers? Slogans like δήμου κρατοῦσα χείρ and δῆμος κρατύνων were just what was needed to signal the coming of a new era, an end to the aristocratic thought-control (Ephialtes could say) of that reactionary body, the Areopagus, a turning away from Cimon and his Spartan friends, who insulted us at Ithome, to our *real* friends, the Argives, "*democratic* like ourselves."

Allusions to democratic procedure in the *Suppliants* are thus seen to be much more than mere anachronisms. They both reflect the political propaganda of the reformers and by a converse process give that propaganda the powerful support of poetry and myth.

CHAPTER V

Oresteia

i

It is not going too far to say that the major theme of the *Oresteia* is that of *Dikê*, the cosmic principle of order which governs the dealings of gods and mortals and whose dictates man ignores to his cost. "Justice's scales weigh wisdom through suffering" the chorus of the *Agamemnon* warns toward the end of its vast parodos (250–251), and again in the first stasimon: "There is no assistance for the man . . . who kicks *Dikê*'s great altar into the shadow" (381–384). Each of the three plays in its own way exemplifies these propositions; one by one the main characters are shown kicking down Justice's altar, and being made to suffer through to an understanding of the magnitude of their crime.

But there is an ambiguity in the term *dikê* which the dramatist was able to turn to good account. As well as the abstract concept which was later to exercise Plato the term in the plural also denoted the concrete proceedings-at-law to which the Greeks had recourse to obtain justice in their everyday dealings. In precisely this ambiguity Aeschylus found the means of solving the problem he had set himself: the Justice of the gods could only become efficacious for men in this world through the workings of Law. By the end of the trilogy the legal sense predominates as the audience witnesses an actual trial, but insufficient attention has been paid to its importance in the two earlier plays. Eduard Fraenkel noted this when he wrote:

> I should like to lay special emphasis on the importance of the legal procedure, for this aspect, duly recognized in the case of the *Eumenides*, has, with a few laudable exceptions, been neglected in the interpretation of the *Agamemnon*, where, from the parodos to the final scene, it is of primary importance.[1]

In his great commentary on the *Agamemnon*, Fraenkel was at pains to show how important is the complex of legal terms and metaphors to an understanding of Aeschylus' thought. Thus, at lines 40 ff. Agamemnon and Menelaus are called Priam's "great adversary-at-law" (*antidikos*), and Fraenkel remarks that the dramatist "uses the juristic word in a prominent place, right at the beginning of the entry song of the Chorus, to give the whole play the colouring which essentially belongs to it."[2] When the expedition against Troy is called *stratiôtin arôgan* (46), "we have both the military conception and the idea of a lawsuit; the expedition is at the same time a demand for legal redress." The chorus opens its account of what happened at Aulis with the words, "I have authority to proclaim . . ." (104) and, as Fraenkel notes, "the phrase has a legal ring." Again, the full meaning of *kyriôs echein* at 178 is "to be in good law." The watchman in the prologue and the chorus in the *parodos* both use formulations which indicate that Aeschylus pictured the sons of Atreus as sharing a single house.[3] Fraenkel's explanation is that Aeschylus made the change to give Agamemnon a *legal* claim to avenge Paris' crime against hospitality: "He felt it important that in the great lawsuit, the Trojan War, the plaintiff should not be solely or mainly represented by Menelaus, but that both the brothers should appear equally as ἀντίδικοι of Priam (40 ff.)."[4]

Both the messenger and Agamemnon himself are shown to have a legalistic attitude to the expedition against Troy. "Paris and the city he represents have no cause to boast that they inflicted more harm than they suffered," the messenger says,

> He was found guilty of plunder and theft
> And both lost his property and wretchedly
> Cut down his father's native house. (534–536)

Here the terminology is obviously borrowed from the courts: Paris has been found guilty (*ophlôn . . . dikên*) of theft, and has therefore lost his *rhysion*, which elsewhere "always denotes a thing which is seized on the ground of a legal claim (actual or alleged), whether by way of securing this claim (as 'pledge' or the like), or with a view to compensation."[5] When Agamemnon arrives his first words are that it is *dikê* to address Argos and its gods:

> . . . joint agents with me
> Of my return and the claims of justice I exacted
> From Priam's city. No merely verbal pleadings
> The gods heard and brought their votes for Ilion's
> Destruction to the bloody urn and unambiguously
> Cast them in. To the opposite urn only
> Hope of a hand approached; it was not filled. (811–817)

Fraenkel explains the legal procedure which inspires the passage: δικαίων θ'ῶν ἐπραξάμην at 812 means "the satisfaction of the legal claims which I have exacted," and the *dikas* of 813 are "the legal claims, pleas, of both parties." The following lines recall fifth-century voting procedure—each member of the jury is given only one pebble, *psêphos*, "which he has to put either into the urn of condemnation, or in the urn of acquittal."[6]

On one level, then, we have the imagery of the courtroom: the Trojan expedition is a lawsuit, with Agamemnon and Menelaus the joint prosecutors and Paris and his city the defendants. Beyond this, the term *dikê* and its cognates are used in other, nonlegal senses, which range all the way from the "personification" noticed at the beginning of the chapter to the almost conventional force of the chorus' assertion, "it is *dikê* to honor the leader's wife when the man is absent from the throne" (259–260). At first sight it may appear that the poet uses the terms indiscriminately, introducing them at random as so many commonplaces. A closer examination of their occurrences, however, shows a careful design: terms referring to the concept "Justice" tend to cluster together at certain points in the play's development, and it is worth trying to trace the pattern which emerges. Apart from the ominous note struck by "Justice inclines for men to learn by suffering" toward the end of the song (250–251), little is made of the nonlegal concept in the *parodos*, for the vivid description of the muster at Aulis and Agamemnon's terrible decision fill the poet's canvas; but in the following choral odes the Elders become spokesmen for a more abstract Justice and warn of the dangers inherent in transgressions against it. In the first stasimon, when Clytemnestra has explained in detail to the old men of Argos the success of her beacon scheme, their mood is more reflective and they can meditate on the larger and more abstract implications of Agamemnon's victory: "The congenital rashness of those who breathe more violently than is just appears (in time)."[7] "Wealth gives no defense against excess for the man who kicks Justice's great altar out of sight" (381–384). In the first antistrophe they sing of the dangers of *Peitho*: when a man comes under Persuasion's power, the fact "cannot be hid . . . but, like bad bronze, from rubbing and wearing he turns black, when he has stood trial. . . ."[8] The central part of the ode is taken up with an evocation of Menelaus' pangs of loss after Helen's departure, and the far more serious losses suffered by Argive widows "on account of an alien woman." But in the final antistrophe, the images of resourcelessness, of darkness and obscurity, and of attrition, which had been related to *Dikê* earlier are resumed in a contrasting picture:

> The black Erinyes at length
> Reverse the fortune of one prosperous without justice,
> Wearing away his life, bringing him to darkness;
> There is no assistance for him among the unseen.
>
> (462–467)[9]

Except for the messenger's description of Agamemnon's razing Troy to the ground "with the pick-axe of *dikê*-bearing Zeus" (525–526) and the elaborate legal imagery noted above (534 ff.), the theme lies relatively dormant in the episode which follows, only to emerge again in the stasimon. The first part of the ode is given to fairly specific reflections about Helen —she was well named, the "Destroyer"—and the woes she brought on Troy. The last three strophes clarify the cosmic principles which are reflected in events. Impious deeds are prolific, begetting a whole flock of ills like themselves, and, likewise, "of houses where justice is straight the destiny is to bear fair children" (761–762). Hybris begets hybris, but "Justice shines out in sooty homes" (772–773). The song closes with anapaests in which the chorus greets the returning king. They will not be like the majority of men, they insist, hypocrites who feign joy or grief to suit the occasion but who in reality feel nothing. Their next words have a special relevance not only to Clytemnestra, but also to Agamemnon:

> Most men give first honor
> To appearances as they transgress justice. (788–789)

And their last words have an ominous importance for what is to follow:

> You will learn in time and at first hand
> Which citizen manages the city justly
> And whose management is inopportune. (807–809)

It is no accident that these more abstract considerations of Justice fall on deaf ears: Agamemnon, like his herald, can think only legalistically of the *dikaia* which he exacted from Troy (812 ff.).

When the theme appears again it is on the lips of Clytemnestra. At the end of her long speech of greeting she orders her servants to strew purple tapestries in Agamemnon's path:

> Straightway let the way be strewn with purple
> That Justice may lead him home against his hopes.

For the rest—my care has not been won by sleep,
But will arrange the gods' decrees with justice. (910—913)

The irony of the repetition is patent; it is, of course, *her* notion
of *Dikê* which will prevail, and nothing more is heard of it in
this scene. It is echoed briefly in the following ode (996), but
does not recur until after the murder. It is noteworthy that
there is not a single reference to justice in the Cassandra scene;
it seems that the poet wished to restrict it to the claims and
counterclaims of the various members of the house of Atreus.

When it does come to the fore again it is in a remarkable
cluster of utterances by Clytemnestra as she gloats over the
bodies of her victims:

If it were fitting to pour libations on a corpse,
For him it would be done justly, more than justly . . .
                                          (1395—1396)

and,

Here is Agamemnon, my
Husband, a corpse by my right hand,
The work of a just craftsman. (1404—1406)

The chorus warns that for her crime she will be an outcast,
"an object of hate to the citizens," to which she retorts, "Now,
your verdict is exile for me" (*dikazeis . . . phygên*, 1412);
"when you listen to my deeds you are a harsh judge" (1420—
1421); the legal metaphor has again come to the surface. This
whole scene, in fact, has something of a lawcourt atmosphere
about it. Clytemnestra tries to defend her action to the chorus,
which acts as a jury trying her case; "it is hard to decide," they
say at 1561. As long as Aegisthus is at hand, Clytemnestra is
without fear, and to testify to her confidence she calls upon her
guardian spirits,

By my daughter's Justice, brought to fulfillment,
And *Atê* and Erinys, with whom I slew this man. . . .
                                          (1432—1433)

But, by her own admission, it is a personal divinity, this *Dikê* of her child to which she appeals. The chorus counters later in the scene with the warning,

> Fate is sharpening justice for further harm
> At other whetstones. (1535–1536)

Measured by a different standard of *dikê*, her act was unjust, and, if she should attempt to bury Agamemnon and sing a dirge over his corpse, she would be acting more unjustly still. The chorus expresses shocked disbelief at the prospect:

> Surely you will not dare to do this,
> You, his murderess, to wail for your husband
> And perform ungraciously a gracious act for him,
> An unjust return for his great deeds? (1542–1546)

When Aegisthus appears the theme returns with renewed force, for he, like Clytemnestra, is anxious to justify his share in the murder. "O kindly light of justice-bearing day" are his first words.[10] He recounts the evil done to his father Thyestes by Agamemnon's father Atreus and the consequent claims which he inherited against his cousin. When Thyestes discovered that his own children had been served up to him, he imprecated destruction against the whole family, "giving the table a kick as a just accompaniment to his curse" (*xundikôs*, 1601). "I am the just contriver of this murder" Aegisthus insists (1604); "when I was still an infant, he drove me into exile with my wretched father, but when I grew up, Justice brought me home again" (1605–1607). He concludes his long speech with the boast that he can face even death, now that he sees his enemy "in the snares of justice" (1611). To his repeated avowal that he acted with justice, the chorus replies, "your head will not escape curses and stones hurled by the people *en dikê*" (1615–1616). The ambiguity of the phrase (= "justly" or "*in iudicio*," "in the hour of justice") is intentional and serves to remind the audience that even when either the abstract or the legal sense of the term is primary, the other is never deeply submerged.

The concept of justice which provides the key to the meaning of the trilogy operates in the *Agamemnon* on several levels. On the first and most obvious, the war against Troy is spoken of repeatedly as a great action-at-law introduced by the sons of Atreus against Priam and his city. Agamemnon and his brother are the prosecutors, the "exactors of justice." But this is justice of a very primitive kind, the mere satisfaction of claims for what is due, raw retribution at its lowest level. In general, it can be said that the principals in the drama never rise above this minimal conception. Agamemnon sees himself simply as an avenger for the wrongs done to him and his brother by Paris; Clytemnestra exacts requital for the wrong done to her child and herself by her husband, while Aegisthus is satisfying the debt owed to him by Atreus and his son.

What the agents in the drama do not see is that in order to satisfy their individual claims they must transgress the rights of others, and the very act of transgression sets up a counterclaim, which must then itself be satisfied. Thus, in order to exact his debt against Troy, Agamemnon must kill his daughter, and this act, in turn, infringes the rights of his wife. She and her lover combine forces to satisfy their separate grievances against her husband, but can do so only at the price of his death, which again sets in motion a conflicting set of claims. It is a never-ending process, from which there seems to be no escape.

This, then, is one defect in the limited view of justice: it is endless and self-defeating. Moreover, in spite of the claims of each of the agents to be working in harmony with a larger and more universal conception of Justice, their individual actions in fact set up a disturbance, create an imbalance, in that larger justice. They act only on the personal, retributory, level; it is left to the chorus to call attention to that cosmic Justice which cannot be contravened: the balance of Justice will right itself again when the guilty learn their error through suffering (250–251), the impious man whose ambitious breaths exceed what is just (376) and who kicks down Justice's altar is beyond help (381 ff.). Him no prayers can save; he is destroyed in his injustice (398). It is no accident that when

Agamemnon, Clytemnestra, and Aegisthus think and speak
only in terms of their narrow, personal "justice," for infringe-
ment of which they are demanding satisfaction, the chorus
dwells on the claims of a larger Justice, claims which the
agents in the drama ignore to their cost, but which will not
long go unsatisfied.

ii

In the next play of the trilogy, the *Choephoroe* (*Libation
Bearers*), we see the gradual development of the concept of a
universal, cosmic Justice which insists on restoration of the
balance upset by Agamemnon's murder. The chorus strikes
the keynote with its mention of the "balance of Justice" (61).
Once again the theme of Justice as a principle of human behavior is developed at some length in the odes. In the first play
the chorus denounced the impiety of the man who "kicked
Dikê's altar into oblivion" (*Agam.* 381 ff.); toward the end of
the first stasimon of this play *Dikê* is said to retaliate by
"trampling to the ground those who unrighteously transgress
every reverence of Zeus."[11] "*Dikê*'s foundation is being firmly
fixed" the women proclaim (646). At the beginning of the
next ode the women say they have "uttered every word in
accordance with justice"[12] and later in the song they pray:
"May the son of Maia with justice lend a hand" (812).

In general Agamemnon's children claim to be following
the dictates of this cosmic Justice. These claims are put forward prominently in the first half of the play, and again—in
significant preparation for the solution—the legal sense is
interwoven with the abstract. The chorus advises Electra to
pray that "some *daimon* or mortal may come for the guilty—"
and she interrupts, "do you mean a judge or bringer of justice?"
(120). Her formulation shows clearly the link between the two
senses: a "dicast" or juryman is a "bringer of justice." At the
end of her prayer she asks her father to send benefits from
below, "with gods and Earth and *Dikê* bringer of victory"
(148), and the personification is amplified by her later in the
scene when she addresses "Might and Justice with the third,
greatest of all, Zeus" (244–245). Both these triads are reminis-

cent of Clytemnestra's earlier appeal to the "*Dikê* of my daughter, *Atê* and Erinys" (*Agam.* 1432–1433).

But the evolution to a higher Justice is a slow and painful process and is only partially achieved in the *Choephoroe*; the more primitive, retributive, sense of *dikê* is not entirely absent from the children's conception of their own role. Some of the time they are simply acting *for* Agamemnon, to satisfy the claims which the dead man has against his wife and Aegisthus, to settle, as it were, an unpaid debt. Thus, the chorus, in the opening lines of the *kommos*, pictures *Dikê* as exacting her due, and shouting loudly as she does it.[13] At line 398 Electra says "I am demanding *dikê* from the unjust," where the legal sense seems to be combined with the retributive. And at 461 Orestes proclaims, "Ares clashes with Ares, *Dikê* with *Dikê*," where the meaning is clearly that Agamemnon's claim is about to meet Clytemnestra's. The chorus, too, although it is generally the upholder of an abstract ideal of Justice, occasionally falls into speaking about the limited, retributive, kind. The serving women ask the gods of the house to "wash away the blood of deeds done long ago with fresh *dikai*" (804–805), where the meaning "penalties" seems uppermost. In the third stasimon, after Orestes has taken his mother within to slay her, the women meditate on all that has gone before in a significant combination of the universal and the retributive senses: "*Dikê* came to the sons of Priam in time, retribution of heavy *dikê*" (*barydikos poina*, 935–936). It is as if the characters in the drama were struggling out of the dark past of vendetta "justice" toward a more enlightened world, where the abstract concept alone is a guiding principle. Orestes, in the course of the prayers at his father's tomb, asks Agamemnon to "send Justice as an ally for friends" (497); but he immediately falls into old modes of thought, "or grant us in turn to take hold of them with the same grip . . ." (498). He is caught between two worlds and it is an ambivalence which the chorus reflects:

> He has come, the one whose business is the wily
> Retribution of secret attack;
> But his hand was held in the fight by the true

Daughter of Zeus—*Dikê*
We mortals call her and so hit the mark. . . .   (946–950)

When Clytemnestra is on stage she makes no further claim
to having acted justly; her distraught condition suggests that
she is beyond this pretense. From her lips there is but one
allusion to the theme, and that an ironical one. When Orestes
knocks at the palace door and pretends to be a Phocian trav-
eler, she assures him that within he will find a warm bath—
so different from Agamemnon's—and a bed, "and the presence
of just eyes" (671). But when Orestes has slain his mother
and Aegisthus he becomes their successor, and he must now
take over their claims to have acted with justice. Thus, he calls
upon the sun to be his "witness in justice" (or, "in the case")
"that I undertook my mother's murder in justice" (987–989);
the blending of legal and abstract senses is once more to be
noted. As for Aegisthus, "he had the *dikê* of a dishonorer, as the
law demands" (990). At the onslaught of the madness which
the Furies inspire, Orestes makes a final pathetic protest: "I
say I slew my mother not without justice" (1027).

The conflict of the first two plays seems beyond resolution.
Claim and counterclaim have been put forward; each side can
appeal, with some reason, to *Dikê*. The king has satisfied his
wife's claims generated by the death of their daughter and
has paid his father's debt to Aegisthus. But his death, in turn,
generates a new claim. The pendulum swings back to Agamemnon's children and, before they exact payment from their
mother and her accomplice, both Electra and Orestes call upon
Dikê to aid them; they act for Agamemnon, exacting vengeance
for his murder, but at the same time appealing to a more
universal principle of Justice. At the end of the play Orestes
is left on stage protesting that he has slain his mother justly.
But it is too late. The Dread Avengers have already been
called up by his mother's blood, to drive him into an exile
from which there seems no possibility of return. Their appearance, archetypal representatives of the primitive justice of

requital, seems to have stifled any chance of realizing the cosmic principle of order in the real world.

iii

Ares clashes with Ares, Justice with Justice (*Cho.* 461). Where will it end? By the old blood-logic of the vendetta, of course, nowhere. Murder calls forth murder relentlessly; each act of vengeance must be revenged in its turn; Justice fights against Justice without victory, without surcease. It is this deadlock which the poet takes as his *datum* at the beginning of the last play of the trilogy, the *Eumenides*. Orestes is shown with the Erinyes on his track, and, although he calls Apollo to witness that it was at the god's bidding that he slew his mother and in spite of his having undergone the ritual purifications prescribed by the god, it is to no avail. The Dread Goddesses press on, insisting that it is their office to track down and destroy such sinners as this. Once more, their appeal is to *Dikê*, which they accuse Apollo of having transgressed:

> By their actions the younger gods
> Exert power entirely beyond justice.   (162–163)

And again there is the counterclaim: "Marriage between a man and woman is greater than an oath and safeguarded by justice," Apollo insists; "I say that you are hunting down Orestes unjustly" (217–218, 221). Both sides in the conflict have appealed to *Dikê*. How are their opposing claims to be resolved? They can be reconciled only through an appeal to an impartial principle of *Dikê* whose validity they both accept and in whose decision both will acquiesce. The method of reconciliation is foreshadowed in the very ambiguity which we have noticed in the earlier plays; Aeschylus brings Orestes to Athens, where he is tried before a special court set up by Athena. The cosmic principle of Justice is brought to earth and made completely efficacious in a court of law, before jurors whose decision is an example of *legal* justice.

The entire central section of the play consists of the procedural details of the trial: the preliminary investigation in which both sides are questioned (408 ff.), the Erinyes stating their case (425) and Orestes his (463 ff.). Athena, like a fifth-century archon deciding which court was competent to hear the case, convokes a special jury of "the best of her citizens" (487). Witnesses are called and Apollo speaks for Orestes as a voluntary codefendant (579). Athena "brings the trial before the court" (582) and the Erinyes cross-examine Orestes, establishing the fact of the homicide (588) and the method (592). The defendant, however, claims justification (610, 612) on grounds that it had been ordered by Apollo. The god then states his (and Orestes') case, and Athena gives her charge to the jury: they are to decide this "first trial for bloodshed" (682) and their court is to abide for all time,

> In future this tribunal of dicasts
> Will exist for all time for Aegeus' folk.   (683–684)

The jurymen then deliberate and cast their ballots.[14]

It is clear that the ambiguity of the term *dikê*, with its emphasis now on the abstract force, now on the legal, is no longer merely incidental or decorative. In the *Agamemnon* the expedition against Troy was portrayed in the elaborate metaphor of a lawsuit, but here the audience sees an actual trial taking place before its eyes. The multivalence of meaning of the term *dikê* is essential to the resolution of the dramatic conflict: *Dikê*, the maiden daughter of Zeus, is embodied and made operative in the *dikai* which assume the center of the stage. Naturally, a great deal is made of the term's equivocal nature, and, although it would be tedious to catalogue every occurrence,[15] several of the more important contexts may be noted. While they are still at Delphi, Apollo tells Orestes to go to Athens and clasp Athena's statue; "there," he says, "we shall discover dicasts" (81)—"jurors" in contemporary usage, but the root meaning, "dispensers of justice," must also have been intended. Apollo promises that "the goddess Pallas will oversee the *dikas* of this case" (224), and six lines later the Furies say "I'm going after *dikas* in Orestes' case." The ambiguity is again present at the end of Orestes' first prayer at

Athena's statue: "I await the *telos dikês*" (243). In the course
of the *anakrisis*, the chorus bids Athena "judge a right *dikê*"
(433)—a "righteous judgment," or "point of legal issue." She
realizes that Orestes has his arms around her statue "trusting
in *dikê*" (439), and the suppliant uses both senses in one line
at 468, when he asks Athena to "judge the *dikê*, whether I
acted justly or no." The goddess' reply echoes the legal note
only: "The matter is too great for a mere mortal to adjudicate,
nor is it right for me to decide the *dikas* of angry murder"
(470–472). And so she goes off to summon dicasts (483) and
the parties to the suit are to call "witnesses and testimony . . .
serviceable safeguards of *dikê*" (485–486).

At this point the Erinyes sing a long threnody to *Dikê*.
Just as the choruses of the first two plays were, in general,
although not exclusively, spokesmen for an abstract Justice,
so, too, here the Erinyes put forward the claims of a cosmic
Dikê. "It will indeed be the overthrow of new ordinances if this
matricide's *dikê* and crime prevail (492). Let no one, when he
is stricken, shout 'O *Dikê*' (511), for the house of *Dikê* is
collapsing (516). Without fear, neither individual nor city will
reverence *Dikê* in future (525)."

> I say to you always
> Reverence the altar of *Dikê*.
> Do not, looking for gain,
> Kick it with godless foot.   (538–541)

It is surely an intentional echo of *Agamemnon* 381 ff. The
parallel continues in the last pair of stanzas: "Whoever freely
and without constraint is just will not be unblessed (550–551),
but whoever proceeds without justice faces shipwreck (554)
and goes aground on *dikê*'s reef (564)," where the "reef of
justice" recalls the "hidden reef" of *Agamemnon* 1006.

We must suppose the Erinyes' solicitude for *Dikê* to be
sincere. Earlier in the play they accused Apollo of using com-
pulsion to get his way against *dikê* (163), but when they boast
that it is their role to see that those who dishonor God or host
or parents are recompensed, "each man getting the deserts of

justice" (273), their concept of *Dikê* is revealed as excessively narrow. For them, Justice is entirely retributive; the sinner must suffer torments, "loppings-off of head, gougings-out of eyes, *dikai sphagai te*—and worse, as Apollo charges (186 ff.). And we sympathize with Athena as she retorts impatiently, "you wish to hear talk of justice rather than act so" (430).

The outcome of the trial is of course Orestes' acquittal. The votes of the jurymen are equal (753) and Athena's vote for the defendant (735) allows him to go free, an "aetiological" explanation of the contemporary "vote of Athena," whereby a drawn jury meant acquittal on grounds that the president of the court was presumed to have voted for the defendant. The Erinyes are left onstage, ostensibly the losers in the case and so embittered, hostile, and dangerous. Their threat before the voting was unequivocal: "If I do not get *dikê* ('obtain justice' and 'win the case') I shall be a harsh associate for this land in future" (719–720). And again, "I shall wait and listen for this *dikê*, as I am uncertain whether to be angered at the city" (732–733). With the freeing of Orestes, the conflict is only partly resolved, for the hostile forces which could set the whole process of retribution working again must be assuaged, neutralized, and brought to rest. To allow the Erinyes to go off unappeased would have brought an only temporary respite from the tensions of the earlier parts of the trilogy; it would have been a conclusion without a resolution, and so unworthy of either the wise goddess of Athens or her playwright. So what we are given instead is a re-education of the Furies and their consequent conversion into resident deities of Athens; the Dread Goddesses become "Well-Wishers" for Athena's people for all time to come. As Aristophanes the grammarian remarked in his Hypothesis to the play, "when Athena mollified the Erinyes she called them '*Eumenides.*'"

It is a *tour de force* of reconciliation and has been worked out principally in terms of the theme we have been considering. The Furies' *dikê* of blood-for-blood has been shown to be inadequate. It has been superseded by a new conception, legal *dikê*, justice achieved through process of law, a human embodi-

ment of the divine exemplar, and at the same time more
humane than the unending vendetta it is devised to replace.
But the Erinyes must be made to yield to this new conception
and reform their old ways. Athena must do nothing less than
persuade them to embrace the new *dikai*. "We think we are
upright and just (*euthydikaioi*)" they boasted in the first
stasimon (312). It is entirely natural, then, Athena argues, that
they should have an honored place in her city:

> I promise to you in all justice seats
> Of honor and sanctuaries in this just land.   (804–805)

If her citizens in turn honor their new deities and the element
of salutary awe they represent, Athena tells them that their
city will prosper and grow in *dikê*:

> If you always give great honor to these kindly ones
> In kindly fashion, you will be conspicuous
> Inhabitants of a country and city upright in justice.
>   (992–995).

The great conflict is at last resolved. The forces summoned
up in the earlier plays of the trilogy, forces whose terrible
destructive power could not be dispelled without bloodshed,
have been channeled. In the full Aeschylean conception the
Dikê which is divine and unchanging takes root in a particular human context; it grows to maturity through nurture in
legal forms and processes and finally flowers as *civic* virtue.
The brute instincts of blind retribution have been civilized
and given a place in human society. The family blood-feud
has been made forever obsolete, to be replaced by the new and
higher morality of the *polis*.

Besides the basic conflict between two kinds of *dikê* the
opposition between Erinyes and Olympians manifests itself in
several other ways, and it is interesting to observe the skill
with which the dramatist resolves these secondary themes. On
one level it is seen as a conflict of functions or fields of competence: the Furies insist that it is their *lachos*, "office," ap-
pointed them by *Moira*, to track down slayers of kin (334 ff.).
They describe their *lachê* as "without privilege, without honor,

separated from the gods by sunless filth" (385 ff.). The sphere of the Olympian gods, represented by Apollo and Athena, is something forever apart. "When we were born these *lachê* were ratified for us: the immortals must keep hands off—no dinner companions they!" (349–351). But at the end of the play, after Athena has persuaded them to accept their new status as civic deities, she gives an immensely widened interpretation of their function: "They have obtained it as their office (*elachon*) to arrange all things in the human sphere" (930–931). On another level, the struggle is seen as one between the old and the new order. "You, a youth, have ridden down aged *daimones*," they say to Apollo (150). "Such are the actions of the younger gods" (162). Apollo had destroyed the "*Moiras* born of old" (172). This conflict is mirrored in the very juxtaposition of words, as the Furies say to Apollo:

You trample on me, your elder, young as you are (731)

and, in their lament after losing their case,

O gods who are younger, ancient laws
You trampled on . . . (778–779)

As this is clearly a delicate point with the Erinyes, Athena, in effecting a reconciliation, is careful to respect their feelings. "I will put up with your bad temper," she says patiently at 848, "for you are older." And again, "I shall never weary of telling you the good things that await you,

That you may never say that you, elder goddesses,
At the hands of me a younger and of my citizens
Went to ruin in dishonor far from this land. (882–884)

Finally, this theme of *atimia* (and we should remember its political overtones) plays an important part in the reconciliation. The Furies are manifestly jealous of their *timai*, which they accuse Apollo of trying to curtail (227). "Leto's son makes us dishonored" they complain (324). What these *timai* are under the old dispensation they tell Athena immediately after identifying themselves: "We drive man-slayers from home" (419–421). While the ballots are being counted Apollo gloats over his adversaries: "Among both young and elder gods you are dishonored" (721–722), and, just before the verdict is announced, the Furies acknowledge what is at stake: they will either "go to ruin, or possess their honors hereafter" (747). The verdict elicits a cry of indignation, "We are dishonored!" (780), but Athena reassures them: the outcome of the trial is "justice of equal votes" and had not been arranged to bring *atimia* on them (795–796). "You are not dishonored" she insists (824); just as a new concept of *dikê* has been substituted for the old, so Athena begins to outline a new form of honor. She promises that they will be "held in reverent honor and coresidents" of her city (833, echoed by the political terms *metoikois* at 1011 and *metoikian*, 1018). They will be sorry, she warns them, if they depart, for "time in its flow will become more laden with honor for these citizens" and the Erinyes will have an "honored seat" near Erechtheus' house if they stay (853–855). At 868 they are described, in an impressive triad, as "doing well, faring well, honored well." "It is possible for you to be shareholders in this land, justly held in honor for all time" (890–891).

Athena's persistent coaxing has at last aroused their curiosity. "And what will this honor be?" (894). "That without you no household shall prosper" (895); and they are won over. Their old office of honor, to drive murderers from home, is replaced by a new position of prominence in the fruitfulness of Athenian civic and domestic life. The play ends with antiphonal prayers for Athens' prosperity by Athena and the Eumenides, who "accept community (*xunoikia*) with Pallas and will not dishonor the city" (916–917). Athena advises her citizens to honor the kindly ones in kindly fashion (992–93), and the closing lines repeat the Eumenides' old character, "lovers of honor" (1033) and their new position, "much-revered with honors and sacrifices" (1037).[16]

iv

At the core of the play stands the foundation of the Court of the Areopagus by Athena, and the presentation before our eyes of the first trial ever for homicide. The acceptance of its decision by the Eumenides constitutes a permanent rejection of the precivilized "justice" of the vendetta, and the victorious enthronement at Athens of a new Justice which is both legal and civic. The foundation-charter of this court receives a prominent place in the action. At the end of the *anakrisis*-scene, after Athena has had the sworn statements of the plaintiff and defendant and the exact nature of the charge has been specified, at the precise point at which an Athenian archon would determine which court was competent to try the case, she states her intention: "The affair is too great for mere mortals to adjudicate; both sides have claim to *dikê*. But since the matter has fallen to me, I shall choose a homicide jury under oath and institute this ordinance for all time to come. You call witnesses, assemble testimony; when I have chosen the best of my citizens I shall return to determine this matter faithfully."[17] Athena fulfills her promise and proclaims her *thesmon* during the trial, after the two sides have been heard and the jury is about to reach its verdict. "Hear, now, the ordinance, people of Athens, who judge the first *dikas* of shed blood. This lawcourt of jurors will abide for Aegeus' people even in the future, on Ares' hill. . . . The Reverence and Fear engendered by this court will constitute a bulwark of the land and a safeguard to the city, such as no Scythian or Peloponnesian ever had. This tribunal I now establish, untouched by thought of gain, revered, quick-tempered, a wakeful guardian of the land for those who sleep" (681–684, 700–706). For those in his audience who would have difficulty coming out of the mythical past into the context of fifth-century politics, Aeschylus underlines the contemporary relevance of Athena's words by making her close her speech with the words, "I have drawn out this exhortation *for my citizens in the future.* But now get up and vote . . ." (707 ff.).

No Athenian in that first audience of Aeschylus' *Oresteia* could fail to see that the poet was calling attention to one of the bitterest political issues of the day, the Ephialtic Reforms of 462/1. A discussion of the constitutional significance of these reforms may be deferred for the moment. What is important here is that they constituted a victory of the radical element at Athens, of whom Ephialtes and Pericles were the leading spokesmen, over the old conservative Cimon and his friends. The radicals had no doubt been biding their time, waiting for an opportunity to put through their program. This opportunity came with the dismissal of the Athenian expedition inspired and led by Cimon to help the Spartans against their Helot revolutionaries. If Plutarch is to be believed, Ephialtes hotly opposed Cimon's proposal to aid the Spartans, but Cimon was determined to carry through the traditional conservative policy of close cooperation with Sparta. After the Athenian forces had helped to besiege Ithome for one campaigning season (at least) the Spartans spurned further Athenian assistance. Cimon returned in humiliation, the conservative policies were discredited, and the radicals saw their chance: the Areopagus was stripped of its power, Cimon was ostracized, and Athens' relations with Sparta, whose chief sponsor Cimon had been, were severed at last.[18]

This *volte-face* had a sudden repercussion on the international scene: Thucydides relates that "immediately upon their return they gave up the alliance with the Lacedaemonians against the Persians and became allies of their enemies, the Argives" (1.102.4). The Argive alliance, then, was part and parcel of the reforms of 462; it was the foreign policy plank of the radical platform, and it, too, is reflected in several passages of the *Eumenides*. Aeschylus, apparently with foresight and originality, transferred Agamemnon's domain from the traditional Mycenae (or Sparta) to Argos.[19] Orestes, heir to the Argive throne, comes as a defendant before Athens' first and greatest court, the Areopagus, and is acquitted. Even before Athena has appeared, Orestes, with his arms about her statue, addresses himself to her: "Now, piously, and with pure lips, I call upon Athena, Queen of this land, to come to my defense. Without her spear she shall acquire myself, my country and the Argive people as a true ally in justice for all time to come" (286–291). During the trial Apollo closes his defense of Orestes with the words, "I sent this man a suppliant to your abode, that a pledge of trust might exist for all time to come; that you might acquire this man and his descendants as allies, O Goddess; and that this exchange of trust might abide everlastingly for their posterity to cherish" (669–673). As if this didn't bring the point home to the audience clearly enough, Orestes' last speech is one long paean of gratitude and praise to Athena and her people:

> I am now going home after swearing
> To this country and your people for all
> The entire length of future time
> That never will a steersman of my land
> Come against them with a well-armed band.
> For even when we ourselves are in the grave
> We shall wreak unavoidable misfortune
> On any who transgress the oaths now made,
> Making their marches dispirited and their paths
> Ill-omened, so that they rue their trouble.
> But with the oaths kept firm, and if they honor
> Pallas' city always with allied might,
> We shall be most benevolent to them.   (762–774)

It seems hardly possible to deny that (to put it most neutrally) Aeschylus approved of the Argive alliance of 461 and was concerned to bring it before his audience in commendatory terms in the trilogy three years later. But the Argive alliance was only the *external* aspect of the liberalization of the Athenian state which also included curtailment of the powers of the Areopagus and it is clear from the prominence of that body in the resolution of the dramatic conflict that Aeschylus also had views on this aspect of the reforms. The difficulty lies in determining what these views were. At first reading, it might appear from the august and reverential tones in which Athena speaks of her new-founded court (especially lines 700–706) that the poet is expressing disapproval of the attacks made on it by Ephialtes and the other reformers. This would indeed fit the still commonly held theory that Aeschylus was a conservative in politics as in religion, who would necessarily disapprove of any such reform of an ancient institution. It was the view

put forward by K. O. Müller.[20] But a reading of the *Eumenides*
as a hymn in support of the Areopagus against the liberal
reforms creates its own difficulties. Müller, writing before the
discovery of the *Athênaiôn Politeia*, was unable to date Ephialtes' reforms securely. Still, he could not help noticing Aeschylus' repeated emphasis on the perpetuity of the Areopagus,
the poet's insistence that Athena was instituting her tribunal
for all time (484, 683–684); so he was misled by his belief in
Aeschylus' conservatism to conclude that the reforms *had not
yet taken place.* "I cannot conceive it possible that Aeschylus
would have put into the mouth of the national goddess herself
the declaration ['this lawcourt will exist for all future time']
if the occurrences of the preceding months had belied the
assertion" (109). But this is precisely the point: the reforms of
462 did *not* belie the praises contained in the *Eumenides* of
458; they were, as we shall see, entirely compatible with them.
Müller wrote: "it is palpably the design of Aeschylus to support the Areopagus in its authority in actions for bloodshed;
consequently it must have been in this quarter that its rights
were attacked" (113). But if there is one thing we can know
with complete certainty about the reforms it is that Ephialtes
did not remove from the Areopagus its "authority in actions for
bloodshed"; it remained after 462, as it had been before, the
chief Athenian court for homicide where cases of premeditated
murder were tried.

Müller's theories were not long left unchallenged. In his
1853 edition of the *Eumenides*, Bernard Drake[21] attacked each
of Müller's arguments in turn and put forward a contrary
hypothesis. Aeschylus "everywhere seems to take it for granted
that *these* rights [jurisdiction in homicide cases] were in per-
fect safety and not likely to be disturbed. Had they been in
danger, he would have mentioned the fact very explicitly.
Wherefore Hermann (*Opusc.* vol. VI, p. 136) argues that the
total silence of Aeschylus on this point proves that the penal
judicature was *not* attacked;—exactly the reverse of Müller's
deduction" (73). Drake quoted with approval a footnote of
Grote's:

[Aeschylus] puts forward the Areopagus prominently and specially as a tribunal for homicide, exercising this jurisdiction by inherent prescription, and confirmed in it by the Eumenides themselves. Now, when we consider that this was precisely the power which Ephialtes left untouched, we may plausibly argue that Aeschylus, by enhancing the solemnity and predicting the perpetuity of the remaining privilege [i.e., jurisdiction in homicide cases], intended to conciliate those who resented the recent innovations and to soften the hatred of the opposite factions.[22]

To Grote's argument Drake adds a shrewd observation of his own:

Had the poet intended to make a decisive stand against Ephialtes and his party,—had it been his object to excite the popular feeling against them by the Eumenides,—he never would have eulogised [the Argive] alliance so openly and entirely; for it was the very point on which Cimon and the oligarchs were most at issue with Pericles and the advocates of democracy (74).

With this much progress made toward what must be the true solution, it is disappointing to find Sidgwick some thirty years later returning to a position both more primitive and confused. He admits that "what the emphasis is laid on all through is the judicial powers in murder cases, like that of Orestes; and these are just what were not touched." At the same time he persists in the view that "Aeschylus, with his conservative and oligarchical instincts, would naturally be opposed to these [reforms], as to the other changes introduced by Perikles."[23]

In this century R. W. Livingstone began by asserting that the play was completely lacking in artistic unity; the last 350 lines of the play were "stitched to its outside."[24] He concluded that Aeschylus was writing political allegory. In Livingstone's view the deadlock between Apollo and the Erinyes represents the impasse reached by radicals and conservatives in the 460's. The early part of this chapter was an attempt to show that the artistic integrity of the *Eumenides*, as of the trilogy, not only

survives but is enhanced by close analysis. The notion of
allegory is completely alien to the spirit of Aeschylean tragedy,
for it implies a political meaning hidden within, posing as,
an artistic form, a view which contradicts the totality of the
dramatist's intention and of the play's impact on the audience.
Furthermore, Livingstone betrays some confusion about what
Aeschylus' own position was, for we are told that Aeschylus
"loyally accepted" the reforms of Ephialtes, but that he "either
believed in his heart, or in fact professed, that the conservatives and reformers of 462 both had irrefragable arguments for
their views and that if the question were put to a human jury,
no decision would be reached."[25]

On the positive side, Livingstone maintained that the
poet's "own political ideals are clearly expressed in Athena's
speech (690 f.). A moderate democracy, τὸ μήτ' ἄναρχον μήτε
δεσποτούμενον (696), which does not push reform to extremes
(693) or go too far in banishing the terrors of restraining law
(698)."[26] It is to Livingstone's credit that he realized that the
picture of Aeschylus the arch-conservative is untenable: "Those
who believe that he took the conservative view must explain
why he gives the Aeropagus the functions which the democrats
left it and gives it nothing more. . . . Even more decisive evidence of the democratic sympathies of Aeschylus is his out-
spoken and repeated approval of the other great change
carried by the democrats in the teeth of conservative opposition
—the substitution of an Argive alliance for friendship with
Sparta (290, 762 ff.)."[27]

A few years later Miss C. M. Smertenko put forward a
new theory of the play's political implications.[28] Starting from
the unobjectionable premise that "the more fully we know the
actual conditions of political and social life contemporary with
the Greek drama, the more explicit seems the applicability of
many plays to specific situations then existing," she professed
to discover a relationship between the mythical Orestes and
the fifth-century Alcmeonids: "The Alcmeonidae, like Orestes,
had suffered enough to expiate their fault, and had been ab-
solved by the oracles of Apollo. The parallelism with Orestes'

wanderings and sufferings is striking. . . [lines 797 ff.] probably refer to the vindication of the Alcmeonidae by Delphi."[29] It is difficult to accept this theory without some solid evidence that the Alcmeonids were in fact purified by Delphi. The main objection to Smertenko's theory, however, is that it rests on a serious misinterpretation of the play. E. R. Dodds pointed out that if Smertenko's theory were correct and Aeschylus were writing propaganda for Delphi's purificatory properties, "he would have made the purification of Orestes at Delphi much more important than it is in our play. As it is, its importance seems deliberately minimized."[30] So far from showing the efficacy of ritual purification, Aeschylus' retelling of the Orestes story shows how ineffectual are traditional expedients against the Furies' wrath. Orestes repeatedly makes it clear that he is ritually pure, undefiled; he has undergone "many purifications" (277), not just at Delphi, as Smertenko's theory requires. He reassures Athena that he is not *prostropaios*, a suppliant in need of purification (445); "long since at other houses have I been purified both by victims and flowing streams" (451–452). But the Furies refuse to accept his plea; they accuse Apollo of having "polluted his sanctuary at its hearth with defilement, at his own bidding, at his own urgence" (169–170) by accepting Orestes. They clearly deny that the ritual ablutions Orestes has undergone have had any cleansing effect whatever: "Our wrath does not creep up to the man who holds out pure hands . . . but whoever having sinned then hides his bloody hands as this man does . . ." (313–317). An odd way to write propaganda for Delphi, or any purificatory shrine.[31] On the contrary, the whole notion of ritual impurity and purification fades into insignificance. Zeus Katharsios is superseded by a new aspect of Zeus: "Zeus Agoraios has prevailed," Athena proclaims (973)—Forensic Zeus, who guides public assemblies, has triumphed.

.   If these criticisms are valid, they will likewise vitiate the second and more specific half of Miss Smertenko's theory, that Aeschylus was giving a mythical prototype for the absolution not only of the whole Alcmeonid clan but principally of its

leading light, Pericles. The grounds on which Athena casts her
vote for Orestes strike us as very odd, it is true. "The mother
is not the child's parent," explains Apollo, "but merely the
nurse of the seed. The father is the begetter, and she merely
preserves the shoot, a stranger for a stranger. Why Athena
here exemplifies this . . ." (658–664). All this is surprising,
even more so when Athena repeats it:

> I cast this vote for Orestes
> For there is no mother who bore me;
> I praise the male in all things except marriage,
> And I am on the father's side with all my heart.
> (735–738)

Livingstone felt this was Aeschylus "in his primitive vein";
for him the overriding problem of the *Eumenides* was why
Aeschylus did not find adequate grounds for Orestes' acquittal.
A totally satisfactory explanation of the incongruity is yet to
be put forward.[32] It will hardly do to say with Smertenko
that Aeschylus is here whitewashing Pericles, who was in-
criminated by the curse of the Alcmeonids only on his mother's
side. Even if her theory of Orestes as a mythical prototype of
the Alcmeonids were correct, there is no evidence that Pericles'
Alcmeonid connection became a political issue until twenty-five
years later, on the eve of the outbreak of the Peloponnesian
War; there is certainly nothing in the circumstantial *potpourri*
of the Plutarchean *Life* to suggest that it did. "It is inconceivable that in the heated controversies of his early political career
so convenient a weapon should not have been used against
him," writes Smertenko (234); but it remains, for all that, an
unproved assumption.

Interest in the political message of the *Eumenides* has
revived in the last ten years. Felix Jacoby seems to have stirred
up a hornets' nest by his extreme statement of the view that
Aeschylus was a supporter of the radical reforms. In his note
on Fragment 1 of Hellanicus[33] he pointed out that Aeschylus
apparently manipulated the myth even more drastically than at
first sight appears, for he ignores the three trials of Ares,

Cephalus, and Daedalus, which, in later Atthidographic tradition, ought to have come before Orestes':[34]

> . . . although [Aischylos] makes the Areopagos later than it was in Athenian tradition, which dated its establishment under the first king, he gives a history of its development which increases the glory of the democratically reformed institution in the view of the Athenians. Personally, I have no serious doubt that Aischylos (to put it roughly) wrote his trilogy because of the Aeropagos; that he composed his poem under the influence and because of (to use a neutral term) the reform of 462/1 B.C. Nor have I any doubt that he (again to put it roughly) defends the democratic restriction of the old Council to jurisdiction in cases of homicide because that was the function Athena had assigned to it, all additional functions falling under the concept ἐπίθετα as Ephialtes terms it and/or Aristotle.[35]

In 1957 K. J. Dover dealt with many of the political aspects of the play in an important paper.[36] He pointed out that *to meson* was not invariably a political slogan. "When someone says, as both the Chorus and Athena do, 'avoid the extremes of anarchy and despotism; the mean between the two is right,' he is not necessarily speaking as a 'moderate democrat' or as a member of a 'centre party.' He is using words which, if we view them from the standpoint of archaic Greek morality in general, merely recommend a reflective rather than a violent attitude to politics" (233). Athena warns her citizens not to upset (text in doubt) the laws, nor "stir up the mud and make bright water unfit for drinking" (693 ff.). This has usually been taken as a warning to the Reformers to go no further. But Dover suggests that just as the "accretions" which the Aristotelian *Constitution of Athens* says Ephialtes stripped from the Areopagus (25.2) may have been a catchword of the democrats themselves to convince the people that they were "purifying" the ancient body and restoring it to its "ancestral" state, so, too, "Athena's words, so far from being a reproach against reform of the Areopagus or a warning against further reform, may well be an adaptation of arguments used by the reformers themselves" (234). Ephialtes may himself, Dover means, have referred to those of the Areopagus' powers which went beyond its homicide jurisdiction as a "pollution" of its pristine dignity. Although Dover finds the political language of the play "neutral, and for that very reason reconcilable with unreserved acceptance of the democratic revolution," for him the deciding factor is Aeschylus' insistence on the Argive alliance: "*Eumenides* differs from all [other examples of political aetiology in Tragedy] in introducing the Argive alliance at so early a stage in the play and in referring to it three times. . . . The alliance was an achievement—or perhaps it would be more accurate to call it a gesture—of the democrats, inseparable from their renunciation of the Spartan alliance to which the conservative elements in Athens gave their loyalty" (235). Dover acutely criticizes Livingstone's conception of the play as allegory; "the participants are not, to a Greek, fictions or abstractions, but real gods, and the issue of the conflict between them is itself a matter of so high an importance that there is no room for allegory" (237). He finds unconvincing any suggestion of contemporary references behind Athena's presence "either in place of the Libyan land . . . or overseeing the Phlegraean plain" (292 ff.).

This last question was taken up by Dodds in a paper whose broad scope is belied by its brevity, for it is a contribution of primary importance to an understanding of Aeschylus' ethical preoccupations.[37] He begins by taking exception to Livingstone's theory that "the last 350 lines of the *Eumenides* are . . . a loosely connected episode, stitched on its outside."[38] For one thing, the political "tone" is not restricted to the *Eumenides*, but is present in the earlier plays. "References to the δῆμος are more frequent than we expect in a Mycenaean monarchy."[39] "We may notice also that the rule of Aegisthus is described in the language of politics: it is repeatedly called a τυραννίς (*Ag.* 1355, 1365; *Cho.* 973), from which Orestes 'liberates' Argos (*Cho.* 1046, cf. 809, 863). . . . The curious circumstance that in the *Eumenides*, alone among Greek tragedies, Athens lacks a king has hardly received the attention it

deserves" (20). Dodds then suggests that in several passages
of the *Eumenides* the audience may have been intended to
perceive a reference to contemporary events. When Orestes
"speculates on the possible presence of Athena in Libya, 'helping her friends' (295), I imagine they asked themselves 'What
friends?' and quickly guessed the answer, 'Of course, our other
ally, those Libyans whose king we are just now helping to
break the yoke of Persia.' "[40] To the suggestion of contemporary references elsewhere in the play (for example, Chalcidice,
295 ff., and the Troad, 398) Dodds remarks that "the supposition can be neither proved nor ruled out."[41]

Dodds then turns to the main political allusion in the
play, the undoubted references to the Areopagus-reform. The
view that Aeschylus was "fighting a conservative rearguard
action" is "virtually excluded by his three emphatic references
to the Argive alliance. . . . But in the light of Athena's foundation-speech I find it almost equally difficult to see Aeschylus
as a consistent and committed supporter of radical reform"
(21). Dodds's misgivings are based on two passages (690–695
and 704–706). He reiterates his theory that the first, a warning
"not to muddy the stream of drinkable water with evil inpourings," is Aeschylus' protest against opening of the archonship to the zeugites, a measure which was in fact passed in
the year after the play, 457.[42] About lines 704 to 706 Dodds
maintains that "the functions of the Areopagus would seem to
be conceived in wider terms than those of a murder-court,
which does indeed protect the security of the individual, but
scarcely that of the country as a whole."[43] He summarizes his
own theory of Aeschylus' political sympathies as follows: "It
looks to me as if the famous saying about the superiority of
τὸ μέσον—which Aeschylus put so oddly into the mouth of the
Erinyes (530)—might in fact be taken, not as a political
catchword of Right or Left, or even as 'recommending a reflective attitude to politics' [Dover's view] but as an honest
and correct description of the author's own position."[44] Dodds
feels that the closing scene, too, must have had contemporary
pertinence. When Athena bids the Erinyes not to instil "in-

testine Ares" in her citizens, and says "Let war be external, not too near at hand" (862–864), the poet

> certainly has his own day in mind, as appears from the allusion to foreign war. . . . And that Aeschylus did at this time fear civil war is plain enough from lines 976–87 [the Eumenides pray for the avoidance of *stasis*: 'may the earth not drink the black blood of citizens . . .'], lines which would naturally be taken by his first audience as a reminder of the fairly recent murder of Ephialtes and an appeal to the radicals not to pursue a vindictive policy.

This is not, however, as Livingstone maintained, political allegory, with the Erinyes "representing" the Athenian oligarchs; rather "what we *can* perhaps say is that their case is *paradeigmatic:* their eventual choice is an *exemplum*, showing that even the bitterest feud can and should end in reconciliation."[45]

The second part of Dodds's paper deals with the larger ethical considerations of the trilogy. The doctrine of "the guilty must suffer" entails the possibility of a real choice, and, one by one, we are shown the various characters of the drama—Agamemnon, Cassandra, Orestes—choosing a certain course of action and suffering the consequences. "The crucial choice [in the *Eumenides*] is surely that made by the Erinyes when they first refuse and then accept Athena's offer . . . [and] it is so presented as to suggest its paradeigmatic value for the poet's own day. The moral issues of the myth are living issues which have still to be faced in the Athens of 458" (29). So it is with the other cardinal tenet of the Aeschylean faith, "wisdom through suffering." The characters in the drama choose and suffer, and through their suffering win a new understanding of the workings of the universe and of their own natures. But in the *Eumenides* Athena voices her confidence in the knowledge which her citizens will gain with the passage of time (line 1000). "I will risk the guess," Dodds writes, "that it was this hope for Athens—the hope of achieving a truer insight into the laws that govern our condition—this, rather than the particular squabble about the powers of the Areopagus, that shaped the composition of the *Oresteia*."[46] The poet's contemporary preoccupations and admonitions are thus shown to be not narrowly political, but ethical and moral as well.

Several recent studies of the politics of the *Oresteia* make no significant advances toward a solution of the problem. S. J. Lurje[47] deals yet again with the references to the Argive alliance and mention of Egypt, the Phlegraean plain, and the Troad. "Aischylos supported the foreign policy of the Athenian democracy completely and entirely." But in internal matters the case changes: "here the poet was not so unquestioning a follower of the democratic efforts as in external policy." Specifically, according to Lurje, Aeschylus is opposing two democratic reforms, the admission of the zeugites to the archonship and "the abolition of the board of *nomophylakes*, to which had been transferred in 460 the right to control legislation and especially the functioning of the democratic institutions, which up to now had belonged to the Areopagus" (297). It is impossible to know, from the summary, on what Lurje bases his argument or how he arrives at his conclusions, but I shall argue below that the purport of Aeschylus' references to the *Nomophylakia* is exactly the opposite of what Lurje conceives it to be, that he is opposing not the abolition of the *Nomophylakes*, but the very institution of that board in the first place and the transference to it of the Areopagus' right of *nomophylakia*. The author takes the protests of Apollo and Athena about primacy of the male parent over the female to indicate that "already in 458 there was intense debate about the draft of the bill according to which children whose mothers were not Athenian citizens were to have no civic rights." In this controversy, according to Lurje, Aeschylus took sides to put forward a mythological example of the fact that "descent on the mother's side could have no significance for civic rights." C. D. N. Costa, in a recent article in *Greece and Rome*, does little more than restate more emphatically and at greater length Dodds's contention that Aeschylus was a "moderate."[48]

Finally, S. Mazzarino put forward in three similar articles[49] the view that the *Eumenides* shows Aeschylus in a pro-

Periclean posture. The contemporary relevance of the play, he believes, is that the poet, as a member of the *genos* of the Eupatridai, was excluded from the festival of the Eumenides, and line 698, "not to throw *to deinon* entirely out of the city," is in reality a protest against the ostracism of the elder Alcibiades, *ca.* 460. As Mazzarino's theories are undocumented and only imperfectly worked out, they can perhaps be passed over.

v

The difference between Dover and Dodds is fundamental, and, in a sense, irresolvable. Both have good arguments on their side. On the one hand the Argive alliance is given repeated emphasis, and the political language, which appears to us highly charged and specific (*to meson* naturally suggesting "middle of the road"), may have been simply neutral; on the other, several passages in the play can only with difficulty, as Dodds remarks, be read in a restrictive sense. It is almost a matter of taste to which of the sets of preferences we give greater weight.

For my own part, while I admit the force of Dodds's objections (certainly his demonstration of the larger ethical application is unimpeachable), I find the prominence of the Argive alliance a decisive objection to the view that Aeschylus had reservations about the reforms of 462/1. It is all very well to believe that "Aussen-" can be separated from "Innenpolitik," but the few glimpses we get into the course of events at Athens suggest the contrary: Ephialtes the prime opponent of Cimon's proposal to aid Sparta, the reforms carried probably in Cimon's absence at Ithome, the latter's ignominious return and the *immediate* (Thucydides is quite specific) rejection of the Spartan alliance and conclusion of a treaty with Argos. While Cimon's ostracism does not figure in the sequence of events which Thucydides says happened "immediately on their return from Ithome" (1.102.4), Plutarch makes it clear that his dismissal by the Spartans gave his enemies a handle against him and that he was ostracized after an unsuccessful attempt to rescind the laws of Ephialtes. At the very least, we may wonder why, if Aeschylus did not support the internal changes of the Reformers, he did not say so unambiguously, and why he gave such repeated and dramatically unnecessary prominence to a major part of their program, the Argive alliance.[50]

In the end it may seem merely a matter of personal preference, but Dodds does not seem to me to present a convincing refutation of Dover's view that the political language of the play is "neutral, and for that very reason reconcilable with unreserved acceptance of the democratic position." To Dover's theory that the slogan "neither anarchy nor tyranny" does not prove that Aeschylus was a "moderate democrat," or a member of a "centre party," but that Aeschylus "is using words which . . . merely recommend a reflective rather than a violent attitude to politics," Dodds simply opposes his own feeling that the words "might in fact be taken . . . as an honest and correct description of the author's own position." Even if Dodds is correct, it does not substantially affect the issue; for even a "radical" would agree that the extremes of tyranny and anarchy were to be avoided. Aeschylus' voicing of these sentiments is not, therefore, convincing proof of his "moderate" tendencies, as Dodds seems to think. As for his unwillingness to accept Athena's foundation-speech as a restriction of the Areopagus' powers to jurisdiction in homicide cases, the difficulty lies in trying to discover what further *specific* powers Athena's words may be alluding to. If they are simply honorific, endowing the Areopagus with unlimited "auctoritas" as the embodiment of *to deinon* in the state, the Reformers might well have approved. If Jacoby and Dover are correct in suggesting that *epitheta* may have been a term of the democrats, then Ephialtes and his supporters would almost certainly have agreed that the Areopagus was to retain all conceivable "moral" influence and prestige—just so long as its actual constitutional powers were cut back to what Athena herself had designed them to be. And Dodds says nothing about Dover's contention that bringing murder into the orbit of the state's legal control was the first step toward, and remained at the heart of, the civilizing influence of the *polis*; that Athena is shown bestowing on her court the one power left to it by Ephialtes, a power not only necessary but also sufficient for it to fulfill its grand function in the state.

In this welter of preference and hypothesis I may perhaps be allowed a conjecture of my own. The reforms of Ephialtes were carried in 462/1 and the Argive alliance concluded very soon thereafter. Aeschylus' support of the alliance has been used to argue to his approval of the reforms. But there is some evidence that Ephialtes' was not the only attack on the Areopagus. If we are able to discover some sign of Aeschylus' dissatisfaction with the contemporary condition of the Areopagus, may not it be taken as referring to this later attempt to remove from it some of its powers? On this hypothesis, the attack would have occurred after the main reforms of 462 but before 458.

First, the passage in the *Eumenides*. Dodds may have been on the right track when he felt that lines 700 to 706 of the foundation speech are not to be read in a restrictive sense:

> If you stand in reverent fear of so august a body
> You would have a bulwark of the country and
> Safeguard of the city as no other humans have,
> Not among the Scythians or in Pelops' land.
> This tribunal, untouched by thought of gain,
> Revered, quick to wrath, for those who sleep
> A wakeful guardian of the land I now establish.

The phrases "bulwark of the country" and "guardian of the land" look suspiciously like a reference to some specific power of the Areopagus. At the very beginning of the Aristotelian *Constitution of Athens*, among the primitive functions of the Areopagus, is included "the office of maintaining the laws" (3.6) and later in the treatise Solon is said to have assigned the Areopagus "to the *nomophylakia*, just as it had been overseer of the constitution before" (8.4). Is it not possible that behind Athena's words *phrourêma gês* lies this constitutional power of *nomophylakia*? That this may have been the power which was the object of a renewed attack on the Areopagus after 462, and to whose removal Aeschylus was objecting in the *Eumenides*? Exactly what the *nomophylakia* consisted in is not clear.[51] But whether it was a specific power, perhaps an earlier safeguard along the lines of the *graphê paranomôn*, or merely a general supervision of magistrates and laws, that there was an attack on it is guaranteed by the mention in Philochorus of a board of *nomophylakes* which was set up at this time.[52] The date of this institution is also unclear; Philochorus says simply that the board was set up "when Ephialtes left only capital cases to the Areopagus," and only a short interval—a matter of weeks perhaps—need have elapsed between Ephialtes' reforms and the renewed attack on the Areopagus' "guardianship of the laws."

I suggest that the man behind this renewed attack on the Areopagus was Pericles.[53] Chapter 27 of the *Constitution of Athens* records several actions of Pericles, but not in any discoverable chronological order. Thus, we are told of his accusation against Cimon which first brought him to public attention. Next, we have the important phrase "and he stripped away some powers from the Areopagites." After this, the outbreak of the Peloponnesian War is mentioned, then Pericles' institution of pay for jury duty. Where the author found a secure date for one of Pericles' measures, he recorded it, as with the citizenship law of 451 (26.4); otherwise, the measure was simply mentioned in a catch-all chapter like 27. Although this absence of a chronological frame makes it illegitimate to argue that the *Constitution of Athens* dated this attack of Pericles on the Areopagus after Ephialtes' reforms, which are discussed in Chapter 25, the fact that the treatise did not associate Pericles' name with the reforms of 462/1 suggests that this was an entirely different stage in the "democratization" of the state. Pericles' absence from the Ephialtic context is important and has not been sufficiently emphasized; the later and more usual tradition, as recorded in the *Politics* and Plutarch, invariably mentioned Pericles and Ephialtes in the same breath.[54] Equally significant in this connection is the *Constitu-*

tion of Athens' later reference to "the laws of Ephialtes and Archestratus" without any mention of Pericles (35.2).

Ephialtes was murdered in the very year of the reforms which were to bear his name.[55] It may be that Pericles, very shortly thereafter, attempted to remove from the Areopagus some of the functions which had been left to it by Ephialtes; among these perhaps was the *nomophylakia*, which Pericles attempted to transfer to a board which had been set up specially for the purpose. It will be this renewed insult to the dignity of the Areopagus against which Aeschylus is complaining through the words of Athena. Her warning to her citizens at 690–695 not to pollute the laws with "evil inpourings," nor to "defile the bright water with mud," lines for which no very satisfactory reference has hitherto been found, can then be taken as a deprecation of this recently instituted board of *Nomophylakes*.

There are two additional indications in the play that Aeschylus is taking a specifically anti-Periclean line. We have already noticed Lurje's suggestion that the argument Apollo and Athena put forward for voting for Orestes' acquittal may show that Aeschylus was denouncing a contemporary proposal of Pericles to restrict Athenian citizenship to those whose both parents were Athenian; if Lurje is correct, it was an unsuccessful attempt to brook the Periclean tide, for the law was passed, as the *Constitution of Athens* relates, in 451. Pericles' other important constitutional innovation was the introduction of pay for jury duty; it was the antiaristocratic measure *par excellence*, substituting remuneration for disinterested public service and, of course, making it possible for men of ordinary means to serve on juries. We would like to know when Pericles instituted it. The measure is mentioned in Chapter 27 of the *Constitution of Athens*,[56] where, as we have seen, no chronological scheme can be detected. Plutarch (*Pericles* 9.3) makes Pericles institute pay for jury duty before *his* attack on the Areopagus, but, as his attack is not clearly distinguished from Ephialtes', Plutarch's testimony is not conclusive. Hignett reviewed the evidence and suggested a date shortly after 462.[57]

With so much uncertainty it is perhaps excusable to put forward a final hypothesis. One of the things Athena emphasizes about her new tribunal is that it is "untouched by gain": κερδῶν ἄθικτον τοῦτο βουλευτήριον (704), and we are reminded that *kerdos* is the motive for the transgression of *Dikê* against which the Furies warn (541). Does not a court "untouched by profit" imply its contrary, one where the members are in paid attendance? So far as I am aware, no one has connected this reference in the *Eumenides* with Pericles' institution of jury pay. But the connection does not seem too farfetched; if it is correct, it will indicate that Plutarch was right to see jury pay and attacks on the Areopagus as part of the same plan of Pericles—and on both of these questions Aeschylus may have felt strongly enough to take a public stand.[58]

We may ask how Aeschylus could bring himself thus publicly to oppose the man who had served as choregus for his *Persians* some fifteen years earlier. The truth must remain forever veiled, but a possible answer can be suggested. Aeschylus' earlier commitment to Themistocles seems, in large part at least, to have been a personal one. Drawn by the magnetic dynamism of the savior of the Persian Wars (as Thucydides was later to be, without the bond of personal contact) the poet took the opportunity in his *Persians* of 472 to remind his fellow countrymen of the great debt they owed Themistocles; the play formed a dramatic protest against their ingratitude. In the course of the next decade Aeschylus was able, in the *Suppliants*, to give a mythical paradigm of a band of fugitives in a similar situation to Themistocles' some years before, refugees sheltered and defended by the same Argive *demos* which had received Themistocles.

In a very real sense, Pericles was Themistocles' successor, but Pericles was not Themistocles. Cool, aloof, haughty even, his enemies could say, the younger man could not have commanded the same warmth of personal devotion as his predecessor; Aeschylus had never fought under Pericles' command. And even politically, Pericles never avowed his debt after he came onto the public scene. As Jacoby well puts it:

> Certainly Themistokles was not a personality to whom an active politician could refer for his policy . . . but Perikles presumably was not a friend of his great (greater?) predecessor, who probably was to blame for the ostracism of his father Xanthippos.[59]

This cannot have been the whole story, to be sure; Pericles' sponsorship of the *Persians* in 472 shows that before he became actively involved in politics, he supported his "greater predecessor"; it was only later that political expediency and latent family feeling caused Pericles to veil over his Themistoclean beginnings.

Beyond the differences in personality between the two men, Pericles' policies were much more radical than his predecessor's, at least in this, his "demagogic" period. If Aeschylus belonged to Themistocles' generation, Pericles was, by any traditional standard, an "upstart." Themistocles had been an Areopagite and, if he would have been in spirit at least a supporter of Ephialtes' reforms,[60] what transformations were to be worked in the following decades might have seemed, even to him, excessive. Jury pay and a separate board of *Nomophylakes* may seem to us a logical development from the Peiraeus walls and creation of a navy, but this did not make them any easier for one of Marathon's generation to accept.

I am suggesting that it was this, a particularly Periclean extreme, which Aeschylus, for all his sympathy with the liberal movement, found it impossible to countenance.

CHAPTER VI

Prometheus Bound

The *Prometheus Bound* can be considered from many points of view: as an anguished cry of the human spirit, a quarrying ground of archetypal images, a Marxian treatise illustrating the class struggle; even as "pure" drama. Here it will be approached from the direction of history, the trends and concepts which make up the political background against which it was written and which help, at least in part, to explain it.

Since Farnell, writing a generation ago, began a study of the religious aspects of the play with the admission that "the student of Greek religion has no more difficult problem to face than that of the *Prometheus Vinctus*"[1] it has been generally admitted that this "problem" is extremely difficult, if not impossible, of solution. Stated briefly, it is this: Zeus in the *Prometheus* is distressingly un-Aeschylean, with not even a trace of Homeric humor to compensate for his unedifying behavior.[2] Admittedly, we have mainly the evaluation of his bitter enemy (because uncompensated former friend), and a dispassionate evaluation of his archenemy is beyond Prometheus in his present circumstances. The chorus of Oceanids, however, corroborates Prometheus' charges, and, although they may be swayed to some extent by Promethean rhetoric, their judgment seems independent enough to insure that his unflattering portrait of his enemy is substantially lifelike. Even the normally politic Ocean once lets down his guard to describe Zeus as "a harsh monarch, whose rule cannot be called to account" (324). Finally, the surly insults and grim bloodthirstiness of Might and Hermes can hardly be said to reflect credit on their employer.

The usual solution is to believe that Aeschylus somehow "rehabilitated" Zeus in the sequel. Todd puts his case for the believers with frank directness: "I have no doubt that in the *Prometheus Unbound* Aeschylus presented not only a wiser and more willing subject in Prometheus, but also a more just, beneficent, and lovable Zeus."[3] Whether Zeus, or, for that matter, any Greek divinity, was ever thought of by his worshippers as "lovable" is another question.[4] Other solutions to the problem, to deny to the play membership in the Aeschylean corpus, or to exculpate Zeus by standing the facts on their heads and putting Prometheus entirely in the wrong, seem far too desperate remedies to be of much use. The most formidable proponent of the first view is still Schmid,[5] to whom two answers are possible: an echo of Rose's reaction that "the notion that [the *P.V.*] is not by him at all, put forward two or three times during the last century, is to me grotesque nonsense over which I refuse to waste time or paper";[6] or a less peremptory attempt to show that the points Schmid makes can be accounted for on other hypotheses than "la non eschileità."[7] The latter expedient, to whitewash Zeus by darkening the character of Prometheus, flies in the face of the obvious meaning of Aeschylus' lines. The most vociferous exponent of this view[8] is forced into absurdities to maintain his position. Along with Prometheus, the Oceanids must also be condemned: "Illusion and pleasure are the central features of their view of life" (57) and they are "indecently inquisitive" (61). "The girls are not only silly, inconstant and envious, but also of a mean sensuality" (63). We have a correlative absolution of the villains; Might and Hermes are simply servants, and "the character of Oceanus is noble and engaging. Wisdom and sincere readiness to help are the most conspicuous features of his character"

(45). Prometheus' benefactions to humanity are "delusions" and Io's sufferings are exaggerated; "for such a glorious future it was, indeed, worth-while to suffer. . ." (59). Verses damaging to the theory (for example, 1063–1079) are excised.

From such farfetched "solutions" of the basic problem, we can return to a chastening admission that, although we are entirely ignorant of the exact lines of the "rehabilitation," Aeschylus must have presented in his sequel an older, wiser and more moderate Ruler of the Gods. Restorations of the lost plays have usually proceeded from this assumption,[9] and there are, to be sure, several indications in the extant play of such a modification. In our play, the newness of Zeus' rule is repeatedly emphasized (35, 96, 149–50, 312, 389, 439, 942); by the opening of the *Pyrphoros*, it seems that 30,000 years have elapsed—time enough for the evolution of brash tyranny to a just and ordered primacy which is Zeus' traditional position.[10] "Zeus will become mild-tempered," Prometheus tells the Oceanids (188):

> He will smooth his stubborn wrath
> To a bond of friendship and will come
> To me at some time, our two wills one. (190–192)

Prometheus himself describes Zeus' part in the birth of Epaphus as a gentle healing process (848–849) and the Oceanids sing of Zeus' power in tones of usual Aeschylean reverence (525 ff.). It therefore seems probable that by the end of the trilogy "the harmony of Zeus," which the chorus mentions in the *Prometheus Bound* (551), was brought to fulfillment. Only we must be clear about this: however necessary such a conclusion appear, it remains an assumption. There are no fragments and very little ancient testimony to support it.[11]

For Zeus, as we see him in the *Prometheus Bound*, is an out-and-out tyrant, a monster of almost melodramatic proportions. The details of his characterization are laid on by the poet with an exaggeration which amounts, at times, almost to parody. Might is a thoroughgoing thug, very much a *doryphoros* in the service of the new Ruler of the Gods. In his opening lines the henchman gloats over the more gruesome aspects of his victim's punishment (especially 55 ff.) and says sardonically that Prometheus must "learn to love" the tyranny of Zeus (10–11). Even Hephaestus, for all his reluctance to comply with Zeus' orders, realizes the dangers of disobedience: "It is a serious matter to neglect the father's words."[12] He concludes his opening speech with an explanation of the severity of Prometheus' punishment: "Zeus' intentions are inexorable (*dysparaitêtoi*) for every new ruler rules harshly" (34–35). This unamenability of Zeus to persuasion is a recurrent theme in the play. The Chorus says that he has made his mind inflexible (*agnampton*, 163). The Chorus reiterates it toward the end of the parodos: "Cronos' son has an inexorable character and a heart which cannot be swayed (*aparamython*, 184–185). Prometheus refutes Ocean's boasts that he will intercede on Prometheus' behalf by pointing out that Zeus is not open to persuasion (333).

Besides harshness and intractability, Zeus is charged with ingratitude to his friends. Thus, Prometheus can say that his rule is afflicted with the usual ailment: "This malady is inherent in tyranny—distrust of one's friends" (224–225). His freedom from external restraint is emphasized: "a harsh monarch, and his rule cannot be called to account" (οὐδ' ὑπεύθυνος κρατεῖ, 324). Ocean is here merely echoing the charge which Prometheus himself had already made when he told the Chorus that he ruled "unrighteously" (*athetôs*, 150). They underline again the idiosyncratic nature of Zeus' rule in the first stasimon when they describe Zeus as "ruling with private laws" (403). Through mere repetition of the word, the audience must have received a stunning impression of Zeus Tyrannos.[13]

It is not too much to say, then, that Aeschylus has gone out of his way to darken his representation of the new "tyrant of the gods," as he calls him. Solmsen, who has studied Aeschylus' debt to Hesiod with great thoroughness, has shown that this heightening is achieved in part by two significant variations on the Hesiodic version of the myth.[14] Although Aeschylus took over the story of Zeus *vs.* the Titans from

Hesiod, Prometheus' assistance to Zeus in the struggle seems to be an addition of Aeschylus' own. The real motive for Aeschylus' innovation, in Solmsen's words, "was clearly his desire to add the charge of ingratitude to the other accusations hurled at Zeus."[15] Second, when Prometheus comes, in his long address to the Oceanids, to explain why he is being thus shamefully treated by Zeus, he begins by saying:

> . . . of long-suffering men
> He took no account, but wished to destroy
> The whole race, and to plant a new one;
> And these schemes no one opposed but I . . .
> (231–234)

This motif of destruction of the human race is not in Hesiod's version of the Prometheus story. "Obviously," as Solmsen writes, "Aeschylus wished to sharpen the conflict and heighten the outrage by using stronger colors than he found in Hesiod."[16]

The Aeschylean Zeus is harsh, not open to argument, suspicious of his friends, not accountable to others for his actions, and above the law. Thomson has shown by an exhaustive collection of the passages describing tyranny in Greek literature that the charges laid against Zeus in the *Prometheus* are all echoed elsewhere in Greek literature in condemnations of *human* tyrants.[17] Of the passages he cites several are especially interesting for the closeness with which they echo lines in the *Prometheus*. In Herodotus' "debate on constitutions" (3.80–83), Otanes condemns *monarchia* on grounds that the tyrant "does what he wants without giving an account" (ἀνευθύνῳ 80.3).[18] Furthermore, "he is jealous of the continued existence of the excellent, while taking joy in the basest of the citizens" (80.4). But of the three greatest charges Otanes levels against tyranny the first is its disregard for ancestral laws: νόμαιά τε κινέει πάτρια (80.5). The charge brought against Zeus that he "ruled with private laws" is repeated almost verbatim in Euripides' *Suppliants*, where Theseus denounces the tyrant as one who is above the law, τὸν νόμον κεκτήμενος αὐτὸς παρ' αὑτῷ (431–432). Another striking verbal parallel is provided by Lucian, to whom the Prometheus story seems to have been of especial interest.[19] The tyrant, he says, is a *despotês aparaitêtos* (*Tyrannicide* 16), which comes very close to Aeschylus' formulation δυσπαραίτητοι φρένες (34). Elsewhere, Lucian remarks that of the cares of the tyrant, the greatest is that "he must suspect most those who are dearest to him and must always expect something terrible to come from them" (*Gallus* 25).

But the most damaging charge against the tyrant was his violence in his treatment of citizens, and especially women. Solon had coupled "tyranny and relentless violence" (fr. 23. 9D); for Lucian, again, he is ὑβριστὴς βιαιότερος (*Tyrann.* 16), and the second greatest charge against the tyrant Otanes formulates thus: βιᾶται γυναῖκας (3.80.5). This charge of wanton violation is precisely the one laid against Zeus in his relations with Io. She is tormented by seductive nighttime visions urging her to offer herself to Zeus. When, finally, driven to distraction, she confides in her father, he consults Delphi and Dodona and is told to drive her from the house and let her roam to the corners of the world. If he does not comply, Zeus will destroy his whole house—

> there would come from Zeus a fiery
> bolt, which would annihilate his whole race
> (667–668)

and the words are a terrifying echo of Prometheus' earlier report of Zeus' plan for the human race ("after having annihilated the whole race. . . ," 232–233). "My father drove me from the house," Io says pathetically, "quite against his will, but Zeus' bridle forced him to do this *pros bian*" (671–672). The words stand as a striking condemnation of the new Lord of Heaven. When Prometheus has finished his first prediction of Io's wanderings, he asks:

> Does the tyrant
> of the gods not seem to you to be violent (*biaios*)
> in all things equally? (735–737)

To this bitter question—addressed primarily to the Chorus, but also to the audience and the Greek world at large—the answer must have been all too shockingly obvious. How can Io thus be blamed for agreeing with Prometheus that she would rejoice to see Zeus deposed? "How would I not rejoice, I who suffer evilly at Zeus' hands?" (759). *Bia*, Violence, though a mute character (addressed by Hephaestus at line 12), makes her presence felt not only in the opening scene, but through almost every line of the play.

In a recent study of the *Prometheus*, Méautis attempts to account for this emphasis on Zeus the Tyrant. He refers repeatedly to "l'arrière-plan politique" of the play and specifies it thus: "This tragedy . . . is an indictment (*réquisitoire*) against tyranny, a regime which Aeschylus could have come to know well during his first sojourn at the court of Hiero of Syracuse."[20] Méautis notes that the whole atmosphere of the opening scene is one of fear and constraint, typical of a tyrant's court. The Oceanids rebuke Prometheus for his unrestrained speech (180), and it is this very absence of free speech which is the hallmark of a dictatorial regime: "Constraint is the characteristic of tyrannies, of dictatorial regimes; freedom of expression does not exist there" (18). Aeschylus had already visited Sicily in 474 or thereabouts, and when, because of his alleged disaffection with the turn political events in Athens had taken, he decided to leave for good, Sicily naturally presented itself to him as a place of refuge. When he went to Sicily the first time, he found himself in a city "dominated by a tyrant. He could sense the atmosphere of terror which reigned there, the absence of liberty, the fear of uttering a free word . . ." (66), and so Syracuse was ruled out as a possible domicile:

> Wishing to return to Sicily since he disapproved of the internal evolution of Athens, Aeschylus could not dream of Syracuse, which recalled to him evil memories of his first stay and where, moreover, he might have been suspect since he had been the guest of Hiero and had celebrated the creation of Aetna. Quite naturally he thinks of Gela which welcomes him warmly. . . .
> *It is at Gela and for Gela that Aeschylus wrote his Prometheia.* These tragedies are, then, his last work and were inspired by

all that Sicily had lived through during the last years when she was removing herself from under the tyrants' yoke   (69).

The facts that Aeschylus, as Méautis notices, wrote his *Aetnaean Women* in honor of Hiero's new city[21] and that he probably arranged a special production of the *Persians* at Hiero's request[22] contradict Méautis' own view that he felt discomfort bordering on horror in the constricted atmosphere of the tyrant's court; and when Méautis concludes that "the *Prometheia* is Aeschylus' testament to Gela, to all of Sicily" (71), we are entitled to ask, Why a testament to Gela? Méautis' alternative explanation of why Aeschylus chose Gela over Syracuse, that his former good services to the tyrant Hiero would have made him persona non grata to the Syracusans, seems more cogent.

Although it is possible to disagree with Méautis on points of detail (as, for example, his *obiter dicta* on the political situation at Athens and Aeschylus' attitude to it), his more general thesis that the *Prometheus* is in some sense "an indictment against tyranny" seems unassailable.[23] In fact, Méautis has not taken his argument as far as he might have done, for he seems to have missed several details of Aeschylus' portrayal of Zeus which can be strikingly paralleled in the career of Hiero. Hiero's "foundation" of Etna for his son Deinomenes sometime after 476 was in fact a resettlement and renaming of Catana. Diodorus (11.49) relates how Hiero, in preparation for the event, expelled the Naxians and Catanians and resettled them at Leontini; he then filled his new city with 5,000 Peloponnesians and 5,000 Syracusans, brought in specially for the purpose. There seems to be a parallel between these upheavals and Zeus' plan to destroy the human race and beget another (*P.V.* 231 ff.). Again, it is clear that when Hiero succeeded Gelon in 478, the tyranny became considerably harsher, the new tyrant taking severe measures to consolidate his rule. Gelon, according to Diodorus (11.38), "had established a beneficent rule over the Sicilian Greeks and was providing their cities with a high degree of orderly government and an abundance of every necessity of life."[24] Hiero's first act upon his accession was to "enlist foreign soldiers and gather about him an organized body of mercenaries, for he expected in this way to get a secure hold on the kingship" (11.48). Diodorus makes the contrast between the old and the new tyrants explicit in Chapter 67:

> Gelon, since he treated the people whom he had subdued with fairness, and, in general, conducted himself humanely toward all his immediate neighbors, enjoyed high favor among the Sicilian Greeks. Thus Gelon, being beloved by all because of his mildness, lived in uninterrupted peace until his death. But Hiero, the oldest of the brothers who succeeded to the kingship, did not rule over his subjects in the same manner; for he was avaricious and violent, and, on the whole, a complete stranger to sincerity and nobility of character.

This worsening of the Syracusan tyranny answers surprisingly well to the "golden days of Cronos" giving way to the harsh and repressive measures of the young Zeus. In fact, this picture of a deterioration from one generation of tyrants to the next, whether true or not, became standard in the Greek view of their own tyrants:[25] we have only to think of Periander and the sons of Peisistratus.

The last point of which Méautis might have made more is the portrayal of Zeus' henchmen in the *Prometheus*. He points out the general resemblance between the character of Ocean and a typical courtier, any one of a dozen flatterers and hangers-on who would have attended the tyrant just as they did a Renaissance prince. "At the court of Hiero," writes Méautis, "Aeschylus must have run into these old courtiers, at the same time cunning and naive, who believed that they had some influence on the mind of the master" (22). What he fails to notice is the striking resemblance between another character in the play and historical persons for whom we have good evidence. In his discussion of the way tyranny is maintained Aristotle remarks that the tyrant must

> try not to be uninformed of what any of his subjects happens to say or do, but there must be spies, just as the so-called *potagôgides* among the Syracusans, and the "Eavesdroppers"

(*ôtakoustas*) whom Hiero used to send out wherever there was an assembly or a conference; for out of fear of such, men use freedom of speech the less . . .   (*Politics* 1313b11—16)

The term *ôtakoustês* exactly describes Hermes' role in the *Prometheus*.

When the remarkable emphasis on tyranny in the play is noted and underlined, the historian's task is only half done. He must then proceed to an interpretation, must try to account for it in terms of the political milieu in which Aeschylus lived and wrote. Even when we have agreed that there were many historical tyrants whom Aeschylus knew either at firsthand or from eyewitnesses—Peisistratus and Hippias, Xerxes, Hiero—upon whom he may have based actual details of his picture of Zeus, we must go on to try to discover why tyranny plays so large a part in the play. It becomes clear at once that no very sound conclusions can be reached until the play is anchored firmly in a chronological context. Otherwise, the historian runs the risk of circularity. From fancied contemporary references or allusions to historical events, conclusions are drawn about date of composition. The play is then examined further and more "contemporary" allusions are discovered. Méautis falls into the circular trap when he calls the play "a veritable indictment against tyranny . . . which enables us to establish, both the date of the work's composition, and the circumstances in which it was written . . ." (59). Unless we can first establish the date from other sources, we are completely unjustified in drawing historical inferences from the allusions to tyranny. We are fortunate in having extrinsic evidence for the dates of Aeschylus' other plays; as for the *Prometheus*, an attempt must be made to date it on other grounds than content. It is now fairly generally held that the *Prometheus Bound* was Aeschylus' last play, and this date is provisionally accepted for purposes of the present discussion; further details are deferred to an Appendix.[26]

On the assumption that the *Prometheus* was composed in 457 or 456, we may return to ask why Aeschylus attacked tyranny so violently in this, his last work. Any attempt to answer the question by saying that he was attacking a particular historical personnage, who stands in a one-to-one relation with Zeus, must be rejected at once. It is one thing to say that Aeschylus drew on real tyrants whom he knew or had heard about for realistic details of portraiture in his treatment of Zeus; quite another to believe that he was writing poetic allegory, that Zeus "is" or "is *really*" Hiero, or Xerxes, or whoever. To give a simple, question-begging refutation: great poetry is not written that way. Furthermore, we have only to look at the attempts which have been made to interpret the play as historical allegory. They are misguided in general conception and ludicrous in the working out of details.[27]

One more recent attempt may be considered at greater length. The equation "Zeus = Xerxes" had been made the basis of an entire volume by the Italian scholar Gaetano Baglio.[28] Baglio states his major premise clearly: Aeschylus might have inserted into the *Prometheus Bound* "individual lines which, apart from their visible mythological meaning, have in addition a meaning which alludes to events and persons of the war between the emperor Xerxes and Greece. . . ."[29] The play is examined by Baglio in painstaking detail, and these "singoli versi" are traced to what the author supposes to be their sources in Herodotus.

Although in theory there is nothing which rules out Baglio's approach on a priori grounds—Aeschylus may, indeed, have been inspired to write the *Prometheus* by certain events in the Persian Wars—in the execution of his plan Baglio falls lamentably short of anything that can reasonably be called critical method; for him, everything in the *Prometheus* is based on something in Herodotus. Several examples will suffice to show the absurdity of Baglio's approach. To serve his view that Zeus is really Xerxes in disguise, he makes much of Herodotus' report that when Xerxes crossed the Hellespont, a certain native of the region cried out, "O Zeus, why did you take the shape of a Persian man and change your name to Xerxes, in your wish to destroy Hellas?" (7.56). In Chapter

220 of the same book Herodotus gives the oracles to the Spartans, in which they were told that their foe could not be resisted, "for he has the strength of Zeus." For Baglio, Prometheus' prediction at line 171 that "Zeus will be stripped of his sceptre and his honors" was intended by the poet to refer to Xerxes' defeat at Salamis and his inglorious flight to Susa. What Baglio ignores, however, is that Prometheus' prediction was proven false in the event: Zeus was not so despoiled, but the two adversaries were (presumably) reconciled in some way. The same glaring discrepancy vitiates Baglio's theory that Prometheus' secret which he intends to play as a trump card against Zeus—his knowledge that if Zeus should be successful in his suit of Thetis the offspring of the union would be greater than the father—is a dramatic echo not only of Themistocles' secret plan (*palamê*, P.V. 166) for drawing the Ionians and Carians away from the Persian fleet at Artemisium (Herodotus 8.19) but also, and mainly, a reference to Themistocles' secret message to Xerxes which led the Persians into the straits of Salamis for their disastrous encounter with the Greeks. But, we want to say to Baglio, Xerxes was *defeated*, and would a Greek audience have tolerated a representation of their arch-enemy Xerxes in the dramatic guise of their Supreme God? Besides, what of these double references? Any case Baglio might have had is weakened by such imprecision, and his lame defense is hardly sufficient: "A great poet accumulates . . . or merges in a single point what occurs in different places, eliminating the intervals of space and of time" (141).

To return to Zeus' predicted suit of Thetis. Baglio believes that it is "based on" the prayers and sacrifices offered by the Persian magi to Thetis and the Nereids before Artemisium (Herodotus 7.191), and Xerxes' pouring of a libation into the sea at the time of his Hellespontine crossing (Herodotus 7.54) "could have offered to the Greek poets the artistic *motif* of imagining the emperor Xerxes as desiring to contract marriage with the western Aegean Sea" (114). But Baglio has overlooked, or is forced to ignore, Xerxes' earlier flogging of the Hellespont, related by Herodotus at 7.35: an odd way to treat an intended bride!

There are numerous other allegorical "equations" in Baglio's study—the two interventions by Alexander, son of Amyntas of Macedon, on the Persians' behalf (Herodotus 7.173 and 8.136) are the "source and inspiration" for Ocean's attempts to persuade Prometheus to submit to the will of Zeus, and Prometheus' boast that he alone withstood Zeus' attempt to obliterate the human race (232 f.) is "inspired by" Athens' aid to the Ionians during the Ionian Revolt, and the heroic resistance to Persia at Marathon in 490—but enough has perhaps been said to show the fatuity of Baglio's method. The rest may charitably be passed over in silence. Baglio's entire effort is stultified because he has ignored a simple but basic fact: plays are not written this way, at least not by competent playwrights. Only a hack could have written the *Prometheus* in the way Baglio assumes it was written, with every motif, every phrase almost, "inspired by" or "derived from" some external source. In addition, Baglio never stops to ask himself how much of what we find in Herodotus is Herodotus', and *not* well-known facts to which Aeschylus might have had access. A paradoxical case might better be made for Herodotus' borrowing of certain motifs from Aeschylus.

It may be that Baglio's very willingness to find minute specific parallels between politics and poetry must lead to his expulsion from the field of sober criticism to the fringe of imaginative fancy. In any case, another more general interpretation of the political "message" of the play commands greater attention. Benjamin Farrington put forward in a provocative chapter[30] the view that "what Aeschylus has dramatized in the *Prometheus* is the political problem of adjusting contemporary institutions to meet the great upheaval of the old ways of life represented by the Ionian enlightenment" (69). The argument is not always easy to follow, but it seems to be that Zeus represents the authority of the old aristocratic families, with their monopoly of the state cults, while Prometheus symbolizes the "Ionian enlightenment," the challenge to authority and alleged aristocratic thought-control in matters of religion which was offered by the speculations of Ionian physicists like Anaxagoras. The teachings of Ionian science, in questioning the traditional religious formulae, threatened the political control which the aristocracy exercised through the state cults. The aristocrats countered by repressing the political instincts of the people: "The aristocratic monopoly of the control of religion had held up the establishment of democracy for the best part of a century after Solon framed his constitution" (81). The attack on Anaxagoras, whom Farrington calls the "ideal embodiment of the spirit of Ionian science" (74), proves "the existence of a habit of exploiting the religious prejudices of the people for political ends" (76).

Aeschylus, as an exponent of democracy, tried in his work to reconcile the opposing sides, to make science compatible with religion and thus prepare the way for a new—and democratic—synthesis. "His purpose in the *Prometheia*, as I understand it (writes Farrington), was to offer the Athenian public a conception of Zeus that would not be incompatible with the Ionian enlightenment" (70). In the *Oresteia* and *Supplices* "the evolution of society is the poet's theme, and it is plain that in the main he is satisfied with the form it has taken in the moderate democracy of Athens" (81). "In his *Prometheia* Aeschylus thought out the problem of the city-state again from the point of view of the conflict between authority and enlightenment"; we are, unfortunately, ignorant of the precise solution Aeschylus found, but it can be assumed that to effect a reconciliation between the opposing forces he brought on stage Prometheus, "the ideal figure of the enlightenment," and showed him learning "to observe caution, to go slowly, to respect authority" (84).

Farrington's argument is general enough to avoid the absurdities into which Baglio and Davison fall, and it has the overriding virtue of being based on what I believe to be a correct view of Aeschylus' political commitment. But it is unfortunate that it is so sketchy. He does not deal specifically with the text of the play to show that his hypothesis can survive close scrutiny. As it is, he outlines a theory about which it is difficult to say more than that it might provide material for further development. On the purely historical side, however, it is an oversimplification to say that the aristocrats' monopoly of religion delayed the establishment of democracy, for the Peisistratid tyranny was surely a much more effective damper on political self-expression. There is, in addition, a major difficulty with his interpretation of the *Prometheus* as a close reflection of the political struggle between democrats and aristocrats. To maintain, as Farrington does, that in the play Aeschylus "gives us the picture of Zeus the tyrant; he is the blind, repressive Zeus of the oligarchic reactionaries" (84) is quite impossible. In the history of Greek tyranny, the aristocrats were the class which suffered most at the hand of a tyrant and they were invariably his bitterest enemies. The tyrant Zeus would then be a most unsuitable representative of the aristocratic old guard with whose entrenched prerogatives Farrington believes the new democratic science to have come in conflict in the figure of Prometheus.

Because it has been necessary to reject all attempts to see "behind" Aeschylus' Zeus, or any of the other characters in the drama, any one historical character, we need not abandon our search for the political importance of the play. For the full-length portrait of Zeus Tyrannos makes the *Prometheus Bound* a supremely interesting document in the history of Greek political theory, and its value as such has been overlooked. The play gives us the first formulation of any length of the new democracy's quarrel with the tyrant, who, as a law unto himself and beyond the check of legal redress, constituted an exact antithesis to the democratic process. When Ocean, in an unguarded moment, says of Zeus

he is a harsh monarch and rules without having to give account
(324)

who in the audience would not have thought at once of the democratic safeguards of the *euthynai*, by which anyone might question the actions of a magistrate at the end of his term of office? The seeds of democracy's quarrel with tyranny must have been planted after the murder of Hipparchus in 514, when the rule of Hippias turned from vague benevolence to repression and terror. After the expulsion of Hippias and his family in 510 the Athenians set up on the Acropolis a monument described by Thucydides as "the stele about the crimes (*adikias*) of the tyrants" (6.55.1). There soon developed what Jacoby called a "publicistic contest" between two sets of rival claimants to the honor of having brought an end to the tyranny, the Alcmeonids, who had been influential in the final expulsion of 510, and their enemies, who claimed the same honor for Harmodius and Aristogeiton four years earlier. The claims of the latter were symbolized in an early statue of the "tyrannicides" by Antenor and given a new lease of life by the dedication of a new group by Kritios and Nesiotes in 477. Although it is impossible to decide the matter with certainty, there are good grounds for believing that behind this recrudescence of support for the claims of Harmodius and Aristogeiton as against the Alcmeonids stood the figure of Themistocles.[31] To the service which visual art rendered politics was added that of poetry; the "Harmodius Song" must have already become a popular after-dinner ditty:

> I shall carry my sword in a myrtle branch
> Just as Harmodius and Aristogeiton did
> When they slew the tyrant
> And made Athens free before the law . . .
> (Attic Skolia, B 10 Diehl)

This anti-Alcmeonid story was to become the "official" version: the "tyrannicides" were given state honors which included a tomb in the Cerameicus, sacrifices offered by the polemarch, and public maintenance in the Prytaneion for the oldest descendant of each.[32] The publicity campaign was so successful that, at the end of the century, we find Thucydides going out of his way to correct the almost universal misconception that Harmodius and Aristogeiton really were responsible for the end of the tyranny.

The precise responsibility for the act of expelling the tyrants—an interesting by-way of history in its own right—

may be taken to illustrate the growth of a more general popular feeling at Athens against the expelled tyrants. No worse
omen nor one more calculated to arouse the Athenians could
be imagined than the arrival of the Persians at Marathon in
the summer of 490 under the escort of Hippias (Herodotus
6.102–103). For, in the twenty years which had intervened
since his expulsion, the Athenians had had their first taste of
the joys of democracy and had grown heady on them. "Athens,"
as Herodotus remarks, "though great before, became still
greater when it got rid of the tyrants" (5.66.1). And as the
democracy grew to a consciousness and appreciation of its own
specific virtues, its quarrel with tyranny as an institution became more bitter. The ostracisms which followed the successful repulse of Xerxes and his tool, the former tyrant of Athens,
were carried through on a wave of anti-tyrant feeling; the
Constitution of Athens calls (rightly or wrongly) the first
three men ostracized "friends of the tyrants."[33] It can plausibly
be maintained that the man behind these ostracisms was
Themistocles. But we need not believe that he simply mobil-
ized the Athenians' latent fear of a reintroduction of tyranny
against his own political enemies. He may also have been
motivated by a genuine hatred of tyranny. At least it seems
fair to assume that Themistocles felt such an antipathy to
tyrants from an anecdote told by Plutarch. "When Hiero sent
horses to compete at Olympia," Plutarch remarks, "and set up
a booth there with very costly decorations, Themistocles made
a speech among the assembled Hellenes, urging them to tear
down the booth of the tyrant and prevent his horses from
competing."[34]

The lines of evidence begin to converge: Themistocles *vs*
the "friends of the tyrants" (Alcmeonids?), Themistocles *vs*
Hiero at Olympia, Themistocles supporting the "tyrannicides"
in 477. In molding his ultra-tyrannical Zeus at the end of his
career, may not Aeschylus have been reflecting—if only inci-
dentally—influences to which he had been exposed decades
before by the politician he so much admired?

It is customary to consider Herodotus' "Persian Debate on

Constitutions" (3.80–82) as the first systematic formulation of
the opposing claims of tyranny, oligarchy, and democracy as
forms of government. In fact, as was noted above, the main
features of Otanes' attack on tyranny, and the correlative
praises of democracy which they imply, had already been anticipated by the charges which Prometheus or other characters
in Aeschylus' play bring against Zeus. By the end of the century the particular strengths and weaknesses of the two forms
of government became stock debating points: witness Theseus'
exchanges with the Theban herald in Euripides' *Suppliants*.
In the succeeding century, political philosophers took up the
question. Both Plato and Aristotle, though not by any means
as committed supporters of democracy, nevertheless formulated
exhaustively the specific evils of tyranny. It is necessary only
to open the *Politics* to Aristotle's treatment of tyranny and scan
several pages, almost at random, to see how closely his picture
of the tyrant echoes certain motifs and even specific lines of
the *Prometheus*.

In Chapter Eight of Book V of the *Politics* Aristotle discusses the reasons for which tyrannies fall. "Tyranny," he says,
"looks to no common good, except for the sake of its own
private interest" (1311a3). Attacks against the person of the
tyrant are brought about by his hybris, which engenders anger,
orgê, in his subjects, "and when men are angry, they mostly
attack for the sake of revenge. . . ." (1311a33 ff.). Later in the
chapter the point is restated. Two causes chiefly lead men to
attack tyranny—hatred and contempt; anger must be considered a part of hatred, and it is very often more effective
of results (*praktikôteron*, 1312b17–28). One of Ocean's pleas
to Prometheus had been, "relax the *orgas* which you have"
(317), and this *orgê* of Prometheus is the dominant note of the
final scene, his bitter exchanges with Hermes. The hybris of
the tyrant, Aristotle continues, manifests itself in shameful
personal treatment of his subjects, who respond by attempting to depose the tyrant:

> Many men also, angered by maltreatment and torture to their
> persons (διὰ τὸ εἰς τὸ σῶμα αἰκισθῆναι πληγαῖς ὀργισθέντες), have

actually carried through assassination, while others have attempted it, because they were treated insolently (*hybris-thentes*) . . . (1311b23 ff.)

A major theme in the play is the torture which Zeus inflicts, in the present and portrayed in bloodcurdling fashion before the eyes of the audience, on Prometheus, in the past on Io. And Aristotle's use of the term *aikisthênai* is noteworthy, for *aikia* and its cognates strike a recurring chord throughout the play. The verb is used by Prometheus of his treatment by Zeus at 168, 227, and 256; by the chorus at 195; the noun *aikeia* rises to Prometheus' lips at 93 and 177, and its variant *aikisma* at 989.[35]

In Chapter Nine, Aristotle proceeds to a discussion of the ways in which tyranny is preserved. Two of these he has already mentioned, "the lopping off of outstanding men, and the destruction of the proud" (1313a40).[36] In fact, the tyrant must guard against all things which might give rise to pride and confidence (*phronêma te kai pistis*, 1313b3). The citizens must be forbidden to join study groups or hold converse with one another, must be kept always in the open, for thus, Aristotle says, "they could least accomplish anything in secret, and would become habituated to thinking humbly, out of constant servility" φρονεῖν . . . μικρὸν αἰεὶ δουλεύοντες, 1313b9). Ocean had suggested snidely that Prometheus was too wise for his own good, *perissophrôn* (328), and he is urged by Hermes to mend his thoughts, *orthôs phronein* (999). "Self-will," says Zeus' henchman, "has no strength of itself in one who thinks not rightly," τῷ φρονοῦντι μὴ καλῶς (1012–1013). Prometheus is urged by Hermes and the Chorus to change his *authadia* for *euboulia* (1031–1038), a convenient euphemism for *phronein . . . mikron*. His refusal to humble his thoughts shows him, in Hermes' eyes, to be among the mad, the *phreno-plêktôn* (1054).

It has already been shown that Hermes exactly fits the description of one of the spies or "eavesdroppers" Aristotle says are employed by tyrants (1313b12 ff.). A further technique of tyranny is "to set men at variance with each other

and make friend clash with friend"; Hermes' attempt to dislodge the Oceanids from their support of Prometheus is met
with a staunch avowal of their loyalty even to death (1063 ff.).
Aristotle continues: "It is characteristic of the tyrant to be
especially distrustful of friends" (1313b31), which seems the
closest possible reminiscence of Prometheus' remark,

> this disease is inherent in tyranny—
> to have no trust in friends   (224–225)

"Behold," Prometheus later says to Ocean with cutting irony,
"this friend of Zeus . . ." (306). Aristotle continues with a
rather odd observation based on his theory that tyranny is the
degeneration of democracy: tyranny is fostered by two excesses
of democracy, dominance of women in the home (*gynaikokra-
tia*), "in order that they may carry reports against the men out
of doors," and lack of discipline among slaves. "For neither
slaves nor women plot against tyrants." Prometheus casts back
Hermes' advice to mend his thoughts with the retort: "Never
suppose that out of fear of Zeus I shall become womanish in
my intent (*thêlynous*) or that I shall beseech the one I hate
to release me from these bonds with hands upturned, woman-
wise" (1002–1006). Among tyrants, Aristotle says, those are in
favor who flatter them and associate with them humbly,
tapeinôs (1314a1): Ocean had complained to Prometheus, "you
are not yet *tapeinos*" (320). "For this reason," Aristotle continues, "tyranny is favorable to the base, for tyrants enjoy
being flattered"; we have only to think of the character of
Ocean.

"It is a further mark of tyranny not to enjoy the company
of anyone who is proud (*semnos*) or free-spirited (*eleutheros*),
for the tyrant thinks that he alone has these virtues, and the one
who answers pride with pride and freedom with freedom (*anti-
semnynomenos kai eleutheriazôn*) takes away from tyranny its
superiority and mastery; therefore tyrants hate such men as
destroying their authority" (1314a6–10). Once again, there are
several remarkable echoes in the play. The Oceanids accuse
Prometheus of harboring knowledge which is *semnon* (521),

and Prometheus uses the term ironically of Hermes' speech (*semnostomos*, 953). Might remarks in the opening scene that "all jobs are burdensome except ruling the gods; for no one is free except Zeus" (49–50). The antithesis of freedom is, of course, the slavery which Prometheus refuses to submit to, especially in speech. "You are too free of speech," the Chorus warns him (180); "your plight," he is told by Ocean, "is the reward of too high and mighty a tongue" (320–321). Aristotle sums up by saying that tyranny aims at three things: (1) to keep its subjects humble, (2) to keep them in a state of distrust of each other, and (3) "lack of power for action (*adynamia tôn pragmatôn*), for no one attempts the impossible, so that no one tries to destroy a tyranny if he does not have the power to do so" (1314a16–25). This last is the precise situation of the *Prometheus Bound:* we see Prometheus being rendered physically powerless—his moral strength grows with his indignation—stripped of the titanic resources he had employed first for Zeus' then for man's benefit, become the plaything of all the forces of nature and of the vindictive hatred of his enemy.

These Aristotelian echoes of Aeschylus have been drawn out at length to show not that the philosopher based his treatment of tyranny on the poet (although that is possible), but rather that the poet anticipated what was to become the standard philosophical view of the tyrant. The infant democracy had begun to try its new powers and to find the exercise of them exhilarating; the *Suppliant Women* was seen to reflect, as well as larger issues facing the democracy, some of the more mechanical aspects of democratic procedure. In the *Oresteia* Aeschylus presented his audience with a vivid exemplar of the incarnation—the embodiment—of an abstract justice in the very real and very human legal processes of his own day. Now, in the *Prometheus Bound,* his testament not to Gela but to the world, he has formulated the specific charges which the maturing democracy was laying at the door of the form of government from which it had evolved. Men like Cleisthenes and

Themistocles had fostered this sense of identity in the fledgling democracy and, now that it had come of age, it could look back on the preceding century with a justifiable pride in its own accomplishments, an excusable sense of superiority. It is this newly blossomed pride and self-assurance which is reflected by Aeschylus in a picture which, if not so systematic as Herodotus' or Aristotle's, is nevertheless dramatically conceived and portrayed with great vigor and beauty.

CHAPTER VII

Conclusion

Aeschylus lived the first fifteen years of his life under the tyranny of Hippias. As a youth he saw the liberation of Athens and the democratic reforms of Cleisthenes. The first years of the fifth century brought Greece under the shadow of Persia, but twice Athens withstood the invader—at Marathon and again at Salamis; in both of these engagements Aeschylus is said to have seen action. With the Persian threat dispelled, power in the Greek world began to polarize toward the two incompatible world views represented by Athens and Sparta. The vigorous adolescence of the new democracy and the confidence in its imperial destiny which the success of 480 had inspired set Athens moving irreversibly to a lofty position which the older and more constricted outlook of Sparta could not help but interpret as a threat. And imperial success itself generated in the ordinary Athenian a brash self-reliance and an eagerness for a real voice in the affairs of his city. The motive which Thucydides attributes to the Spartans for their dismissal of the Athenians from Ithome is significant: they "feared the Athenians' audacious vigor and readiness to make changes" (1.102.3). The men of Marathon had to yield in the end to the self-assertiveness and sheer thrust of Pericles and his generation.

It was an exciting time. Is it any cause for surprise that Aeschylus, who had lived through these years of danger and victory, of feverish activity abroad and political revolution, more or less peaceful, at home, should have taken an interest in public affairs and should have reflected that interest in his plays? Is his work any the less impressive for being firmly rooted in a definite historical context? Are his universal themes the less moving for at times being applicable to the particular issues with which his contemporaries were concerned?

The relevance of Aeschylus' dramas to the political life of their day seems considerable. Indeed, it is probable that much of that relevance has escaped us, who are so far removed in time and temperament from the men who watched them and from the movements with which the dramatist and his audience were involved. But here and there a glimmer has come through. The influence of their political background on the plays has been shown to be various. If Zeus in *Prometheus Bound* is not Xerxes, or Hiero, or, for that matter, Hippias, touches of realistic detail from all of these sources—and more besides, now, unfortunately, lost to us—may have influenced the final portrait of the young Olympian tyrant. In a more general way the whole play betrays a preoccupation with tyranny as a political system, and it formulates, perhaps for the first time, many of the charges which the young democracy must have been making against the tyrants, both its own and those around it. Many of the details which characterize Zeus became, within a short time, stereotyped features of the tyrant, which ultimately appeared, in more abstract guise, in the philosophical thought of the fourth century. The *Seven Against Thebes*, on the other hand, is the least political of the surviving plays. Aeschylus may, it is true, have taken his description of Amphiaraus as an opportunity to defend the probity of Aristeides, whose honesty seems (surprisingly) to have been under attack at the date of the play, but it is at best a doubtful hypothesis. There is an additional interesting, though decidedly less important, suggestion that the details of the siege of Thebes by the Seven were drawn by Aeschylus from memories of the Persian invaders. Beyond this we cannot go. Attempts to see real persons "behind" the characters of either drama are thoroughly unconvincing. Eteocles is not Pericles, nor Prometheus Protagoras.

In the remaining plays the political interest is both greater and more precisely definable. The *Persians* and the *Suppliants* can be called "Themistoclean" dramas in the sense that they have, in addition to their dramatic themes, a particular application to the career of Themistocles. The *Persians* was written in 472, probably on the eve of Themistocles' ostracism. Featured prominently in the play is the victory of Salamis for which his strategic genius was largely responsible. On the dramatic level the defeat of Xerxes assumes the center of interest, but that defeat was itself brought about by the men in the audience under the guidance of one of their number whose enemies were now mustering their forces against him. Aeschylus throws great emphasis on Salamis by introducing its name throughout the play in a threnodic refrain. He has the messenger describe the actual battle in extended and breathtaking detail. It was here (almost here alone, the dramatist seems to be saying) that the Persians' hybris was finally thwarted by the gods. From here the Great King beat a hasty retreat to his eastern dominions in humiliation and despair. And the details of the ruse by which Themistocles was said (whether truly or not does not matter) to have lured the Persian fleet into the straits are placed by Aeschylus at the beginning of the messenger's account of the actual battle. The choice of subject, the method of its development, and its presentation at just this time, when Themistocles' career was being threatened, lead ineluctably to the conclusion that in the *Persians* Aeschylus was reminding the Athenians of the debt they owed to Themistocles—was, in fact, issuing a subtle rebuke to their ingratitude in now doubting the loyalty of the savior of Salamis. It is a typically Athenian paradox that the trilogy of which the *Persians* formed a part should have won first prize in the dramatic competitions but that Themistocles himself was ostracized and later declared an outlaw on a charge of collusion with Pausanias' alleged advances to the Persian king.

In the *Suppliants* we have a band of fugitives received

and given official protection by the Argive state, after a unanimous vote in a thoroughly democratic mass meeting of the people. Here Aeschylus seems to be reminding his audience that it was Argos which had given protection to Themistocles after his ostracism some years before—and the Argive *demos*, although the democracy at Argos had since fallen on evil days with the return to power of the "Sons of the Slain," had apparently been restored or was on the verge of restoration at the probable date of the play's production, 463. Beyond this reminiscence of the Argives' services to Themistocles, the play had a more immediate relevance to the whole political situation of the 460's. It was at this time that the Athenian liberals were pressing for a realignment of Athens' external commitments. Cimon and the conservatives had always favored Sparta, Athens' "yoke-fellow," as Cimon was said to have called her, but the more foresighted Athenians (Themistocles among them, for he had probably been organizing anti-Spartan feeling in the Peloponnese after his ostracism) knew that Athens' imperial design would have to be forged in opposition to Sparta. By the end of the decade Cimon's pro-Spartan policy was sharply repudiated and Cimon himself ostracized; as a sign of the new challenge which Athens felt herself strong enough to offer to Sparta, an alliance was formed with Sparta's inveterate enemy and traditional competitor for Peloponnesian hegemony. The alliance with Argos was probably being debated some years before its actual conclusion, and, if that is correct, the extremely favorable light in which the *Suppliants* casts the Argive democracy and the praises heaped on their benefactors by the daughters of Danaus will show that Aeschylus was looking not only backward to the Argive reception of Themistocles but forward to the coming alliance as well. The concept of democracy is here formulated explicitly, perhaps for the first time. It is even possible that this formulation was encouraged by the slogans issuing from Ephialtes and his circle.

Part and parcel of Athens' reorientation toward Argos were Ephialtes' reforms of the powers of the Areopagus in 462/1. This was the sign·that the new era in the development of

Athenian democracy had arrived: the conservative old guard of Athenian public life, steeped in traditional privilege and wielding great moral influence as a senior Board of Censors, was stripped of all its judicial powers except in certain capital cases: murder, arson, and religious questions concerning the sacred olive trees. "Some of these Ephialtes gave to the Five Hundred, some to the *demos* and the lawcourts," the *Constitution of Athens* remarks. What precisely these powers were is nowhere made clear, but what is important for our purposes is the reflection of the reforms in the *Oresteia*. There we see the grim blood-feud of the house of Atreus played out before our eyes: Agamemnon falls victim to the claims of Clytemnestra and Aegisthus, they in turn are slain by Orestes, and all the members of the doomed family insist that they are merely acting as agents of Justice. By the final play, the *Eumenides*, claim and counterclaim have been put forward and the opposing forces have reached an impasse. Clytemnestra's ghost drives on the Erinyes to seek retribution for her murder by Orestes, while he protests that he only carried out Apollo's commands. At this point Athena steps in and resolves the dispute by instituting the lawcourt of the Areopagus—a human tribunal composed of the "best of her citizens"—whose verdict she persuades the Erinyes to accept. At the end of the play, in a tour de force of reconciliation, the Dread Goddesses are transformed into "Eumenides" and the bestial forces let loose in the earlier plays are civilized and brought to rest. The claims of cosmic Justice are satisfied through the application of legal justice, at once civic—organized by the *polis* as a whole and exercised for the benefit of its members—and. more humane than the blood vengeance it has been designed to replace. In this sense the *Eumenides* can be said to be the most political of Aeschylus' plays.

The prominence of the Areopagus in the resolution of the conflict makes it clear at once that Aeschylus was adverting in 458 to Ephialtes' reforms of some years before, although the precise stand he takes in the dispute is less clear. At first sight the prestige with which Athena endows her new court might be taken to indicate that Aeschylus disapproved of the reforms, but a closer reading shows that the one specific judicial power she assigns to her newly instituted court is jurisdiction in homicide cases, such as Orestes'. When we discover that it was precisely this power which was left untouched by Ephialtes, we may begin to wonder whether Aeschylus' attitude to the reforms was not, after all, more subtle than at first appeared. May he not here portray Athena bestowing on the Areopagus this power and this power only, because (to adapt a remark of Jacoby's) it was the very power left undisturbed by Ephialtes? In other words, is it not possible that Aeschylus was trying to disarm opposition to the reforms in conservative circles by composing a mythical charter for the Areopagus which authorized it as possessing for all time exactly the field of competence which the Reformers allowed it to retain? That this was in fact Aeschylus' message to his compatriots is made extremely probable by the triple reference in the *Eumenides* to the Argive alliance, which formed, as we have seen, a major part of the reform program.

Some critics have felt that beyond the actual constitutional powers of the Areopagus referred to in the play, the body is shown to be endowed by Athena with a *moral* authority, an *auctoritas*, which was threatened by the Reformers' attacks. Thus, the court is described as a "bulwark of the country," a "guardian of the land." Since it appears that Aeschylus gave wholehearted approval to the curtailment of its legal powers by Ephialtes, it may be that he is here going on to protest a further attack against this moral prestige of the Areopagus. If a notice in Philochorus is correct that a board of *Nomophylakes* was set up about this time and if the vague phrases in Athena's speech can be taken as referring to this "guardianship of the laws" (perhaps merely an honorific title without constitutional significance), Aeschylus may be rebuking an actual or proposed transfer of this *Nomophylakia* from the Areopagus to a special board. The quarter from which this alleged attack came is unknown, but we hear of a separate (undated) attempt of Pericles to strip power from the Areopagus. The hypothesis that it was Pericles' attempt to remove from the Areopagus its *Nomophylakia* which Aeschylus is opposing in the *Eumenides* is given some confirmation by Athena's remark that her new court is "untouched by gain"; we know that Pericles, at an unspecified date, introduced pay for service on the popular juries, and Aeschylus seems to be going out of his way to emphasize that service on the Areopagus is, by contrast, disinterested. If the dramatist took the trouble to oppose a known measure of Pericles it is possible that Pericles was responsible for another measure, institution of a separate board of *Nomophylakes*, against which Aeschylus also seems to be issuing a protest in the play.

Aeschylus was a *Marathōnomachos*, a veteran of the Persian Wars, who had come within the magnetic field of the author of the victory of Salamis. Two of his plays manifest his support of Themistocles, and his only extant trilogy shows him on the side of the liberal reforms of 462/1. But Pericles was of the younger generation, and Pericles lacked the personal attractiveness of Themistocles. It is not difficult to see where Aeschylus drew the line in his support of the liberals: one innovation which he is seen to have opposed is firmly attributed to Pericles, and the hypothesis is not inconsistent with this that he raised his voice in the *Eumenides* against institution of the *Nomophylakes* as another Periclean extreme.

Aeschylus on Salamis

In the *Persians* we have a contemporary and firsthand account of the battle of Salamis, the messenger's report of which takes up the whole central section of the play.[1] Modern historians are generally agreed on the unique value of Aeschylus' testimony. Macan puts it well:

> To Aischylos belongs indisputable priority in this case; and, making all allowance for poetic treatment, and dramatic situation, Aischylos must remain the regulative witness in regard to the actual battle, of which he, and he alone, writes as a contemporary and eyewitness for eyewitnesses and contemporaries. In case of contradiction between Aischylos and Herodotus, in regard to matter of fact, and failing a harmony or explanation, the historian must succumb to the poet.[2]

Unfortunately, Macan does not later adhere to this admirable program, but it is to his credit that he underlined clearly the significant differences which exist between the accounts of Aeschylus and Herodotus. A recent tendency has manifested itself (in the work, for example, of Hammond, and, to a lesser extent, Burn) in a particularly distressing brand of syncretism: when "authorities" disagree, they must all be correct; they are "supplementing" one another. The first step is to examine Aeschylus' account:

A Hellene, from the Athenian host, came to thy son Xerxes and told this tale: that, when the gloom of sable night should set in, the Hellenes would not hold their station, but, springing upon the rowing benches of their ships, would seek, some here, some there, to preserve their lives in stealthy flight. But Xerxes, on hearing this, not comprehending the wile of the Hellene nor yet that the gods grudged him success, straightway gave charge to all his captains to this effect—that, when the sun had ceased to illumine the earth with his beams, and darkness had covered the precincts of the sky, they should bring up in serried order the main body of the fleet, disposed in triple line, to bar the exits and the sounding straits, and station other ships in a circle around the island of Ajax; with the warning that, should the Hellenes escape an evil doom, finding by stealth some means of flight for their fleet, it had been decreed that every captain should lose his head.

(355–371; text and trans. Smyth)

We may note the time indications; the messenger must have come in the afternoon of the day before the battle; he announced that "when night fell" the Greek fleet would attempt to escape; Xerxes ordered his admirals to embark "when the sun had set." According to Aeschylus the contents of the message to Xerxes were as follows: "The Greeks will not stay but will try to save their lives in disorderly (ἄλλος ἄλλοσε) and secret (κρυφαίῳ) flight." Equally specific were Xerxes' orders to his men "to station the main body of ships in three columns to keep the Greeks from sailing out and guard the 'pathways of the roaring sea,' but for others to encircle the isle of Ajax."

The messenger continues:

Our crews then, with no lack of order but with an obedient spirit, prepared their evening meal, while each sailor looped his oar about its thole-pin so that it fitted well. But when the light of the sun had faded and night drew on, each master of an oar and each man versed in arms went on board. The long galleys cheered each other, line by line; and they held their course as each captain had been ordered, and all the livelong night the commanders of the fleet kept their whole force cruising to and fro across the strait.

(374–393; text and trans. Smyth)

They had an orderly supper and embarked only "when the sun's light waned and night came on." The ships formed three columns as they had been instructed, and the men were kept at the oars all through the night. "Night departed and the Hellenic force was very far from sailing out secretly; but when it was light (to paraphrase and abridge the rest of the speech somewhat) first the Greeks were heard to be singing noisily and in good spirits. . . . Fear seized all the barbarians that they had been mistaken in their judgment, for the Hellenes were raising the paean not in flight, but rushing to battle with high hearts" (384–394).

The order of the events which followed is clearly indicated by the messenger: the trumpet's blare (395), then the *sound* of oars striking the water (396–397), and finally "all came quickly into view" (398), the Greek right wing leading, and in good order; then followed the entire force (399–400). After an exhortation from the Greek side and an answering shout from the Persian, "immediately ship drove brazen beak on ship" (408–409), and the actual fighting had begun.

However the account stands up to a comparison with others which claim to be more properly "historical," and whatever reconstructions of Persian strategy are brought to bear, it is obvious that Aeschylus' retelling of the preliminaries and first encounter is clear, internally consistent, and, so far as we can judge, complete. If we now turn to the narrative of Herodotus, we see that it differs from Aeschylus' account in almost every detail. First, the time of the message: according to Aeschylus, the man crossed to Xerxes before supper, therefore at some unspecified time in the afternoon or early evening. In Herodotus, night had already fallen (8.70) when Sicinnus delivered Themistocles' message to Xerxes (8.75). There is a discrepancy in the two accounts as to the sender and receiver of the message. Aeschylus says a "Greek man," and the message is apparently delivered to Xerxes in person, while Herodotus says that Themistocles' slave Sicinnus took his message "to the generals of the barbarians" (8.75). It should be noted that Aeschylus' account, by omitting the intermediary slave, throws greater emphasis on Themistocles as the author of the message;

"a man went and said" is poetic shorthand for "his slave took the message and went." Whether Sicinnus spoke to Xerxes' commanders or to the king personally seems impossible to decide. Probably, Xerxes himself would have to decide about so important a matter as the credibility of the message and how the fleet was to be disposed as a result of it.

The message itself, simple and to the point in Aeschylus, is considerably expanded in the Herodotean version—"the Athenian commander has sent me without the knowledge of the other Greeks"—not a word of this in Aeschylus; Herodotus' whole motif of the wily Themistocles outwitting not only the Persians but his fellow Greeks as well, by forcing them to fight against their will, is belied by Aeschylus' description of the good order (εὐτάκτως . . . κόσμῳ) and good spirits (εὐψύχῳ θράσει) of their advance. This is in fact unwittingly confirmed by Herodotus' incidental remark, ". . . since the Hellenes had fought in orderly arrangement and as they had been assigned" (8.86), although this detail is in conflict with his earlier statement that the Greeks "backed water" (8.84), a detail otherwise unexplained and leading up (suspiciously) to the report of the miraculous apparition of a woman who asked—in a voice so loud the whole army could hear—how long they would go on backing water. The kernel of the message is the same in both authors; as Herodotus puts it, "the Hellenes, though affrighted, are planning flight." But he continues it as follows:

> . . . . Now you can accomplish the most spectacular feat of all, if you do not sit back and watch them run off; for they do not agree among themselves nor will they any longer withstand you, and you will see them fighting each other, those who think the same as you and those who do not. . . .
>
> (8.75)

Now Munro interprets this "second part" of the message as indicating that Themistocles "really" assured Xerxes that the *Athenians* were ready to Medize and come over to his side; it was precisely this promise of a quick surrender, he maintains, that lured the Persian fleet into the straits. This alleged Herod-

otean "variation" of the content of the message has become
something of a modern myth. Munro's theory is accepted, and
the "Herodotean version" preferred to the Aeschylean, by Tarn,
Macan, and How and Wells, who write, ". . . the full message
must have sounded to the King as follows: the Peloponnesians
are so completely cowed that they wish to flee, and we Athenians are so disgusted at being deserted that we are ready to
Medize; attack this dispirited and divided fleet and you will
end the war in a blaze of glory."[3] Now, Themistocles' "real"
message to Xerxes may have sounded like that, but Herodotus'
obscure wording does little to help prove it. The promise of
Athenian surrender has been seized on by modern historians
as the only thing which will explain the Persians' entry into
the straits; this may be correct, but we should be clear that
such an interpretation rests only shakily on the authority of
Herodotus. It might be supposed, however, that if Herodotus
felt a different version of the message was necessary to explain
the entry of the fleet into the straits, he would have made
clearer what exactly the bait was that lured Xerxes' ships into
the trap. As it is, we have simply an expansion of the Aeschylean version without a clarification of the point which modern
historians feel to be unacceptable in it.[4]

   The effect of the message is clearly stated by Aeschylus:
Xerxes ordered the main part of the fleet to deploy in three
columns (*stoichoi*) in order to "guard the exits and channels
of roaring sea" (367), while some other ships were to sail
around Salamis (368). According to Herodotus the effect of
Themistocles' message was not that the Persians initiated
action, as Aeschylus indicates, but that they were led by this
new development to modify an existing plan, for we are told
that earlier in the day on which the message arrived, "they
put the ships out toward Salamis and in leisurely fashion drew
them up posted for battle" (παρεκρίθησαν διαταχθέντες); they
were only prevented from giving battle by the intervention of
night (8.70). The natural meaning of the Greek is that the
Persian fleet was "drawn up along the shore" *of Attica*, that is,
from Mount Aigaleos to Munychia Bay; but if that is what

Herodotus meant, he must have been mistaken. What could have induced the Persian fleet to sail into the narrows? And how could they have done so under the very noses of the Greeks on Salamis? Herodotus' confusion in this respect notwithstanding, historians like Macan take his account as evidence that the Persians had an "original plan" which was somehow modified as a result of Themistocles' message; the nature of this plan remains obscure.

In Chapter 76 Herodotus describes the Persian reaction to the message. "First they landed many men on the islet of Psyttaleia; next, in the middle of the night, they advanced their western wing circling towards Salamis." Both these actions are thought to be mentioned by Aeschylus, but the differences are noteworthy. Aeschylus states definitely that Xerxes gave orders that "other ships were to circle around Salamis" (368). If it was this movement to which Herodotus is referring, as How and Wells maintain,[5] he does his best to obscure the point by his phrasing: "circling with the west wing towards Salamis" is not a satisfactory way of referring to a *separate* contingent which was to circumnavigate the island.[6] The Persian detail on Psyttaleia is likewise troublesome, not least because the island has not been identified with complete certainty.[7] Herodotus makes this move follow immediately on the receipt of Themistocles' message; Aeschylus is less definite. The messenger completes his account of the disastrous naval battle and destruction of the Persian fleet. There are several exchanges between him and the Queen, and he proceeds to his account of a "greater horror": "There is an island. . . ." Aeschylus does not specify when the Persian troops were landed on the island, but it seems a safe inference that he thought it was after the message had been delivered, whether in the late afternoon, that night, or some time the following morning. Almost the only point on which Aeschylus and Herodotus agree is the purpose of these troops: "so that when the shipwrecked enemy should try to get to safety on the island, they might kill them easily and save their friends from the watery waves. . . ." (451–453); "to save the one group and destroy the other" (8.76).

When we come to the actual battle, neither Aeschylus nor Herodotus gives a very full account.[8] But there are some precious indications of the order of events at the beginning in Aeschylus. First, the sound of oars striking the water, then the Greeks come quickly into sight, the right wing leading and in good order (399); finally, "the entire force followed the advance" (400–401). A Greek ship struck first, breaking off the beak of a Phoenician (409–411). The Persian fleet was thrown into confusion; their ships were knocked together and damaged by one another's rams (415–416), and the Greeks took this opportunity to encircle and strike (417–418). The scene then dissolves into a series of rapidly sketched pictures: ships overturned, the sea and neighboring shores full of wreckage and corpses, the Persian fleet in full flight and the survivors struck with bits of flotsam like tunnyfish, the whole sea "possessed" by shouts and groans. We get a series of quick impressions vividly suggesting destruction and carnage, but little help in reconstructing actual events of the battle.

Herodotus' account (8.84–95) is not much more helpful.[9] His report of how it started is less specific than is Aeschylus': "Then the Hellenes put their ships out to sea, and as they were doing so the barbarians immediately attacked them." Some say Ameinias of Pallene, an Athenian, was the first to charge, but the Aeginetans claim this honor for themselves.[10] Chapter 85 opens: "Against the Athenians were arrayed the Phoenicians (for they held the wing towards Eleusis and the west), against the Lacedaimonians, the Ionians." This apparently straightforward account is not without its obscurities. "In strictest accuracy the wing, or column, towards Eleusis could not be the west wing," notes Macan, and it is not clear that Herodotus has distinguished this "west wing" from that in Chapter 76.[11] In Chapter 86 he reports that "the majority of the ships were destroyed at Salamis, some by the Athenians and others by the Aeginetans." There follows a series of anecdotes: Artemisia's exploits (88–89, to illustrate Xerxes' *mot*, "my men have become women and my women men"), the Phoenicians' unsuccessful attempt to impugn the loyalty of the Ionians (90),

Athenians and Aeginetans again (91), Polycritus of Aegina and Themistocles (92), Greek *aristeiai* (93) and Corinthian cowardice (94), Psyttaleia (95).

It is clear, then, that of the two earliest accounts of the events of the day preceding the battle, the disposition of the Persian fleet during the night, and the preliminaries and first encounter of the actual engagement, Aeschylus' is the more complete and the more internally coherent.[12] He cannot have been in a position to know with any precision the course of events during the battle, and so he limits himself to a few quick but telling impressions. There is only one obscurity in Aeschylus' account. Why did the Persian fleet enter the straits? The secret message of Themistocles, as most authorities ancient and modern agree, can alone explain this disastrous move, and yet the message as reported in the *Persians* does not seem to do so. "The Greeks will attempt to escape under cover of night" was the essence of the message, and Xerxes reacted appropriately by stationing the main body of his fleet to guard the "exits and channels of the roaring sea" (367). The Persians kept at their stations all night long (382) and in the morning were surprised that the Greeks had not attempted to sail out secretly (385). When it was completely light, they heard the Greeks raise the paean; fear gripped their hearts and the next thing they knew the Greeks came streaming out to give battle (394). It must have been at this point that a definite decision was made by the Persian fleet to answer the challenge; they raised a shout:

> And it was high time to delay no more.
> At once ship struck brazen beak
> Against ship.   (407–409)

That the main encounter took place within the straits is certain from the messenger's words, "when the main body of ships had collected in the narrows" (413–414), and the implication of the phrase "the stream of the Persian force" (412) seems to be that when the Persians perceived the Greek fleet rushing to the attack, they responded by surging into the straits themselves—to their cost.[13] Although it has been assumed (by, for example, Macan) that the three *stoichoi* were in parallel rows south of Lipsokoutali, it is possible that they were stationed separately (say) one south of Lipsokoutali, another between the island and Cynosoura, and—perhaps—a third stretching partly into the straits from Peiraeus.[14] Something of the sort may be indicated by the messenger's words "all night long the lords of the ships kept the naval host διάπλοον" (382–383).[15] If this conjecture is correct, much of the Persians' confusion will have been due to the attempt of the other two *stoichoi* to rush to the defense of the one that stretched partly into the straits and was the direct objective of the Greek fleet as it streamed from Salamis harbor. Herodotus also suggests that the confusion was compounded by the efforts of the rear ranks of ships to rush forward to perform a memorable exploit before the eyes of the king; in so doing they fell afoul of the retreating front ships (8.89.2). Themistocles, then, must simply have gambled that the Persians, in their expectation of finding the Greek ships easy prey as they tried to escape secretly by night, would be taken off their guard by a sudden, well-ordered attack at dawn; that the frustration of the Persian commanders, cheated of their easy prey, would incite them into entering the straits to join battle, and that their crews, exhausted from having been kept at the oars all night, could be defeated by a refreshed and high-spirited Greek offensive. Certainty in the matter is impossible, but some such explanation as this seems preferable to the view that Herodotus is reporting (quite unintelligibly) the "real" message, a promise of Athenian surrender.

Recently, the whole question of Themistocles' message and its influence on the Persian movements was reopened by Hignett.[16] He attempts to show that it was not authentic but a "historical fiction" which "may have grown out of a claim made by [Themistocles] that he had been responsible for compelling the Persians to fight in waters favourable to the Greeks" (407). For him, Persian entry into the straits at dawn would have been "an act of stark lunacy"; "it is incredible

that the Persians should ever have ventured to take such a
frightful risk on the bare word of a lying Greek" (228). This
movement, according to Hignett, would have been so lacking
in motivation that the message (and the message in its Herodotean version) had to be invented to account for it, for "the
message in its original [Aeschylean] form provides no explanation for the decision of the Persians to enter the straits . . . on
the morning of the battle" (228). But Hignett's solution to the
impasse, to prefer Herodotus' account of the Persians' entering
the straits *by night*, in reality solves nothing; it simply moves
the difficulties back in time by a few hours. In addition to the
minor inconcinnity of the "Herodotean" version of the message
invented to account not for Herodotus' own report of the
movement of the fleet (at night), but for Aeschylus' (at dawn),
Hignett's confidence that Persian entry by night needs no false
bait to explain it seems misplaced. It is not enough to suppose,
as Hignett does, that the Persians had to attack because they
knew they could not turn the position of the Greek land army
at the Isthmus without first precipitating an encounter with the
Greek fleet which was flanking their advance. For the question
remains, Why now and in these unfavorable waters? To assume, with Hignett, that the Persians allowed themselves to
be lured in simply by the prospect of the advantages to be
gained by deploying under cover of darkness gives little credit
to the Persians for good sense; it would not have taken an
Aristeides or a runaway Tenean ship to tell the Greeks that
the Persians were coming up the channel under their very
noses. And the assumption—that the Persians were seeking
the advantage of a secret deployment—is itself vitiated by
their actions at dawn; on Hignett's own admission, they "allowed the Greek fleet to form in line undisturbed at daybreak
on the morning of the battle when they were separated from
them by not much more than a mile of sea" (225–26). Hignett's
own parry to this objection is ineffectual: "Perhaps they were
tired after the strain of their nocturnal movement and failed
to realize the need for prompt action if they were to exploit
to the full the advantage which that movement had given

them" (227). They risked entry into the channel by night, on Hignett's hypothesis, precisely to throw away their opportunity because of fatigue!

But what if Hignett were justified in suspecting the authenticity of the message? In that case, an even stronger argument could be made for the *Persians* as propaganda for Themistocles. The message is displayed prominently in Aeschylus' account of the battle and Themistocles is all but named, the mediation of his slave Sicinnus being conveniently ignored; if the story of the message originated in Themistocles' circle, as Hignett believes, who could say with confidence that it was not Aeschylus who originated it? At the very least he would have given it the stamp of his approval and started it on its long life as a snare to historians through the ages, by including it in his play at extended length and in the emphatic position at the very start of his report of events leading up to the battle.

APPENDIX B

The Date of the
Prometheus Bound

There is a *consensus sapientium* that the play was written later
rather than earlier in Aeschylus' career, but this gives considerable leeway. Focke held that the play was written about
470, and he is followed by Vandvik, who believes that "the
Prometheia is probably written not long after 475." Wilamowitz argued from what he supposed to be an echo in the lost
Sphinx of 467 that the Prometheus must have been written
before that date.[1] Croiset and Mazon place it, somewhat un-
helpfully, between the *Seven* and the *Oresteia*.[2] Among English-speaking scholars, the orthodox tendency has been to place
it very late, perhaps last, in the poet's *oeuvre*. Thus, Farnell,
". . . the *Oresteia*, composed at a date not far removed from
that of the *Prometheus Vinctus*"; Thomson: ". . . the *Prometheia* was composed during the last two years of the poet's
life"; and Rose: ". . . the play was produced during the poet's
second visit to Sicily, after 458 B.C., during which visit he
died."[3]

To inspire confidence a proposed date must be based on
more than personal preference, and those scholars who suggest a late date adduce stylistic arguments for their choice;

they profess to see similarities of structure or diction between the *Prometheus* and the *Oresteia*. Thomson bases his conclusion on an examination of the words which are found in the *Prometheus* and the *Oresteia*, but nowhere else in Aeschylus, or words which occur only in the *Prometheus* and in Sophocles, but not elsewhere in Aeschylus.[4] Méautis discerns structural similarities between the *Prometheus* and the Orestes-trilogy. He argues from a similarity between the geographical sections of the *Prometheus* and *Agamemnon* 281-316 that "they must not be separated in time." From the evidence of two passages in Athenaeus, it would seem that at the end of the succeeding play Prometheus crowned himself with a wicker headband in symbolic admission of his guilt and prophesied that men would wear such crowns in future as a mark of "solidarity and gratitude" to him.[5] Méautis suggests that this prophecy is an echo of the promise of honors to the Eumenides, and that the reconciliation of Prometheus and Zeus is paralleled by that between the Erinys and the Olympians in the *Eumenides*; "The close relationship of this ending with that of the *Eumenides* . . . would allow us to affirm that the *Oresteia* and the *Prometheus* were composed at almost the same date."[6]

To any argument based on the occurrence or absence of certain words it can, of course, be maintained that this is pure accident, or that a poet chooses his words to suit his subject, while an approach like Méautis' is weakened not only by the conjectural nature of his reconstruction, but also by the circularity of his argument. It will hardly do to fill out the *Prometheia* by assuming similarities with the *Oresteia*, and then date them together because of the assumed similarities. Even if Méautis were right, it would be rash to maintain that Aeschylus could not have written a trilogy ending with a prophecy of future honors to one of its characters before 458. The Danaid-trilogy, written at least five years before, may have ended in just this way.[7] On the other hand the argument can be converted to show that a good poet would not have repeated such an obvious plot-device within two years.

More probative is the evidence drawn from unconscious

variations of certain formal techniques for which no other reason can be found than the development of a poet's individual style. One such test is based on metrical resolution. E. C. Yorke examined the frequency of trisyllabic substitution (tribrach, anapaest, or dactyl) in the iambic trimeters of Aeschylean dialogue and found a striking similarity between the figures for the *Prometheus* and the *Oresteia:* one in 20 for *Agamemnon* and *Eumenides*, one in 21 for *Prometheus*. He concluded that "the P.V. should be very close in time to the Oresteia."[8] Several other such stylistic tests point in the same direction. Denniston examined exceptional sense-pauses in the trimeters of the three tragedians and found several striking affinities between the *Prometheus* and Sophoclean technique.[9] He also noted "a greater variety of particles . . . in the later plays than in the earlier ones" with "a number of usages confined to *Prometheus* and the Trilogy."[10] Recently, C. J. Herington has shown that in the dateable plays the tendency of the chorus to speak in quatrains steadily increases, from no instances in the *Persians* and *Seven*, and only one in *Suppliants*, to ten occurrences in the *Oresteia*, and nine in the *Prometheus* alone. The quatrain becomes, in fact, the only means of dialogue utterance of the chorus apart from one couplet and stichomythic single lines.[11]

If we were to plot the occurrences of these phenomena on a graph, the similarities between the *Prometheus* and the *Oresteia* might convince us that the *Prometheus* was Aeschylus' last play. But what of the statistics which would seem to take the play right out of the Aeschylean orbit? Yorke, in another study, this time of "enjambement" (runover of verses) found one example in *Persians*, seven in the plays of the trilogy, and eighteen in 733 trimeters of the *Prometheus*, which thus turns out to be "overwhelmingly Sophoclean."[12] The differences, too, in several of the sense-pauses examined by Denniston between the *Oresteia* and the *Prometheus* are difficult to account for in two works written, *ex hypothesi*, within three years of each other. So far from confirming Aeschylean authorship, several of the stylometric findings would seem to point to post-, or at least non-Aeschylean reworking of a core of genuine material.

There is one serious obstacle to acceptance of a late date for the play: some scholars have supposed that it contains unmistakable references to a fairly solidly dateable event, the eruption of Mt. Etna, dated by Thucydides 474 B.C., and by the Parian Marble 479.[13] Complications arise from some close similarities between Aeschylus' description and a passage in Pindar's *First Pythian* describing the same event. Suspicion is further aroused by a discrepancy in speaker-attribution of the lines in the *Prometheus* which has suggested that they were added hurriedly and ill-fittingly to their present context.

The disputed lines are *Prometheus* 347–372, a description of Zeus' punishment of Prometheus' brothers Atlas and Typhos, and the Pindaric parallels are as follows:

Aeschylus	Pindar
Prometheus Bound	*First Pythian*
349–350. κίον' οὐρανοῦ . . . ὤμοις ἐρείδων (Atlas)	19. κίων δ' οὐρανία συνέχει (Typhos)
351–352. Κιλικίων . . . ἄντρων	17. Κιλίκιον ἄντρον
352. δάϊον τέρας	26. τέρας μὲν θαυμάσιον προσιδέσθαι
353. ἑκατογκάρανον	16. ἑκατοντακάρανος
354. πᾶσιν ἀντέστη θεοῖς	15. θεῶν πολέμιος
368. ποταμοὶ πυρὸς and	21–22. ἀπλάτου πυρὸς ἁγνόταται ἐκ μυχῶν παγαί
371. ἀπλάτου . . . πυρπνόου ζάλης	
369. τῆς καλλικάρπου Σικελίας	30. εὐκάρποιο γαίας

The parallels[14] seem close enough to rule out complete independence of the two descriptions, but which was the original and which the reminiscence it is impossible to decide merely from examination of the lines. It is usually supposed that the passage in the *Prometheus* was modeled on Pindar, but the possibility that both poets drew on a third source for some of their phrasing cannot be excluded.[15]

There is, in addition, some textual suggestion that the lines were felt in antiquity to be a later insertion. The Medicean is the only manuscript which assigns the lines to Prometheus; all other manuscripts and the non-Medicean scholia attribute them to Ocean. According to this arrangement one speech of Prometheus ends at 346 and another begins at 373, where the manuscripts are careful to indicate a change of speaker. It may be that an early scribe felt that the transition at 347 was not as smooth as it might be, and, however relevant the examples of Atlas and Typhos may be to the dramatic situation, it can be maintained that the length of the digression betrays an extra-dramatic motive for its insertion. The scribe's remedy (if it was such) is hardly successful, but it shows at least that he recognized the difficulties.

Arguing from the fact that lines 347–373 have the appearance of being an interpolation (what he calls their "Einschub-Charakter"), as well as from certain metrical peculiarities which they manifest, Focke concluded that they were "inserted by the poet himself into a preexisting unity."[16] The *First Pythian* can be dated to 470 B.C.,[17] and Focke suggested that Aeschylus heard or read the ode at the court of Hiero in this or the following year and was inspired by Pindar's vivid description of the eruption of Etna to include a parallel passage in his already completed play. From the peculiar interest the Sicilians would have found in this "mythical heightening" of a major event in their recent history, Focke concluded that "every likelihood supports the view that this [insertion] was made not only in Sicily, but also for Sicily."[18] The *Prometheus*, he therefore inferred, was completed and produced in Sicily during Aeschylus' sojourn at the court of Hiero, in 470/69.

Focke's case deserves to be resuscitated, for it is closely argued and has the advantage of pinning down the elusive date and explaining certain other phenomena: the relatively simple structure and meters of the choral odes would have been necessitated by the unavailability of a trained tragic chorus in Sicily, while indications of Orphic doctrines and Sicilian vocabulary may also point to a Sicilian setting.[19] Unfortunately, the firmness of Focke's suggested date is weakened by his dependence on a historical event—the dangers of such argumentation have already been emphasized—although close imitation of Pindar might suggest that the two works were written at about the same time. The strength of Focke's arguments for an early date is further impaired by the alternative hypothesis that the play was composed during a *later* visit by the poet to Sicily, after 458, a view put forward most recently and vigorously by Rose and Méautis. It must be admitted that a reference to so famous an event as Etna's eruption might whet a Sicilian audience's interest almost as much at twenty years' remove as at five, and the argument from the Pindaric parallels to a chronologically close connection between the two works must perhaps bow before the statistics of the stylistician.

Fragments, Titles, and Theories

We can infer the date of the *Aetnaean Women* from the occasion for which it was written, the foundation of Hiero's new city ca. 475.[1] Some light has been thrown on the contents of the play by a recently discovered papyrus fragment, but there is little in it that shows the work to have been specifically political,[2] although Aeschylus' purpose in writing it certainly seems to have been such—"as an augury of a good life for (Aetna's) settlers."[3]

The *Persians* was produced in 472 and is Aeschylus' most obviously historical play. What of the rest of the trilogy? Evidence for the content of the other plays is meager. A glance at the titles, *Phineus, Persians, Glaucus*, should have been enough to classify all attempts to find connections between them as so much misplaced ingenuity. Only one theory is relevant to a political study of Aeschylus' works. Welcker put forward the view that the third play was *Glaucus Pontius*, and assigned to a speech in which Glaucus describes his arrival in Sicily, a fragment preserved in the scholia on Pindar, *Pythian* 1.79:

I washed (or 'having washed,' Heyne) my body in fair baths;
I came to Himera built high on a montain.

> (fr. 32 Nauck = 64 Mette)

Welcker further argued that the play contained "an account
of the victory of Gelon over the Carthaginians at Himera,
and, at the end of the play, some prophecies on the future of
Greece followed by choral jubilations over the victory."[4] Need-
less to say, this is pure conjecture; not even the identity of the
speaker is certain. But if Welcker's theory could be shown to
have any truth in it, it might be important for our purposes.
A tradition reported by Herodotus (7.166) had it that Hamilcar
and the Carthaginians were defeated at Himera by Gelon and
Theron on the same day as the Persians at Salamis. A possible
link between *Glaucus* and *Persians* might then be provided by
the two battles, and it would be necessary to ask whether the
subject of *Glaucus* had also suggested itself to Aeschylus for
political reasons.

Unfortunately, it is not at all clear that the third play was
Glaucus Pontius. M, the best manuscript, gives the title simply
as *Glaucus*; P, V, and R expand this to "*G. Potnieus*." Most
scholars believe that this is correct and that the *Pontius* was a
satyr play. In that case it is difficult to see what connection
the *Glaucus Potnieus* can have had with Sicily. Potniae is in
Boeotia and this Glaucus, son of Sisyphus and Merope, was
torn apart by his flesh-eating mares; a very different person
from the genial (and itinerant) sea-god. It is from this latter
play that Freeman took a fragment

> Chariot with chariot, and corpse with corpse,
> Horses with horses were all confused
>
> (fr. 38 Nauck = 446 Mette)

and assigned it, along with the Himera fragment, to the
Glaucus of the *Persians* trilogy. He suggested that the lines
described the battle of Himera.[5] Now Freeman, who believed
that the first fragment described the wanderings of Heracles
to Sicily, pointed out (correctly) that the Pindar scholia which
preserve it do not specify which *Glaucus* it comes from, but

it seems to fit the *Pontius* and so has generally been assigned to that play. The second fragment is clearly ascribed to the *G. Potnieus* by its source, Scholia M V S of Euripides' *Phoenician Women* 1194.[6] Freeman seems to be aware of this discrepancy, but he persists (by an obscure argument which is either very elliptical or very naive) in assigning the two fragments to the same play. "Let us for a moment fancy to ourself the sacrifice of Hamilkar told in the verse of Aeschylus. . . ."[7] This would indeed have been impressive; but there is no solid evidence to justify Freeman's conclusion "that there once was a contemporary picture of the battle of Himera from the hand of Aeschylus."[8]

Beyond these poor remains there is only a handful of tantalizing titles. It would be interesting, if true, if "Aeschylus was moved to select the subject of his *Oreithyia* by the founding of the temple of Boreas."[9] Herodotus reports that the Athenians built this temple in thanksgiving for the North Wind's help before Artemisium, and we may recall Themistocles' part in the engagement and his consequent interest in having its memory perpetuated; Boreas seems to have played an important part in Simonides' poem "The Sea-Fight at Artemisium."[10] Another obvious candidate for such speculation is the *Eleusinians*,[11] which told the same story as Euripides' *Suppliants*. According to Plutarch the difference between the two versions consisted in that in Euripides, Theseus had to fight the Thebans to effect the surrender of the corpses of the "Seven," while in Aeschylus this was achieved "by persuasion and under a truce."[12] A play in which Theseus consented to the burial of the Argive chiefs at Eleusis, "doing a favor for Adrastus," as Plutarch says, would obviously fit into a context of close Athenian-Argive relations, and such a theme causes no surprise coming as it does from the author of the *Suppliants* and the *Eumenides*. Whether it is significant that the Thebans were portrayed as open to persuasion (reflecting, perhaps, an attempt to realign Sparta's allies), and the drama's importance to the cult of "Theseus' bones," are moot points. Hauvette[13] put forward an elaborate theory that the *Eleusinians* was part of Cimon's attempt to "rehabilitate the memory of his father" by giving currency to the old legends about Theseus and by emphasizing that hero's connection with the victory of Marathon.[14] Unfortunately, Hauvette's argument is weakened by its circularity: he reconstructs the play's content and significance from its supposed political context, and then places it in that context ("in the years which followed 475") on the basis of his reconstruction. Furthermore, if the picture presented above of Aeschylus as the dedicated liberal and pro-Themistoclean carries conviction, it will be distinctly odd, not to say inconceivable, that he would be found volunteering support to Cimon's propaganda program. The possibility of dating the play securely would seem to doom us to ignorance of its political significance, but a date different from Hauvette's has been proposed by Jacoby.[15] He suggested that Pindar, in twice insisting on burial of the Seven at Thebes (*Nemean* 9.21 ff., *Olympian* 6.15 ff.) is specifically contradicting Aeschylus' version, in which the heroes are buried at Eleusis. If that is correct, Aeschylus' presentation of the myth must have become well known by the time of *Nemean* 9, which can be dated ca. 475 from the reference to "new-founded Aetna" in line 2. Cimon's exhumation of "Theseus' bones" was later than 476/5, the year in which, according to Plutarch,[16] the Athenians were told by Delphi to effect the transference of Theseus' bones to Athens. Chronological considerations, then, would make it extremely unlikely that the *Eleusinians* formed part of this Delphic-Cimonian program.

Notes

Note on the Text: The text followed is generally that of Murray's second edition (Oxford, 1955), with an admixture of Denniston-Page (Oxford, 1957) and Fraenkel (Oxford, 1950) for the *Agamemnon*. For the *Persians* I have used the new edition of H. D. Broadhead (Cambridge, 1960).

Translations, unless otherwise indicated, are my own.

Chapter I: Introduction: Life of Aeschylus

1. ". . . biographi Graeci veteres mendacissimum fuerunt genus hominum," C. Dindorf, *Poetarum Scenicorum Graecorum . . . Prolegomena* (Leipzig, 1869) 1.

2. Put forward most recently by A. Lesky, *Die tragische Dichtung der Hellenen*[2] (Göttingen, 1964) 50.

3. Dindorf, 1, n. 1.

4. 1.21 D-F, 22 A; 9.428 F. At 375 D, Athenaeus quotes three fragments of Aeschylus which he says were cited by Chamaeleon. (The fragments of Chamaeleon are collected and commented on by F. Wehrli, *Die Schule des Aristoteles* [Basel/Stuttgart, 1957] vol. IX, frgs. 39-42. For an earlier discussion cf. E. Köpke, *De Chamaeleonte Peripatetico* [Berlin, 1856] 33-36.)

5. An important collection of *testimonta* supplementary to the *Life* is that of F. Schöll, in Ritschl's edition of the *Septem* (Leipzig, 1875). More accessible, if less full, is the collection of Wilamowitz in his edition of the plays (Berlin, 1914, repr. 1958) 9-19. Reference will be made to the ancient sources and to the appropriate paragraph (not page) in Wilamowitz, who cites the *testimonia* as "Vitae Supplementa" and numbers them accordingly; thus, "Athen. 9. 402 B, W30." The text of the *Vita* is likewise Wilamowitz's.

Modern treatments are few. Still worth consulting are E. J. Kiehl, "Aeschyli Vita," *Mnemosyne* 1 (1852) 361-74, and J. van Leeuwen, "De Aeschyli itineribus Siculis," *Mnemosyne* n.s. 18 (1890) 68-75. See now the abundant and up-to-date collection of 165 *testimonia* to all aspects of Aechylus' life and art in Stefan Radt, *Tragicorum Graecorum Fragmenta* vol. 3, Aeschylus (Göttingen: Vandenhoeck und Ruprecht, 1985) pp. 31-108.

6. The Parian Marble (*IG* XII, 5, 444 = *FGH* 239) ep. 48

makes him thirty-five years old at the time of Marathon (W49, no. 4) and sixty-nine at the time of his death in 456/5 (*Marm. Par.* ep. 59, W49, no. 7).

7. *Vita* 1, Schol. Aristophanes *Frogs* 886, W20.

8. Lesky (see note 2) 50–51 and W21. His sister's son Philocles was victorious over Sophocles' *Oedipus Tyrannus* (Dicaearchus in Hypoth. to *O.T.*), and a later descendant, Astydamas the Younger, won many victories in the fourth century.

9. *Vita* 3 (Pindar and Aeschylus contemporaries); Eustathius, Prologue to *Commentary on Pindar* 25, W23 (association and *megalophônia*).

10. *Vita* 4.

11. If we can believe the anonymous commentator on Aristotles' *Nicomachean Ethics* (p. 145 Heylbut), who seems to be quoting Heracleides Ponticus, Aeschylus sustained many wounds at Marathon and had to be taken from the field on a stretcher, W44, no. 3.

12. Scholiast on *Persians* 429, W26. An anecdote connecting Aeschylus and Ion (at the boxing matches of the Isthmian games) is related by Plutarch *Mor.* 79 E. (The remark, "The man who is hit keeps silent, but the spectators cry out," is attributed to Aeschylus at the games without mention of Ion at *Mor.* 29 F.)

13. Pausanias 1.14.5, W24.

14. Herodotus 6.114, W25.

15. Herodotus 8.84, 93; not as straightforward as it appears: Plutarch *Themistocles* 14.3 calls him a Decelean.

16. Diodorus 11.27 (presumably following Ephorus) says that Herodotus' Ameinias was Aeschylus' brother. "Ephorus' stupidity made him Aeschylus' brother, Diod. XI 27, which has drawn many into error" is Wilamowitz's comment; one of the "many" was presumably Aelian, who tells the story of how *Ameinias* effected the acquittal of Aeschylus on a charge of impiety by showing the jury the stumps of his arms (*V.H.* 5.19: an obvious reference to the mangled, but deceased, Cynegeirus).

17. Eusebius' entry under ol. 71.1 (= 496; ol. 70.4 in the Armenian version), "Aeschylus the tragic poet was becoming known," may point in this same direction. For the notices, in Eusebius, W49 (p. 17 bottom); for "Suidas," W50 (pp. 18–19).

18. *Vita* 2.

19. *Marm. Par.* ep. 50, W49 no. 5.

20. *kataspoudastheis*: the transitive use is late and the exact

sense here obscure. *LSJ* (ed. 9) gives "to be troubled" from the Septuagint Book of Job and "to be oppressed" from Vettius Valens (2d cent. A.D.).

21. *Marm. Par.* ep. 59, W49 no. 7.

22. Diodorus 9.48 dates Hiero's change of name of Catana to "Aetna" in the archonship of Phaidon, 476/5. P. Mazon offered an alternative which has been adopted by Lesky (see note 2, 52): the *Aetnaean Women* was not produced until 470, the time of Aeschylus' alleged reproduction of the *Persians* (*Eschyle*[2], [Paris, 1958] I, intr. iv, n. 1). Kiehl, however, notes that the *Life's* "*Hierônos tote . . . ktizontos*," taken strictly, would seem to indicate a visit by Aeschylus closer in time to the only date we have for Hiero's transference of population from Catana and "foundation" of Aetna, 476/5 (see note 5, 363–64).

23. *Cimon* 8, W28.

24. Kiehl (see note 5) 365; Simonides' victory: *Marm. Par.* ep. 54 (477/6), commemorated by himself in frgs. 77D and 79D.

25. Cited by the Scholiast on Aristophanes' *Frogs* 1028 as from Book 3 of Eratosthenes' *On Comedy*. For the Scholiast's *dedidachthai* the *Life* (no. 18) has *anadidaxai*, which implies that the Sicilian production followed the Athenian première.

26. The theory of another version is not demanded by Aristophanes' reference at *Frogs* 1028 to *Darius'* death which, as has been noted by scholars since Didymus, does not occur in our version of the play; Aristophanes may have simply forgotten what did occur in the play. (For a full discussion see the introduction to Broadhead's edition of the *Persians*, Sec. C, xlviii–lv, and van Leeuwen [see note 5] 69–70. Van Leeuwen discusses the evidence for Aeschylus' Sicilian visits and attempts to account for several of the confusions.)

27. "Suidas" in Hesychius' epitome, *s.v.* "Aischylos," W41.

28. W50 no. 4, p. 19.

29. *Frogs* 807.

30. *Vita* 10; clearly an *aition* for the oracle recorded in the same chapter, "a heavenly projectile will slay you." (Further references at W32.) Eventually, of course, an appropriate epitaph was invented, *Vita* 17. Van Leeuwen put forward the ingenious theory that a comic poet made up this ridiculous story of Aeschylus' death as a parody of Aeschylus' own invention concerning the death of Odysseus in the satyric *Psychagôgoi*.

31. *Vita* 11. The first couplet is quoted by Plutarch *de exilio*

15 (*Mor.* 604 F) and by the anonymous commentator on Aristotle's *Nicomachean Ethics* (p. 146 Heylbut), the latter with two variants. Athenaeus 14.627 D cites the second distich (W33).

32. W33, p. 11.

33. The usual formula is *mnêma* + name(s) of deceased in the genitive. See, e.g., W. Peek, *Griechische Versinschriften* I (Berlin, 1955) numbers 85, 86, 87, 90, 94, 95, 96, 98. Against Wilamowitz's "Gelae positum monumentum Gelam non nominaret" may be adduced Peek no. 46 (*IG* II/III² 5220), "wide-wayed Athens once buried this man . . . ," from the Cerameicus.

34. Ep. 59, W49 no. 7. The *Life* is therefore mistaken when it says he "lived sixty-three years" (*Vita* 13).

35. *Vita* 13.

36. The question has been discussed most recently by M. Untersteiner, "Quanti drammi scrisse Eschilo?," *In Memoriam A. Beltrami* (Univ. di Genova, Inst. de Filol. Class., 1954) 244–45. Untersteiner attempts to salvage the *Life*'s authority by drastic emendation.

37. *Vita* 12.

38. *Vita* 13. Posthumous productions and victories are mentioned also by Quintilian *Inst. Orat.* 10.1.66 and Philostratus *Life of Apollonius* 6.11; productions only by the Scholiast on Aristophanes *Acharnians* 10, and *Frogs* 868. (These passages are cited by W34.)

Chapter II: Persians

1. Phrynichus, Aeschylus' older contemporary, wrote historical tragedies: we have only the title of one, *The Capture of Miletus*, and several lines of his *Phoenician Women*. It is impossible to tell how much of Aeschylus' *Aetnaean Women* was based on recent history.

2. Richmond Lattimore, "Aeschylus on the Defeat of Xerxes," in *Classical Studies in Honor of William Abbott Oldfather* (Urbana, 1943) 87.

3. Lines 865–866 are contradicted by Darius' Scythian expedition, and the whole motif of Darius' shock at his son's attempt to bridge the Hellespont (lines 723, 725, 744–750) requires the audience to forget that he performed a similar impiety when he bridged the Thracian Bosporus (Herodotus 4.83).

4. Other references: 347–348, 473–474 (not altogether ap-

propriate: Atossa calls it "famous Athens" and yet she had not known where it was in the earlier scene), 716, 824 ("remember Athens and Hellas" ∽ Herodotus 5.105, and cf. line 285).

5. Lattimore (see note 2) 91.

6. Reading δᾷαν in 271 (Blomfield and *cod. rec.* for δῖαν).

7. Cape Tropaea is identified by Hammond ("The Battle of Salamis," *JHS* 76 [1956] 34, n. 3 and p. 54) as Cape Kamatero; by others as Cape Varvari.

8. Reading, in 553, βάριδές τε πόντιαι (m) and retaining, in 563, the mss διὰ δ'Ἰαόνων χέρας.

9. With mention of the "Dorian spear" at line 817 inserted as "a sop to historical actuality" (see note 2, 91–92).

10. This message and other details of the battle of Salamis are discussed in Appendix A.

11. So Gomme: ". . . it is probable that he was not yet ostracized when the *Persae* was produced, spring 472; not certain by any means, for Aeschylus was capable of praising a man who had lately been rejected by his countrymen, but probable" (*Commentary* I.401).

12. This point is made in passing in an uneven paper by F. Stoessl, "Aeschylus as a Political Thinker," *AJP* 73 (1952) 121, and in his introduction to a revision of Droysen's translation of Aeschylus (Zurich, 1952), 32 and 159.

13. Polygnotus was said to have had illicit relations with Cimon's sister, Elpinice, whose face later appeared on the picture of the Trojan Laodice in the Stoa Poikile (Plutarch *Cimon* 4.5).

14. See an interesting paper by Erika Simon, "Polygnotan Painting and the Niobid Painter," *AJA* 67 (1963) 43–62.

15. Pierre Amandry, in a provocative paper ("Sur les 'Epigrammes de Marathon,'" Θεωρία, *Festschrift Schuchhardt*, [Deutsche Beiträge zur Altertumswissenschaft 12/13, Baden-Baden, 1960], pp. 1–8) outlines the nature and extent of this publicistic contest, and suggests that the second of the two "Marathon epigrams" was part of Cimon's later sponsorship of the Marathon victory as a rival to Salamis.

16. Plutarch (*Themistocles* 5) gives the date as the archonship of Adeimantus (477/6). Although he does not name the play, that it was the *Phoenician Women*, as first suggested by Bentley (*Opusc.* p. 293), seems an all but necessary inference (after 480 and before 472).

17. E. O'Neill, Jr., "Notes on Phrynichus' *Phoenissae* and Aeschylus' *Persae*," *CP* 37 (1942) 425–27, makes the interesting suggestion that Themistocles may have used ship-timbers captured from the Persians at Salamis for the *ikria* of his restored theater.

18. Wade-Gery, *Essays in Greek History* (Oxford, 1958), 177–78, dates the performance to March 493, in the year before Themistocles' archonship, July 493/2 (Dionysius Halicarn. A.R. 6.34). He thus accounts for Phrynichus' 1000-drachma fine. W. G. Forrest remarks that "if Miletus fell in Nov./Dec. 494, there wasn't much time to write a play for March 493."

19. Herodotus 6.21. If we follow Wade-Gery in dating the play to 494/3, the year before Themistocles' archonship, Phrynichus' condemnation may have been due to "the resentment of the anti-war party then in power" (Dodds). The political tendency of the "Capture of Miletus" was denied by G. Freymuth, "Zur ΜΙΛΗΤΟΥ ΑΛΩΣΙΣ des Phrynichos," *Philologus* 99 (1955) 51 ff., against the patent meaning of Herodotus' phrase *oikêia kaka*.

20. *Ox. Pap.* II, 59. That the phrase $<ὀψί>ην$ ἐς δειέλην refers to Salamis (perhaps borrowed from Simonides? See Plutarch *Themistocles* 15.2) is cogently argued by Pohlenz, *Griechische Tragödie*[2] (Göttingen, 1954) Erläuterungen, p. 24, against F. Marx, "Der Tragiker Phrynichus," *Rheinisches Museum*, n.s., 77 (1928) 357 ff., followed by F. Stoessl, "Die Phoenissen des Phrynichos und die Perser des Aischylos," *Museum Helveticum* 2 (1945) 158–59, who refer the fragment to the battle of Mycale.

21. The Hypothesis notes Aeschylus' victory with the tetralogy "in the archonship of Menon," whose year was 473/2, according to the *Fasti Theatri Atheniensis* (*I G* II. 2318, v. 9), where the entry reads, "Tragedies: Pericles of Cholargos was choregus, Aeschylus the producer."

22. Accepting, with Broadhead, Trendelenberg's transposition of 237–238 to follow 239–240 (but the point is the same with the ms order).

23. The late Prof. Wallace noted that the usual view that the "mines in Maroneia" were discovered in 483/2 is mistaken. What *Ath. Pol.* 22.7 is actually dating is Themistocles' act of preventing the distribution of the increased income. (See W. P. Wallace, "The Early Coinages of Athens and Euboia," *Numismatic Chronicle* 7 ser. 2 [1962] esp. pp. 28–32.)

24. Line 349. R. W. Macan, *Herodotus VII-VIII-IX* (London,

1908) I.ii, cites these lines in his note on the Herodotus passage, but draws no conclusions. That a city's men were her *herkos asphales* may have been a commonplace (Alcaeus fr. 35, 10 D = E 1, 10 L-P, Soph. O.T. 56–57, Thuc. 7.77); which does not mean that Themistocles could not have appropriated it as a maxim of his own. See Thuc. 1.143.5, where Gomme draws attention to the parallel with Herodotus 8.61.2.

25. Hignett, *Xerxes' Invasion of Greece* (Oxford, 1963) 443, suggests that Themistocles and the Athenian envoys at Delphi may have applied pressure on Delphi to produce a second, more favorable response.

26. Broadhead, 44.

27. Broadhead, 194 top, at lines 770, 771.

28. Broadhead, 213, note to 852–908. It should be noted that Broadhead's implication that the cities of Cyprus were lost to Persian control by 472 is unfounded. (Cf. B. D. Meritt, H. T. Wade-Gery, and M. F. McGregor, *The Athenian Tribute Lists* [Princeton, 1950] III, 207–8.) Have they been introduced to allow the poet another reference to the "metropolis" of Cyprian Salamis, "cause of these laments" (894–895)?

29. Herodotus 8.44; but the Athenians disliked the title (Herodotus 1.143).

30. Euripides' *Ion* provides the most elaborate mythical working out of the relations between Athens and Ionia (cf. esp. lines 1581–1588).

31. How and Wells, *Commentary on Herodotus* (Oxford, 1912, repr. 1950) II.72, at Herodotus 6.21.2.

32. As Lattimore (see note 2) 88 supposes: ". . . this minor engagement (fought by Aristeides and *Athenians*, Herodotus VIII.98) has been magnified into a major battle by land." Hignett (see note 25) 238 likewise suggests that Aeschylus exaggerated the importance of Psyttaleia because "he wanted the hoplites to have their share in the glory of the Greek triumph."

33. W. W. Tarn, "The Fleet of Xerxes," *JHS* 28 (1908) 226, goes so far as to claim that Aeschylus fabricated the whole incident: "one is sorely tempted to believe that it is all a mistake of our anti-Themistoclean tradition, and that the only contribution made that day by the just Aristeides to the cause of Greek freedom was the butchery of a few shipwrecked crews."

34. See How and Wells, Introd. No. 31, pp. 42–43, and F.

Jacoby, *Atthis* (Oxford, 1949) 376, n. 43 on Herodotus' anti-Themistocles bias.

35. C. Hignett, *A History of the Athenian Constitution* (Oxford, 1952) 188–89 (cf. 183, n. 4), following Beloch and de Sanctis.

36. J. B. Bury, "Aristeides at Salamis," *CR* 10 (1896) 414–18 (lines 45 ff. of the "Themistocles Decree," which probably do not refer to the first recall of the exiles, may point in the same direction). I cannot refrain from quoting Bury's comment on Herodotus' "sensational" description of Aristeides' return: "This incident is one of those excellent stories of Herodotus, in reading which one cannot forbear entertaining the suspicion that they are incidents which ought to have occurred if real life were only artistic, but which, since real life is nothing if not inartistic, never did" (415).

37. Gomme, *Commentary* I.259. See also *Ath. Pol.* 23. 3–4, and Wilamowitz, *Aristoteles und Athen* (Berlin, 1893) II.86–87, with note 27.

Chapter III: Seven Against Thebes

1. Thucydides 1.98.1–2, gives the bare facts, with additional details in Plutarch *Cimon* 7–8 (three herms with epigrams purportedly honoring Cimon for the Eion victory). Diodorus 9.60.1–2 misdates these exploits to 470/69.

2. T. G. Tucker, *The Seven Against Thebes of Aeschylus* (Cambridge, 1908) xlvi.

3. J. T. Sheppard, "The Plot of the *Septem Contra Thebas*," *CQ* 7 (1913) 77.

4. H. J. Rose, *Commentary* I.176, at lines 169–70.

5. Sheppard suggests that the "barbaric blazons" of the Argive invaders are specifically Persian, and cites Plutarch *Themist.* 8.1 (where, however, it is not clear whether the *episêmoi* are shield blazons or ships' ensigns). He notes later that "the blazon of Tydeus we only half understand: there as elsewhere in this scene, if we knew more of the Persian equipment we should perhaps find more significance" (81). The symbolism of the shield designs is discussed in an interesting article by Helen H. Bacon, "The Shield of Eteocles," *Arion* 3 (1964) 27–38.

6. *Classical Weekly* (now *Classical World*) 44 (1950) 49–52.

7. For the "Curse of the Alcmeonids" see Herodotus 5.71

and Thucydides 1.126, and G. W. Williams' discussions "The Curse of the Alkmaionidai I, II, III," in *Hermathena* 78 (1951) 32–49, 79 (1952) 3–21, 80 (1952) 58–71.

8. Herodotus 6.131 for Pericles' parentage, and Thucydides 1.127 for the Spartan demand.

9. Gilbert Murray, *Aeschylus, the Creator of Tragedy* (Oxford, 1940) 140, cited by Post (see note 6) 51.

10. See my paper, "The Character of Eteocles in Aeschylus' *Septem*," TAPA 95 (1964).

11. Alfred von Domaszewski, *Die attische Politik in der Zeit der Pentekontaetie* (Sitz.-ber. der Heidelberg. Akademie, Phil.-hist. Kl., 1924/5, Abh. 4) 4.

12. "The most violent of his accusers," remarks Plutarch (*Cimon* 14.4) quoting Stesimbrotus. After recounting an unsuccessful attempt of Elpinice to intervene with Pericles on her brother's behalf, Plutarch notes that in the course of the trial, Pericles was "very gentle and got up to accuse only once, as if for appearances' sake."

In this same period (perhaps this same year) would be placed an early generalship of Pericles, although the source is not above suspicion (Plutarch *Cimon* 13.4, quoting Callisthenes [= *FGH* 124, fr. 16]: "Pericles with 50 ships and Ephialtes with 30," therefore in or before 462, the year of Ephialtes' death).

13. At that, the *Ath. Pol.* seems to indicate that the prosecution of Cimon in 463 was something of a political "inaugural" for Pericles: "When Pericles came forward to lead the *demos* and first distinguished himself . . . although still a young man. . ." (27.1).

14. Franz Miltner in *R-E* art. "Perikles": "His birth must be placed at the end of the first decade of the fifth century around 490" (748). Domaszewski (see note 11) 4: "He was born around the year 490."

15. Plutarch *Aristeides* 3.4–5, trans. B. Perrin (Loeb Class. Lib., London and New York, 1914).

16. Prof. Dover notes that "since it was written while Hiero was still alive, it *must* antedate the *Seven*, as 468 was the last Olympic games in Hiero's lifetime."

17. See Eric Bethe in *R-E* art. "Amphiaraos." According to the Scholiast on Pindar *Ol.* 6.15 ff., Adrastus' description of Amphiaraus, "good both as a prophet and at fighting with spear," is a direct quotation from the *Thebais*.

18. Léon Legras, *Les Légendes thébaines dans l'épopée et la tragédie grecques* (Paris, 1905) 70.

19. Plutarch *Aristeides* 26.1–2 (= Craterus, *FGH* 342, fr. 12), trans. Perrin.

20. Jacoby remarks that Craterus' source must have spoken of the "just" and "poor" Aristeides: "therefore the matter need not be genuine; it can (in view of the relatively low fine, which even so Aristeides cannot pay) stem from a pamphlet which censured the Athenians for their ingratitude towards their best men. . ." (*FGH* III b², 104).

21. According to Nepos, "he died about four years after Themistocles was expelled from Athens" (*Aristeides* 3.3).

22. Tucker, although he postulates a reference to Aristeides later in the scene (at 605 f.), doubts that line 592 was intended by Aeschylus to refer to him. He notes that Plutarch quotes the line with *dikaios* substituted for *aristos* and suggests that "it is altogether more probable that the lines were applied to Arist. by others, with the adj. so changed as to suit ὁ δίκαιος ἐπικαλούμενος" (see note 2, 120–121). The identification of Amphiaraus with Aristeides is accepted by E. G. Harman, *The Birds of Aristophanes in Relation to Athenian Politics* (London, 1920) 40–45.

23. For the fallacy in the view that the two men were invariably opposed, see Chapter II, pp. 24–25.

24. Prof. Dodds comments: "I find the equation Amphiaraos = Aristides wholly unconvincing. Yet the lengthy praise of Amph. does call for some explanation. I should explain it by the contemporary importance of Amph. as an oracle-giver (cf. Hdt. 1.52, 8.134). This made him interesting both to Thebes where his oracle was at first situated and to Athens which from 506 onwards controlled Oropus, the later seat of his oracle. The Oropus oracle existed in Aristophanes' time, but unfortunately we do not know the date of its foundation. There may well be a lost bit of history behind the praise of Amph., though no political allegory." (Personal letter, August 14, 1964.)

25. Post's theory (put forward only tentatively and somewhat confusedly in the paper cited above, note 6, p. 50, and reiterated in his book *From Homer to Menander* [Berkeley, 1951] 73) that Polyneices in the play is "really" Themistocles was taken over, with embellishments, by Stoessl, "Aeschylus as a Political Thinker," *AJP* 73 (1952) 132–33, and his edition of Droysen's translation of

Aeschylus (Zurich, 1952) 36. The implausibility of the identification leads me to prefer Sheppard's *obiter dictum:* "Cadmeia is a
Greek city besieged by wicked invaders; Polyneices like Hippias is
an exiled prince on whose behalf these invaders come . . ." (see
note 3, 77).

26. Tucker (see note 2) xliv.

27. Prof. Wallace informed me that "what is involved is the
south wall of the Akropolis—this was a retaining wall, not a fortification wall."

28. Tucker suggests in a footnote (xlv,n.2) that "it may
even be suspected that [Aeschylus] also intends a good word for
Themistocles" in lines 449–450, where we find mention of Artemis
the Protrectress, for, Tucker recalls, "the chosen guardian deity
of Themistocles was Artemis Aristoboule." The theory is not so
farfetched as it might first seem if we consider the strength of the
identification between Themistocles and Artemis. At Chapter 22 of
Plutarch's life we are told that Themistocles built a temple to her
near his house in Melite; he surnamed her "Aristoboule," according
to Plutarch, "on grounds that he had given the best counsel to the
city and the Hellenes." Plutarch further notes that a small portrait
of Themistocles stood in this temple down to his own day. For the
recently discovered remains of this temple, now unfortunately again
covered over, see J. Threpsiades and E. Vanderpool, "Themistokles'
Sanctuary of Artemis Aristoboule," *Archaeol. Delt.* 19 (1964)
26–36.

Chapter IV: Suppliants

1. The papyrus text can be consulted most conveniently in
Murray's second edition of Aeschylus (Oxford, 1955) 2, and in
Lloyd-Jones' appendix to the fragments in the Loeb edition (repr.
1957) 595–98, with a useful short discussion of the issues and
difficulties, and extensive bibliography. Cf. also the bibliography
in A. Lesky, *Die tragische Dichtung der Hellenen*[2] (Göttingen,
1964) 59, n. 1.

2. Lobel remarked that ἐπὶ ἀρ["is prima facie ἐπὶ ἄρχοντος"
(his dotting of the *rho* seems hyper-conservative; there is no dot
in Murray and Lloyd-Jones). But it should be noted that *Ox. Pap.*
2256, fr. 2, which immediately precedes our Hypothesis and seems
to be written in the same hand, contains part of the Hypothesis to
the *Oedipodea* (whose accuracy is confirmed by the Hypothesis of

the *Seven* in *Laurentianus*). In it there does not seem to be room for the formula *epi archontos* – –, and Lobel restores ἐδιδάχθη ἐπὶ Θεαγενίδου. . . . Since we may assume that the scribe was consistent, it seems all but certain that he also wrote ἐπὶ ᾿Αρχεδημίδου.

3. It is somewhat surprising to find H. D. F. Kitto, in the third and latest revision of his *Greek Tragedy* (London, 1961) saying incautiously, "if we limit ourselves to the period immediately preceding Aeschylus we may form a general impression by arguing backwards from the *Supplices* . . ." (23), for he had already accepted the evidence of the papyrus, "though without any burning conviction" (3).

4. F. R. Earp, *The Style of Aeschylus* (Cambridge, 1948).

5. *Ibid.*, 7.

6. F. R. Earp, "The Date of the *Supplices* of Aeschylus," *Greece and Rome* 22 (1953) 119.

7. A. Diamantopoulos ("The Danaid Tetralogy of Aeschylus," *JHS* 77 [1957] 220–29) argued from fancied political allusions to a date of composition in the nineties, 493/2 (but the play was suppressed until 463!). Other diehards who believe that Aeschylus kept the play in his drawer for thirty years include J. T. Kakridis, "Classical Tragedy in the Light of New Texts," *2d Int. Cong. of Class. Studies* (Copenhagen, 1958) I.151, and E. Wolff ("The Date of Aeschylus' Danaid Tetralogy, Continued," *Eranos* 57 [1959] 22). Murray, in his Preface to the second edition (Oxford, 1955), held out for a posthumous production (p. vi).

8. Lesky (see note 1), 60.

9. *IG* II.2325; see E. C. Yorke, "Mesatus Tragicus," *CQ*, n.s., 4 (1954) 183–84.

10. This theory was suggested by E. G. Turner, rev. of *Oxyrhynchus Papyri XX*, *CR*, n.s., 4 (1954) 22: "The name might be that of the tragedian Phrynichus, son of Melanthus (Suidas, s.v.), distinguished as μεσατος from his great predecessor Phrynichus, son of Polyphrasmon, and the later Phrynichus *comicus*." Against this Lloyd-Jones objected "μέσατοσ as an equivalent to μέσοσ was a poetic word, and cannot possibly have stood here" (see note 1) 597.

11. H. D. F. Kitto, *Greek Tragedy* (2d ed.; London, 1950) 29. In the most recent (third) edition (see note 3), Kitto notes "with some complacency" that he had rejected some of the stylistic arguments for an early date even before the papyrus was discovered.

12. Walter Nestle, rev. of Kranz's *Stasimon, Gnomon* 10 (1934) 413–15; N. Wecklein, *Äschylos, Die Schutzflehenden* (Leipzig, 1902) 22. (The latter was drawn to my attention by Prof. Dover.)

13. For some more or less plausible conjectures see D. S. Robertson, "The End of the *Supplices* Trilogy of Aeschylus," *CR* 38 (1924) 51–53; M. L. Cunningham, "A Fragment of Aeschylus' Aigyptioi?" *Rheinisches Museum* 96 (1953) 223–31, and, most recently, R. P. Winnington-Ingram, "The Danaid Trilogy of Aeschylus," *JHS* 81 (1961) 141–52.

14. The obscure phrase *aneu klêtêros* is explained by the Scholiast as referring to fifth-century constitutional practice: " 'without a summoner' means 'before the herald said *whoever assents, let them raise their hands.*' "

15. Murray's text; the exact reading of 698 is open to doubt, but its meaning is clear from the marginal note in M, *asphalias*.

16. Prof. Dover notes that in the third century B.C. "*aliaia teleia* is a technical term in Argive decrees, and may be much older."

17. See also H. G. Robertson, "Δίκη and Ὕβρις in Aeschylus' *Suppliants*," *CR* 50 (1936) 104, n. 3, for a not quite complete list.

18. Kitto, *Greek Tragedy* 2d ed., 10.

19. *Ibid.*, 9 and 16.

20. *Ibid.*, 9. This has been reformulated in the new edition as "the centre of his thinking in this play, as it certainly is the centre of its tragic feeling" (3d ed., 10).

21. *Ibid.*, 10.

22. See Viktor Frey, *Die Stellung der attischen Tragödie und Komödie zur Demokratie* (diss. Zurich, 1946) 5 ff. The king's absence from the Danaids' prayer is also noted by B. Daube, *Zu den Rechtsproblemen in Aischylos' Agamemnon* (Zurich and Leipzig, 1938) 34.

23. The date for Themistocles' ostracism is arrived at by assuming that he was not yet ostracized when the *Persians* was presented in 472, and that Diodorus, who places Themistocles' ostracism and flight under the year 471/0 (11.55) is to be taken as dating the ostracism only.

24. Who Themistocles' "enemies" were is clarified by Plutarch, who names "Leobotes, son of Alcmeon, of the deme Agraule" as the mover of the indictment against him for treason (*Them.* 23.1):

an Alcmeonid, but also perhaps an agent of Cimon, who later prosecuted a certain Epicrates for getting Themistocles' wife and children out of Athens (Plutarch *Themistocles* 24.6, citing Stesimbrotus).

25. "When he saw him thus banished from his state and in great bitterness of spirit," *Themistocles* 23.2, trans. Perrin.

26. For Elis and Mantinea, Strabo 8.3.336–7 (Mantinea specifically "synoecized *by the Argives*"); synoecism of Elis dated to 471/0 by Diodorus 11.54.1. For Themistocles' efforts, cf. A. Andrewes, "Sparta and Arcadia in the Early Fifth Century," *Phoenix* 6 (1952) 2–3.

27. The war motif is curious. Although it is absent from Thucydides' very circumstantial account of Themistocles' supplication of Admetus' wife and son, it is prominent in Diodorus' story. The Spartans (alone, not with the Athenians) send to Admetus to demand Themistocles' surrender, and they threaten "to make war on him with all the Hellenes" if he does not surrender him (11.56.2). The similarities between Pelasgus and the historical Admetus suggest that Aeschylus may have included details of the actual demand to Admetus in his fictional account. Themistocles' supplication by Admetus' son seems to have furnished material for another famous tragedy, Euripides' *Telephus* (N. Wecklein, "Ueber die dramatische Behandlung des Telephosmythus," Sitz-ber. bayerischen Akademie, phil.-hist. Kl., 1 Abh. [1909] 18–19).

28. Cunningham (see note 13) 228. See C. Bonner, "A Study of The Danaid Myth," *HSCP* 13 (1902) 129–73 for a lengthy account of the variations in the Danaid myth.

29. This point was suggested to me by Prof. Dodds.

30. E. Cavaignac, "Eschyle et Thémistocle," *Rev. de philologie* 45 (1921) 103–4.

31. Cavaignac, "A propos d'un document nouveau: la fin de Thémistocle," *Nouvelle Clio* 7–9 (1955–7) 123–25.

32. F. Stoessl, "Aeschylus as a Political Thinker," *AJP* (1952) 125–26, and his revision of Droysen's translation of Aeschylus (Zurich, 1952): "There can be no doubt that Aeschylus' Danaid trilogy, which testifies to such a great and warm sympathy for the democratic state in the Peloponnese, likewise must have worked in the direction of a *rapprochement* (Annäherung) with Argos. Aeschylus has in any case approved of Themistokles' foreign policy and supported it by his own means, those of tragic poetry" (30). Stoessl, however, misdated the play to 476.

33. W. G. Forrest, "Themistokles and Argos," *CQ*, n.s., 10 (1960) 221–41.

34. *Ibid.*, 239. I include Forrest's judicious note: "Not, of course, a political masquerade . . . Danaos and his daughters are faced with Themistokles' problem, but they do not, in any real sense, represent Themistokles. Even so one might expect to find in some lines direct comments on some aspects of Themistokles' position, even if irrelevant to the main theme. . . ."

35. *Ibid.*, 240.

36. V. Ehrenberg, "Origins of Democracy," *Historia* 1 (1950) 517.

37. *Ibid.*, 524.

38. Contrast, for example, the relative clumsiness of Euripides *Suppl.* 346 ff.: "I shall either convince the Thebans to surrender the bodies," Theseus says, "or force them to do so in battle." Then he adds, "I want the entire city to decree this, and it will so decree, since I wish it." This reference to the city is really without importance for the plot, and Theseus' next words show that he, and the dramatist, are uncomfortable about it: "I would have a more favorably disposed *demos* if I give them a reason. For I set up the *demos* under a single rule after freeing the city and giving it an equal vote" (350–353). Contrast the way Theseus accepts Oedipus' petition completely on his own authority in Sophocles' *Oedipus at Colonus* (see esp. lines 636 f., 639, 649, 655 f.).

39. Forrest, 240. The supposed allusion to the Argive alliance had already been used in their argument for a late date by August Boeckh and K. O. Müller. According to George Mueller, *De Aeschyli Supplicum tempore atque indole* (diss. Halle, 1908) the latter followed Boeckh, who, on the basis of the prayers for the safety of the Argives at lines 625 ff., "considered it certain that Aeschylus was, in these verses, looking to the treaty between the Argives and Athenians as either concluded or to be concluded" (p. 5. K. Müller's arguments are put forward in his *Dissertations on the Eumenides of Aeschylus* [Engl. trans., Cambridge, 1835] 118–19. G. Mueller himself unfortunately rejected this argument in favor of stylistic "evidence" of an early date, pp. 50 ff.).

40. Forrest, 227.

41. Nepos remarks, for what it is worth, that Themistocles heard of his condemnation for treason *in absentia* and left for Corcyra "because he knew that he was not sufficiently safe at Argos" (*Themistocles* 8.2–3).

42. If anything, they indicate a date later in the decade: Amandry's date for the statues, which Forrest follows Pomtow in interpreting as an offering by the "sons of the slain" (the Argive aristocrats) is "shortly before 460," and Bowra's opinion is that to *Nemean* 10 "the nearest parallels are Ol. VII and Ol. XIII, both from 464" (Forrest, 227–28, with p. 228, n. 4).

43. The only "firm" date is Diodorus' for the Mycenae campaign, 468/7 (11.65); but, as he connects it with the earthquake at Sparta and the Helot revolt, it is usual to accept Diodorus' synchronism and lower the date to 465/4 (e.g., Andrewes [see note 26], 3 with n. 10). On Forrest's view the Argive democracy fell during the Mycenae campaign; how soon after its beginning the change took place we do not know. It seems that either Forrest's sequence "Mycenae—fall of Argive democracy—flight of Themistocles" or his date for the last event ("c. 465") must be abandoned.

44. Forrest, 240. If Herodotus' *douloi* really are the Argive democrats, the rest of the chapter (6.83) is embarrassing. The *douloi* after their expulsion seized Tiryns, and after an unspecified period of peace were incited to attack Argos by the seer Cleandrus. "As a result of this there was war between them for a considerable time, until the Argives with difficulty got the upper hand," says Herodotus. *Ex hypothesi* the war was over by 464, and so could not have lasted very long (to allow for a period of peace after "c. 468")—hardly "a considerable time"; and a restoration of democracy ought to have meant, in Herodotus' terms, victory for the *douloi*, not the Argives.

45. Rose, *Commentary* I, at line 254.

46. Not, of course, that Aeschylus is making specific geographical claims for Argos. It was a long-standing quarrel between Argos and Sparta, and Aeschylus simply puts forward, in the grand manner, claims to Argive hegemony over "all Greece."

47. From Ion of Chios, cited by Plutarch *Cimon* 16.10.

Chapter V: Oresteia

1. Eduard Fraenkel, "Aeschylus: New Texts and Old Problems," *Proceedings of the British Academy* 28 (1942) 256. One exception is B. Daube, *Zu den Rechtsproblemen in Aischylos' Agamemnon* (Zurich and Leipzig, 1938). See pp. 4 ff. for "Metaphors from Political Life and Criminal Law."

2. Eduard Fraenkel, *Aeschylus, Agamemnon* (Oxford, 1950) II.27.

3. "In the halls of the Atreidae" (3), "when Paris came to the house of the Atreidae" (399–400).

4. Fraenkel, *Agamemnon* II.210, at line 400.

5. *Ibid.*, II.271, at line 535. Fraenkel believes that the word is here used in a nontechnical sense to mean simply "plunder," "spoils," but even he admits that "the half-technical tone of the word, recalling the phrasing of legal claims, must have appealed to the poet particularly in this sentence which abounds in juridical terms" (272).

6. *Ibid.*, 376, at 11.816 ff.

7. 374–376, a makeshift rendering of Murray's makeshift text; "more violently than is just" is, however, beyond suspicion.

8. 385 ff. I can find no parallel for this meaning of *dikaiôtheis* in 393, but it seems required by the context. Fraenkel favors the more usual "legal" meaning, "condemn, punish." In my view, the wear and tear on the bronze is identified with a legal trial, a characteristically complex image. Fraenkel elsewhere (above, note 1, 251–252), approves Sewell's rendering, "to sentence is he brought," which is very close to my interpretation.

9. οὗτις ἀλκά (467) ∼ οὐ γὰρ ἔστιν ἔπαλξις (381) ἀμαύρον, ἐν δ'ἀίστοις (466) ∼ εἰς ἀφάνειαν (384) τρίβῳ (391) ∼ τριβᾷ (465).

10. 1577. Fraenkel remarks: "Here again one of the fundamental motifs of the *Oresteia* is stressed. It is significant that in the very first sentence he utters Aegisthus insists upon his δίκη. . . . As Paley observes, the speech begins and ends (1604, 1607, 1611) with the δίκη-motif."

11. 641 ff. (accepting Ahrens' πατουμένας for Murray's πατούμενον).

12. 787, reading, with Hermann, καδ'δίκαν from the scholium's κατὰ δίκαν (although the meaning is similar with Murray's text, διὰ δίκας [Pauw]).

13. 310–311. See also, in this section, 308 and 330.

14. R. J. Bonner and G. Smith, *The Administration of Justice from Homer to Plato* (Chicago, 1930), note several discrepancies between the trial scene and actual fifth-century procedure. "While the voting proceeds, the Erinyes and Apollo alternately address the jury in an attempt to win their votes. From a legal standpoint this

is entirely irregular" (127). "Aeschylus does not reproduce the regulation set speeches of an Athenian homicide trial. . . . The method used by Aeschylus is reminiscent of the time when the trial took place before a single magistrate who had final jurisdiction" (128). H. T. Wade-Gery put forward the interesting theory that the *Eumenides* reflects the recent change (by Ephialtes, he suggests) by which magistrates lost their power to render judicial decisions and became mere *eisagôgeis*, deciding which court was to hear a particular case (*Essays in Greek History* [Oxford, 1958] 176, 183 n. 2).

15. A rough count gives seventy-six occurrences of the term *dikê* or its cognates in 1047 lines.

16. How contemporary Athenians observed the goddess' injunction to honor the Erinyes is suggested by the Scholiast on Demosthenes 21.115 (p. 607 in Dindorf's edition), where we learn that the three men who managed the sacrifices to the Eumenides were chosen *by the Areopagus*. We do not know when this practice was instituted, but the play's emphasis on "honors" may indicate that its connection with the Areopagus was a recent innovation.

17. 470–485; I have paraphrased and slightly abridged the text.

18. Cimon's expedition and its humiliating dismissal are mentioned by Thucydides (1.102.1–3), but the exact chronology remains a mystery. Plutarch's more circumstantial account (presumably devised to solve some of the chronological problems) mentions two expeditions, the first in "the fourth year of Archidamus' reign" (465). It is of this that we are told that "Ephialtes opposed the project and besought the Athenians not to succour nor restore a city which was their rival, but to let haughty Sparta lie to be trodden under foot of men. . . . And Ion actually mentions the phrase by which, more than by anything else, Cimon prevailed upon the Athenians, exhorting them 'not to suffer Hellas to be crippled, nor their city to be robbed of its yoke-fellow' " (Plutarch *Cimon* 16.8, trans. Perrin). In the next chapter Plutarch says that the Spartans called on the Athenians again (*authis*); he then gives an account of the expedition and its dismissal similar to Thucydides'. Plutarch's story is usually rejected (by, e.g., Gomme, *Commentary* I.411, n. 1), but it has recently been defended by N. G. L. Hammond, "Studies in Greek Chronology of the Sixth and Fifth Centuries B.C.," *Historia* 4 (1955) 374–79.

19. C. M. Bowra, "Stesichorus in the Peloponnese," *CQ* 28 (1934) 115–19, suggested that Stesichorus, who had already in the sixth century relocated Agamemnon's kingdom in Sparta, did so for political reasons (although, as Prof. Dodds points out, "the reference at *Odyssey* 4.514 to Agam. rounding Cape Malea on his way home from Troy shows that his location at Sparta is older than Stesichorus"). The Scholiast on Euripides' *Orestes* 46 notes: "Homer says the seat of Agamemnon's kingdom was at Mycenae, Stesichorus and Simonides say in Lacedaemon." On this point P. Mazon speaks of "the invention of a common royal house of the two Atreidae at Argos, created only for the needs of the drama and of politics" (*Eschyle* Tome II [Paris, 1955] xi).

20. K. O. Müller, *Dissertations on the Eumenides of Aeschylus* (Engl. trans., Cambridge, 1835).

21. Bernard Drake, *Aeschyli, Eumenides, the Greek Text with English Notes, etc.* (Cambridge, 1853).

22. *Ibid.*, 73, quoted from G. Grote, *History of Greece* (edition unspecified) V.495 note.

23. A. Sidgwick, *Aeschylus, Eumenides* (Oxford, 1887) 25.

24. R. W. Livingstone, "The Problem of the Eumenides of Aeschylus," *JHS* 45 (1925) 123–24.

25. *Ibid.*, 127; not the only contradiction in Livingstone's views. We are told both that "Aeschylus does not, of course, allow his moral to spoil his story" (125) and that "in writing this play, Aeschylus was interested far less in Orestes than in the political issues of his own day" (129). This, if true, could not help but "spoil the story."

26. *Ibid.*, 124.

27. *Ibid.*, 124–25.

28. Clara M. Smertenko, "The Political Sympathies of Aeschylus," *JHS* 52 (1932) 233–35, reprinted in *Studies in Greek Religion* (U. of Oregon Studies in the Humanities 1, 1935) 25–27.

29. *Ibid.*, 234.

30. E. R. Dodds, "Morals and Politics in the *Oresteia*," *Procs. of the Cambridge Philological Society* 186 (1960) 23. Smertenko's theory was restated by A. Plassart, "Eschyle et le fronton est du temple delphique des Alcméonides," *REA* 42 (1940) 293–99; he maintained that *Eum.* 12–16 recall the group of *kouroi* with Apollo on the east pediment (fragmentary; note the circular argument: Plassart would restore hatchets in their hands from Σ *Eum.* 13).

31. Pierre Amandry, "Eschyle et la purification d'Oreste," *Rev. Archéologique* 11 (1938) 19–27, maintained that the "purifications by slain swine" of *Eum.* 283 are certainly *not* Delphic, because there purification was by laurel and flowing water, although Prof. Dover notes that "the painter of Louvre K710 obviously thought purification by pig's blood was Delphic." Amandry's view, that Aeschylus was writing propaganda for a brand of specifically Eleusinian purification, seems untenable if my arguments are valid.

32. The mother as mere receptacle was Anaxagoras' view of the matter, according to Aristotle (*Generation of Animals* 763b30 ff.). Prof. Herington informs me that the argument seems to have been acceptable in legal circles until the eighteenth century, which makes it less surprising on the lips of Apollo and Athena.

33. F. Jacoby, *FGH* IIIb Suppl., i.22–25.

34. See Hellanicus (*FGH* 323 a) frag. 22.

35. Jacoby, *op. cit.*, i.24–25.

36. K. J. Dover, "The Political Aspect of Aeschylus' *Eumenides*," *JHS* 77 (1957) 230–37.

37. E. R. Dodds (see note 30) 19–31.

38. R. W. Livingstone (see note 24) 123–24.

39. Dodds, *op. cit.*, 20. He cites *Agam.* 456 ff., 640, 938, 1409, and 1616.

40. *Ibid.*, 20. Dodds offers a convincing refutation of Dover's objection that the Egyptian campaign took place not in Libya but in the Delta: "Probably neither the poet nor the majority of his audience would be in a position to know just where the battles were taking place; what they would know is that many of their kinsfolk were overseas, fighting for the Libyans" (21).

41. *Ibid.*, 21, with n. 2, "Cf. *Ath. Trib. Lists* III, 321, n. 88: 'Very possibly lines 295–6 will refer to some sort of trouble in Pallene, and this would surely mean Poteidaea. It is not impossible that Poteidaea remained recalcitrant till Kimon made his Five Years' Truce in 451.' As for the Troad, Sigeum seems to have been threatened by Persian encroachments in 451/0 (*IG* I³ 17, and B. D. Meritt in *Hesperia* V [1936] 360 f.), and it is *possible* that the trouble began earlier."

42. "In the sixth year after the death of Ephialtes," *Ath. Pol.* 26.2. Dodds first argued for this view in "Notes on the Oresteia," *CQ*, n.s., 3 (1953) 11–21. (This theory had already been put forward by Friedrich Cauer, "Aischylos und der Areopag,"

Rheinisches Museum 50 [1895] 354–55.) In his paper of 1960 Dodds noted Jacoby's objections to this view, but did not do them full justice. In an *addendum* to his note on Hellanicus fr. 1 (*FGH* IIIb, Suppl. ii.528) Jacoby argued that, as it was from the great mass of middle-class zeugites that the reformers drew their support for the change from Sparta to Argos (for it was these, the hoplites, whom the Spartans had insulted at Ithome), it would have been inconsistent, if not contradictory, for a supporter of the Argive alliance to refer to them as "evil inpourings" and "mud" (*Eumenides* 694).

43. Dodds, 22. He does not seem to me to take sufficiently into account Dover's observation that ". . . the Greeks did not put murder and stasis into separate compartments; they clearly perceived that an authority which restrains and punishes homicide is the first step in progress from the life of beasts to the life of a human community, and upon the preservation of that authority the continued existence of the community ultimately depends" (see note 36, p. 234).

44. Dodds, 22–23; he is then seen to be reviving the notion of "Aeschylus the Moderate," the view held by, *inter alios*, Livingstone, A. W. Verrall (*The 'Eumenides' of Aeschylus* [London, 1908] xlix) and G. Thomson (*The Oresteia of Aeschylus* [Cambridge, 1938] II.357).

45. Dodds, 24. This view of the political import of lines 976 ff. had already been put forward by Wilamowitz, *Aischylos Interpretationen* (Berlin, 1914) 227 and *Aristoteles und Athen* (Berlin, 1893) II.342.

46. Dodds, 31; but who can say that what to us appears a "particular squabble" may not have been as important to a fifth-century Athenian as any "insight into the laws that govern our condition"?

47. Lurje's paper, the Russian original of which is summarized in the *Bibliotheca Classica Orientalis* 5 (1960) 295–97, was given the German title "Die politische Tendenz der Tragödie 'Die Eumeniden.'" This review indicates that it formed part of a doctoral dissertation (Leningrad, 1943), and so Lurje and Dodds must have formulated their theories about admission of zeugites to the archonship independently.

48. C. D. N. Costa, "Plots and Politics in Aeschylus," *Greece and Rome*, 2d ser. 9 (1962) 22–34. Costa's treatment of the

Suppliants offers a good occasion to speak out against the insidious tendency to explain away "political" features of the story on grounds that these were "demanded by the myth." As if Aeschylus had to write about Argive acceptance of the Danaids in 464/3! Only slightly less distressing is the tendency to ascribe peculiar features of a story to "alternative versions" of the legend; it is apparently always easier to attribute mythical innovations to anonymous authors.

49. Santo Mazzarino, "Echilo, Pericle e la storia dell' Areopago," *Rivista di cultura classica e medioevale* II (1960) 300–306; Santo Mazzarino, "Introduzione alle 'Eumenidi' di Eschilo," *Dioniso* 23 (1960) 67–71; Santo Mazzarino, " 'Incontro con le Eumenidi,' gli Eupatridi, Eschilo e Pericle," *Orpheus* 7 (1960) 119–22.

50. This point has recently been reiterated by J. H. Quincey ("Orestes and the Argive Alliance," *CQ*, n.s., 14 [1964] 190–206); he examines the relevant passages and shows that emphasis on the alliance "exceeds the requirements of the plot" (190). On the other hand the references Quincey finds in *Eumenides* 767–774 to the late sixth-century invasions by the Spartan king Cleomenes strike me as being, at best, very tenuous. An allusion so remote (in time and place) would seem to require something more explicit to catch the audience's attention.

51. The lexical notices, collected by Jacoby in his note on Philochorus frag. 64, are in agreement that the *nomophylakes* "forced the magistrates to exercise the laws, and prevented a vote on a measure which was illegal or disadvantageous to the city," but such details of their functions may refer to the reinstitution of the office in the 320's. It should be noted that the suspect Constitution of Draco (*Ath. Pol.* 4.4) gives such a verbal explanation of the *nomophylakia;* according to it the Areopagus "was guardian of the laws and kept close watch over the magistrates to see that they ruled according to the laws." By the fourth century a trial of impeachment of a magistrate "for not using the laws" was held before the *Boulê* (with appeal to the law courts in case of conviction, *Ath. Pol.* 45.2). If, therefore, the *lexica* are referring to the later *nomophylakes*, this function of seeing to it that magistrates "used the laws" must have been transferred to that board from the *Boulê* some time after the composition of the *Ath. Pol.*

For a desperate (and, to me, unconvincing) attempt to explain the content of the *nomophylakia*, cf. C. Hignett, *A History of the Athenian Constitution* (Oxford, 1952) 208–10.

52. *FGH* 328 Fr. 64 b (*a*) Lex. Cantabr. p. 351 10 N:
"*Nomophylakes* . . . they were seven, and were established, as
Philochorus says, when Ephialtes left to the Areopagus only
capital cases." This notice does not seem to me to entail *simul-
taneity* of establishment of the board with Ephialtes' reforms. Jacoby
doubts the number, *FGH* III b, Suppl. ii. 244–45, nn. 23, 24.

53. It may be objected that the *Ath. Pol.* implies that it was
Ephialtes himself who attacked the Areopagus' *nomophylakia*: "He
stripped off all the *epitheta* through which it was guardian of the
constitution and gave some to the 500, others to the *demos* and
the lawcourts" (25.2). It is a confused notice: it implies that the
nomophylakia was not a separate power; to call this *epitheta* is
contrary (if not contradictory) to the early chapters of the treatise
which indicate that it preexisted Solon (*Ath. Pol.* 8.4, cf. 3.6). On
my hypothesis the implied connection of the attack on the *nomophylakia* with Ephialtes' reforms must be rejected.

54. Aristotle *Politics* 1274 a 8, Plutarch *Pericles* 9.4. The
Ath. Pol., in distinguishing the attacks of Ephialtes and Pericles,
may be "correcting" the *Politics* from an *Atthis*.

55. The admission of the zeugites to the archonship in 457
is placed in "the sixth year after Ephialtes' death" (*Ath. Pol.* 26.2).

56. With the inevitable motive, "seeking to gain popular support against Cimon's wealth." This cannot, even if true, be used
to date the measure to before Cimon's ostracism (or, for that matter,
to the period after his return).

57. C. Hignett, *A History of the Athenian Constitution* (Oxford, 1952) App. IX, 342–43: "Whether the reform was carried
before Ephialtes' death is doubtful; the fact that such an important
measure was sponsored by Perikles suggests that Ephialtes was no
longer alive, but it was a logical consequence of the revolution of
462 and cannot have been long delayed" (343).

58. I will note here that the latter part of my hypothesis does
not depend on acceptance of the earlier. The reference to jury pay
seems to me to stand firm even if my identification of Pericles as
institutor of the *nomophylakes* does not find favor. My suggestion
is also independent of the exact date of Pericles' introduction of
jury pay. Aeschylus could criticize it whether it came before, at
the same time as, or after, Ephialtes' measures.

59. F. Jacoby, *Atthis* (Oxford, 1949) 396 n. 43; see also
340–41, n. 64: "[Herodotus] evidently was prejudiced against
Themistokles . . . [for] apparently Perikles, who took up the policy

of Themistokles with the peace of Kallias at the latest, had no love
for the author of that policy; in any case the end of Themistokles'
career made it impossible to refer to him."

60. Themistocles' actual cooperation with Ephialtes (*Ath. Pol.*
25.3–4) is one of the more hopeless of the treatise's many confusions.

Chapter VI: Prometheus Bound

1. L. R. Farnell, "The Paradox of the *Prometheus Vinctus,*"
JHS 53 (1933) 40.

2. The difference between the Zeus of the *P. V.* and the other
plays is evident, in spite of Lloyd-Jones' argument for a consistent
Zeus, assimilated to the god of the *P.V.* ("Zeus in Aeschylus," *JHS*
76 [1956] 55–67).

3. O. J. Todd, "The Character of Zeus in Aeschylus' *Prometheus Bound,*" *CQ* 19 (1925) 67.

4. Lloyd-Jones (see note 2, 66) aptly cites Aristotle's *dictum*:
"it would be strange (*atopon*) if someone said he loved Zeus"
(*Magna Moralia* 2.11.6, 1208 b 31).

5. Wilhelm Schmid, *Untersuchungen zum gefesselten Prometheus* (Tübinger Beiträge 9, Stuttgart, 1929) and again in
Christ-Schmid-Stählin, *G.G.L.* I.iii (Munich, 1940) 281–308.

6. H. J. Rose, "On an Epic Idiom in Aeschylus," *Eranos* 45
(1947) 99, n. 2.

7. The phrase is Del Grande's (*Hybris* [Naples, 1947] App.
IV, 435–57); he offers an elaborate defense based on "coherence
of thematic composition." For a short but sensible answer to some
of Schmid's arguments, see Louis Séchan, *Le Mythe de Prométhée*
(Paris, 1951) 58–64, an admirably concise and useful work.

8. Eirik Vandvik, *The Prometheus of Hesiod and Aeschylus*
(Oslo, 1943).

9. George Thomson, for example, maintains that in the *Unbound,* the Titans "urge [Prometheus] to submit to his old enemy,
not merely because he is the ruler of the world, but because he
now rules it well" (*Aeschylus. Prometheus Bound* [Cambridge,
1932] 20). Although I accept the traditional place of the *Desmotês*
at the opening of its trilogy, the exact position makes no difference
to the political background. Welcker's view that it was preceded
by the *Pyrphoros* has recently been revived by Fitton-Brown
("*Prometheia,*" *JHS* 79 [1959] 52 ff.) and C. Kerenyi, *Prometheus*

(Engl. trans., London, 1963) 75–76. For an interesting attempt to reconstruct the trilogy on the basis of the theme of the four elements and from Aristophanic analogies see C. J. Herington, "A Study in the *Prometheia*," I, *Phoenix* 17 (1963) 180–97 and II, *ibid.* 236–43.

10. Scholiast on *P.V.* 94, not, perhaps, to be taken literally; see Herington (preceding note) I, 194, nn. 53 and 54.

11. As Rose puts it, "the only supposition at all resembling a solution of the difficulty, that Aeschylus represented Zeus as having learned wisdom and gentleness with experience of rule, is completely devoid of positive evidence on its behalf, though in itself not at all impossible" (*Handbook of Greek Literature* [New York, 1960] 154). Lloyd-Jones (see note 2), 56, n. 21, gives an extensive bibliography of scholars who believe in an evolving Zeus.

12. Line 17, *bary*, echoed by Kratos at 1.77, "the severe appraiser of the work" (*epitimêtês* a "political" word).

13. See also lines 305, 310, 357, 736–737 (*tyrannos . . . biaios*), 756, 761, 909–910, 942, 957–958, 996. Herington notes that "the word τύραννος (or derivatives) occurs thirteen times in the *P.V.*, on all but one occasion (957) with direct reference to Zeus; it occurs eight times in the other works of Aeschylus, never with reference to Zeus" (see note 9, II.239, n. 16).

14. Friedrich Solmsen, *Hesiod and Aeschylus* (Ithaca, 1949).

15. *Ibid.*, 138. Others have taken this too far in an effort to absolve Prometheus. A close reading of *P.V.* 206 ff. shows that Prometheus had originally been on the side of the Titans. When he saw that they were unwilling to follow his advice to use guile against Zeus, then and only then did he transfer his allegiance to Zeus; he was merely making the best of a bad job (216).

16. *Ibid.* 140, n. 80.

17. George Thomson, "ZEYΣ TYPANNOΣ, A Note on the *Prometheus Vinctus*," *CR* 43 (1929) 3–5; expanded in his edition (above, note 9) 6 ff.; additional references in his *Aeschylus and Athens* (London, 1941) 452, n. 9.

A short but penetrating paper by N. F. Deratani, "La Figure du tyran dans 'Prométhée Enchaîné' d'Eschyle," *Comptes rendus de l'Academie des Sciences de l'URSS* (1929) 4.70–74, has left no mark on English-speaking scholarship. Deratani analyzes the play to show that Zeus is a typical tyrant and concludes "that from the first in Greek poetry, the traditional portrait of the tyrant was already reflected in Aeschylus," and that "this depiction by Aeschylus includes details fixed in later philosophico-political theory and reiterated in the tragedies of Sophocles and Euripides." (The paper is in Russian; I quote from an English translation kindly supplied by my former pupil, Mr. L. Senelick.)

18. Prof. Herington reminds me that at *Persians* 213 Atossa points out that Xerxes is *ouch hypeuthynos polei.*

19. Two of Lucian's dialogues, "Prometheus" and "Prometheus and Zeus" (the first of the "Dialogues of the Gods") sometimes figure in reconstructions of lost plays of the *Prometheia.*

20. Georges Méautis, *L'Authenticité et la date du Prométhée Enchaîné d'Eschyle* (Univ. de Neuchatel, recueil de travaux, etc., 29, Geneva, 1960) 46–47.

21. The notice in the *Life* implies that Aeschylus produced the play as a tribute to the city's new settlers and its "founder": "as an omen of a good life for those who settled in the city" (*Vita* 9).

22. The Scholiast on Aristophanes' *Frogs* 1028 says clearly, "the *Persians* was presented by Aeschylus in Syracuse, at the urging of Hiero," and the source of this information is given as Book 3 of Eratosthenes' work "On Comedy." The date for this Sicilian production would have been some year between Aeschylus' victory in the Dionysia of 472 and the *Seven* of 467.

23. Eugenio Leone's attack on Méautis, "Il Prometeo Incatenato una requisitoria contro la tirannide?" (*Paideia* 17 [1962] 16–24) flies in the face of the obvious, although Leone is right to question Méautis on details, e.g., the latter's argument drawn from the word *aulê* at *P.V.* 122 (Leone compares *Odyssey* 4.74).

24. The translations of Diodorus are, with minor changes, those of C. H. Oldfather (Loeb Classical Library, London, 1946).

25. See, e.g., Aristotle's *Politics* 1312 b 23.

26. See Appendix B.

27. E. G. Harman, *The Prometheus Bound of Aeschylus* (London, 1920) Chap. II, "The Allegory and the Characters," 12–25, and J. A. Davison, "The Date of the *Prometheia*," *TAPA* 80 (1949) 66–93; these two scholars' views are self-refuting.

28. Gaetano Baglio, *Il 'Prometeo' di Eschilo alla luce delle storie di Erodoto* (Rome, 1952), reissued, apparently without change, as *Il 'Prometeo' di Eschilo e la storia Ellenica e Persiana fino all 'invasione Persiana di Atene* (Rome, 1959). (Cf. A. Lesky, in *Anzeiger für die Altertumswissenschaft* 14 [1961] 14).

29. Baglio, 6.

30. Benjamin Farrington, *Science and Politics in the Ancient World* (London, 1939) Chap. 7, "Prometheus Bound; the Clash Between Science and City-State," 67–86.

31. See my article, "The Political Significance of the Athenian 'Tyrannicide-Cult,'" *Historia* 15 (1966).

32. Honors to "tyrannicides": tomb (Paus. 1.29.15); sacrifices by polemarch (*Ath. Pol.* 58.1); meals in prytaneion (*IG* I². 77).

33. *Ath. Pol.* 22.6. Was this more Themistoclean propaganda? We know the names of only two of the three: the younger Hipparchus, a relative of Peisistratus, and Megacles the Alcmeonid, nephew of Cleisthenes and uncle of Pericles.

34. Plutarch *Themistocles* 25.1 (trans. Perrin), quoting Theophrastus, *On Royalty*.

35. *aikeia* used by Io of her own treatment, *P.V.* 599; the adjective *aeikês* by Prometheus at 97, 525; ironically at 1042; by the chorus at 472.

36. It is curious that the somewhat rare word Aristotle uses, *phronêmatias*, "high-spirited," should be used by Pollux (1.194) of a horse, for the simile is used of Prometheus by Ocean (323).

Appendix A: Aeschylus on Salamis

1. The more important studies in English of the battle of Salamis are:

W. W. Goodwin, "The Battle of Salamis," *Papers of the American School at Athens* 1 (1882–83). 237–62.

J. A. R. Munro, "Some Observations on the Persian Wars," *JHS* 22 (1902) 294–332, esp. 325 ff.

W. W. Tarn, "The Fleet of Xerxes," *JHS* 28 (1908) 202–33, esp. 219–26.

R. W. Macan, *Herodotus VII-VIII-IX* (London, 1908) II, App. VI, "Salamis," 287–325.

W. W. How and J. Wells, *Commentary on Herodotus* (Oxford, 1912, repr. 1949) App. XXI, "Salamis," 378–87.

Most recently:

N. G. L. Hammond, "The Battle of Salamis,"*JHS* 76 (1956) 32–54.

W. K. Pritchett, "Toward a Restudy of the Battle of Salamis," *AJA* 63 (1959) 251–62.

H. D. Broadhead, *The Persae of Aeschylus* (Cambridge, 1960) App. VI, "Salamis," 322–39.

A. R. Burn, *Persia and the Greeks* (London, 1962) Chap. XXI, "The Battle of Salamis," 450-75.

C. Hignett, *Xerxes' Invasion of Greece* (Oxford, 1963) Chap. IV, "Salamis," 193-239.

These will be cited by author's name only.

2. Macan, 290.

3. How and Wells, 381.

4. So, too, Hignett, who notes that the Aeschylean version "seems to be the original nucleus of the message, while the Herodotean addition reads like an awkward excrescence which has no organic connection with the rest of the message and is hardly consistent with it" (405).

5. "In ch. 76 the words κυκλούμενοι πρὸς τὴν Σαλαμῖνα read like a misunderstood reference to the circumnavigating squadron" (II. 383).

6. That *Persians* 368 must refer to circumnavigation of the island and not, as in Diodorus, to a blockade of the western channel by Megara is made clear by W. Marg, "Zur Strategie der Schlacht von Salamis," *Hermes* 90 (1962) 116-19, who argues from a rise in water level since antiquity that a blockade of the western channel would have been unnecessary.

7. Hammond tried to revive Beloch's thesis that Psyttaleia was not Lipsokoutali but St. George, and succeeded in convincing Broadhead; but the issue remains open.

8. "Of ordered movements in the battle we hear little or nothing, Aeschylus giving a vivid picture of the mêlée and Hdt. isolated exploits in the general scene of confusion" (How and Wells, II.385).

9. "[Herodotus'] conceptions of the strategy are vague or erroneous, while all real account of the tactics is conspicuously absent" (How and Wells, II.378-79).

10. For this Ameinias see Chapter I, p. 4.

11. Macan, *ad. loc.* Hammond attempts to reconcile 8.76.1 and 8.85.1: "It means that at midnight the Persian right wing was not pointing in that direction [toward Eleusis] but next morning it was" (47, n. 57).

12. ". . . the poet's account is simple and logical: the Greek message, placed at the start of the action, is the element that sets it moving. Herodotus' account, contrary to that of the dramatist, is confused and does not provide an explanation which answers to

the exigencies of logic," G. Smets and A. Dorsinfang-Smets, "La Bataille de Salamine: les sources," *Mélanges Grégoire* (1952) 415.

13. That the Persians entered the straits at dawn is the obvious implication of Aeschylus' account, in spite of Hignett's contention that the dramatist's testimony is "ambiguous" on this point. (Hignett must reject the connotations of *rheuma* in line 412 and interpret it simply as "a natural metaphor for a host of men," 224). We have here another discrepancy between Aeschylus and Herodotus, for the latter clearly, as Hignett emphasizes, places the entry of the Persian fleet into the straits during the night (8.76).

14. That one of these *stoichoi* was intended to block the western channel by Megara, as maintained by Munro (327) and Broadhead (328–9), is ruled out by the narrowness of that channel in antiquity and is in clear violation of the indications of the ms order of lines 366–368: τάξαι . . . στίφος μὲν ἐν στοίχοις τρισὶν ἔκπλους φυλάσσειν . . . ἄλλας δὲ κύκλῳ. . . . Hammond (44) somewhat improbably maintains that "the 'three columns' probably refers to the three squadrons, Phoenician, Ionian and mixed, each being under one admiral."

15. Hignett notes that "the word διάπλοος does not occur as an adjective except in this one passage; elsewhere it is a noun which means a 'voyage across' or 'room to sail through, a passage'" (224). (His explanation of the phrase, however, differs from mine.)

16. Hignett, Chap. IV, 193–239 *passim*, and App. IX (a) 403–8.

Appendix B: The Date of the Prometheus Bound

1. F. Focke, "Aischylos' Prometheus," *Hermes* 65 (1930) 259–304; Vandvik, *The Prometheus of Hesiod and Aeschylus* (Oslo, 1943) 49, n. 3; U. von Wilamowitz-Moellendorff, *Aischylos Interpretationen* (Berlin, 1914) 242, n. 2. Wilamowitz's argument is based on fr. 235 N (= Mette 181) and is taken over, with some elaboration, by Mette, 256–57.

2. Croiset, cited by Séchan, *Le Mythe de Prométhée* (Paris, 151) 117, n. 93; Mazon, *Eschyle I* (Paris, 1958) 151: "The style has an ease and firmness which bring it rather close to that of the *Oresteia*. . . ."

3. Farnell, "The Paradox of the *Prometheus Vinctus*," *JHS* 53 (1933) 45; Thomson, *Aeschylus, the Prometheus Bound* (Cambridge, 1932) 46; H. J. Rose, *Commentary* I. 9–10. The date has

been accepted most recently by Fitton-Brown, who follows his Anglo-Saxon predecessors ("Prometheia," *JHS* 79 [1959] 60).

4. Thomson, 43–46.

5. Athenaeus 15. 672 and 674 D; only in the latter is the *Unbound* mentioned specifically: "Aeschylus says clearly in the *Unbound Prometheus* that in honor of Prometheus we put the crown (of wicker) on our heads as a requital for his bonds." That the custom was *foretold* by Prometheus himself seems to be an inference of Méautis.

6. Georges Méautis, *L'Authenticité et la date du Prométhée Enchaîné d'Eschyle* (Univ. de Neuchatel, Recueil de travaux, etc., 29, Geneva, 1960) 58. See also Thomson's theory: "[*Prometheus Pyrphoros*] was partly ritualistic, ending with the inauguration of the Prometheia, just as the *Oresteia* ended with the inauguration of the Court of the Areopagus, and the *Supplices* trilogy, probably, with the inauguration of the Thesmophoria" (35).

7. Herodotus 2.171.2, reports that the daughters of Danaus brought the rite of Demeter called "Thesmophoria" from Egypt, which led D. S. Robertson to conclude that the trilogy ended with the foundation of this festival ("The End of the *Supplices* Trilogy of Aeschylus," *CR* 38 [1924] 51–53).

8. E. C. Yorke, "Trisyllabic Feet in the Dialogue of Aeschylus," *CQ* 30 (1936) 116–19, confirmed and in part corrected by E. B. Ceadel, "Resolved Feet in the Trimeters of Euripides," *CQ* 35 (1941) 85. Some of Yorke's other findings may surprise confirmed Aeschyleans: "Out of 37 trisyllabic feet in the trimeters of this play [*P.V.*], 12 are first-foot anapaests. There is nothing approaching this proportion elsewhere in Aeschylus or in Sophocles or in Euripides" (117).

9. J. D. Denniston, "Pauses in the Tragic Senarius," *CQ* 30 (1936) 73–79, with several corrections on p. 192. (I owe this reference to Prof. Dodds.)

10. J. D. Denniston, *Greek Particles*[2] (Oxford, 1954) lxviii.

11. C. J. Herington, "A Unique Technical Feature of the *Prometheus Bound*," *CR*, n.s., 13 (1963) 5–7.

12. E. C. Yorke, "The Date of the *Prometheus Vinctus*," *CQ* 30 (1936) 153–54.

13. Thucydides 3.116.2, *Marmor Parium* (*F. Gr. Hist.* 239) 52. Rose began by accepting the argument: "The date of the *Prometheus Bound* is uncertain, though it probably was written not long after the great eruption of Aetna in 479/8; it is a not improb-

able hypothesis that the allusion to this which the play contains arises from its having been composed, or revised, while the author was in Sicily" (*Handbook of Greek Literature* [New York, 1960] 151). He later recanted (see note 3).

14. Kerenyi (*Prometheus* [Engl. trans., London, 1963] 107–8) notes the close parallels between *Isthmian VIII* 35–38 (? 478 B.C.) and *P.V.* 921–924, particularly "the mention of the trident side by side with the thunderbolt."

15. "Aeschylus however, in referring to Mt. Aetna, like Pindar echoes an archaic epic which coloured the ancient saga of Typho with the experiences of the first Greek settlers on the shores of Sicily" (G. Zuntz, *The Political Plays of Euripides* [Manchester, 1955] 59, with note 2).

16. Focke (see note 1) 289. He finds three of the twelve first-foot anapaestic resolutions in these lines (see note 8).

17. See Camille Gaspar, *Essai de chronologie Pindarique* (Brussels, 1900) 129 ff. If H. C. Bennett's persuasive arguments for reinstating the old "Pausanian" system of Pythiad-dating be accepted, the twenty-ninth Pythiad—and with it Pindar's *First Pythian*—must be moved back to 474 (cf. H. C. Bennett, Jr., "On the Systemization of Scholia Dates for Pindar's Pythian Odes," *HSCP* 62 [1957] 61–78, esp. 75–77).

18. Focke, 294.

19. For the Orphic influences, especially in vocabulary and in the theory of development of culture, see J. R. Bacon, "Three Notes on Aeschylus *Prometheus Vinctus*," *CR* 42 (1928) 115–20, supplemented by Thomson, "Notes on *Prometheus Vinctus*," *CR* 23 (1929) esp. 161–63.

Sicilian vocabulary: Athenaeus 9.402 B, "it is not surprising that Aeschylus should use many Sicilian expressions since he spent time in Sicily," but cf. *contra*, the remarks of Ed. Fraenkel in *Agamemnon* III, 712 ff.

The case for the prominence of both elements in Aeschylus' work has been restated by Q. Cataudella, "Eschilo in Sicilia," *Dioniso* ann. 37, vol. 26 (1963) 5–24.

Appendix C: Fragments, Titles, and Theories

1. See Chapter I, p. 5.

2. *Ox. Pap.* XX. 2257, fr. 1, from a Hypothesis to the play, shows it to have been in five parts, with the first and third taking place at Aetna, the last at Syracuse. *Ox. Pap.* XX. 2256, fr. 9 (a)

is plausibly ascribed to the *Aetnaean Women* by E. Fraenkel, "Vermutungen zum Aetna-Festspiel des Aeschylus," *Eranos* 52 (1954) 61–75. The most recent treatment of the fragment is that of Ph. J. Kakridis, "Der ΠΑΙΣ ΜΑΡΓΟΣ im Dike-Fragment des Aischylos," *Eranos* 60 (1962) 111–21.

3. *Vita* 9.

4. This summary of Welcker's views is given by Broadhead in his introduction to the *Persians*, lvii.

5. E. A. Freeman, *History of Sicily* (Oxford, 1891). The argument is rather scattered: see I.414, n. 2, but esp. II.279–80, and Appendix XX, 522.

6. Although it is also preserved—with a variant reading—by Scholium R on Aristophanes' *Frogs* 1403, and which *Glaucus* it is from is again not specified.

7. Freeman II.280.

8. Freeman 522.

9. The suggestion is quoted by Fraenkel as "worth considering," *Aeschylus, Agamemnon* (Oxford, 1950) II, 116, n. 1. Of the literature cited there the most accessible is perhaps W. Schmid, *Geschichte der griechische Literatur* II (1934) 203, n. 9.

10. Wilamowitz, *Sappho und Simonides* 207, cited by Fraenkel, preceding note.

11. Not the play for which Aeschylus was believed in the fourth century to have been brought to trial for revealing secrets of the mysteries. The detail is mentioned by Aristotle *Eth. Nic.* III.2 (1111a); further information is collected by Wilamowitz (W44) who, apropos the list of titles compiled by Aristotle's anonymous commentator, remarks "the grammarians looked for this tragedy in vain."

12. *Theseus* 29.4 f.

13. A. Hauvette, "Les 'Eleusiniens' d'Eschyle et l'institution du discours funèbre à Athènes," *Mélanges Henri Weil* (Paris, 1898) 159–78.

14. See pp. 13–14.

15. In a long and valuable discussion on Philochorus, frs. 112–113 (*FGH* IIIb, Suppl. i, 442–448, esp. 447).

16. *Theseus* 36.

Index